# AN ABC FOR THE PCC

# Mowbray Parish Handbooks

# AN ABC
# FOR THE PCC

## A HANDBOOK FOR
## CHURCH COUNCIL MEMBERS

John Pitchford

MOWBRAY

Mowbray
A Cassell imprint
Wellington House, 125 Strand, London WC2R 0BB
387 Park Avenue South, New York 10016–8810

First published 1979 by Wyche Publications
Second edition published 1985 by A. R. Mowbray & Co. Ltd
Third edition first published 1993
Reprinted 1995

British Library Cataloguing-in-Publication Data
A catalogue record for this book is available from the British Library.

Library of Congress Cataloging-in-Publication Data
Available from the Library of Congress

ISBN 0–264–67280–1

Typeset by Colset Private Limited
Printed and bound in Great Britain by
Biddles Ltd, Guildford and King's Lynn

# Foreword

*By the Right Reverend Mark Santer, the Bishop of Birmingham*

John Pitchford's *An ABC for the PCC* has been valued since its publication in 1979 by churchwardens and Parochial Church Council members up and down the country. A mine of factual information and practical suggestions, it has sold over 14,000 copies and, alongside the *Handbook for Churchwardens and Parochial Church Councillors*, it has informed a generation of PCC members. The current revision has taken account of recent changes in General Synod legislation, bringing it up to date with current church practice. I commend the *ABC* to churchwardens and PCC members and congratulate Mr Pitchford on an excellent revision of a really useful compendium.

✠ *Mark Birmingham*

# Commendations of former editions

I warmly commend Mr Pitchford's *ABC* to all priests and Parochial Church Councils. The book fills a long-felt need, and I hope it will be widely read.

*The Late Right Reverend John Eastaugh,*
*Bishop of Hereford (1979)*

Mr Pitchford's *ABC* is a magnificent compendium of basic factual information, a host of practical hints and suggestions, and questions for discussion, all of them intended to help Parochial Church Council members and, indeed, everyone in the parish, to work together more efficiently – above all, to be more effective in mission. Mr Pitchford's book should take its place side by side with the *Handbook for Churchwardens and Parochial Church Councillors* as a constant reference point and as a welcome source of fresh ideas. Here indeed is a book full of 'wise saws and modern instances'.

*The Reverend Sir Derek Pattinson,*
*Secretary General of General Synod (1979)*

This is not a book for the complacent and it is not only the clergy and PCC members who will find much to interest them. Mr Pitchford quotes the saying 'if you fail to plan, then you plan to fail'. He wants every parish to have a clear and definite policy worked out by the clergy and the PCC, and the congregation.

*Canon Michael Hocking in the* Church Times *(1985)*

I am very happy indeed to commend *An ABC for the PCC*. Fr Pitchford is an experienced parish priest who has served both in the country and in London, as well as being a member of the General Synod for the Hereford diocese.

The advent of synodical government has brought new opportunities for the Church and clearly demonstrates the need for real partnership between clergy and laity.

I hope this most helpful guide for clergy and people alike will be very widely read.

*The Right Reverend and the Right Honourable*
*Graham Leonard, Bishop of London (1985)*

*For my wife Valerie*

# Acknowledgements

The author thanks and acknowledges the courtesy of the following for their kind permission to use copyright material:

The Bible Reading Fellowship for *The People of the Book*.
General Synod of the Church of England for Canon Law material; The Central Board of Finance for the quotation from *The Christian Stewardship of Money*; Her Majesty's Stationery Office for the Synodical Government Measure (No. 2); The University Presses of Oxford and Cambridge for quotations from the New English Bible; extracts from the Authorized Version of the Bible, which is Crown copyright, are used with permission; SCM Press Ltd for the quotation from *Ministry and Sacrament* (1937); Dr Donald Coggan (formerly Archbishop of Canterbury) for quotations from his Enthronement Sermon at Canterbury Cathedral, and also his Christmas Sermon 1977; Hodder and Stoughton, for the quotation from *Convictions* (1975) by Dr Donald Coggan; SPCK for the quotation from *Ministry and Ordination – an Agreed Statement of the Anglican–Roman Catholic International Commission* (1973) and the Lambeth Conference Encyclical Letter (1958).

The author also wishes to thank the following for their kind help – Mr Derek Pattinson, Secretary-General of General Synod; Mr Brian Hanson, Legal Adviser to General Synod; Barbara England, formerly Publishing Manager of the Church Information Office, and the members of the CIO Publishing Committee.

The following read the manuscript, and the author also wishes to thank them for their kind help and comments – The Right Reverend B. J. Masters, Lord Bishop of Edmonton; The

Reverend Canon George Smith, Rector of Leckhampton, Cheltenham; The Reverend Malcolm Grey, Vicar of Holy Trinity, Winchmore Hill, London.

The author is very grateful to the following for their helpful comments on the typescript of the third edition: Mr Brian Hanson, Legal Adviser to General Synod; Mr Tim Robinson, Secretary of the Central Board of Finance; Miss Alice Wilkinson, Secretariat of the Church Commissioners; Mr Robin Stevens, Central Stewardship Officer of the Church of England; Mr Martin Howe, Commissioner of the Royal School of Church Music; Mr Jonathan Goodchild, of the Council for the Care of Churches.

Last, but not least, is to acknowledge the considerable help from Mrs Ruth McCurry and Miss Fiona McKenzie of Mowbray, and also Ms Ann Grindrod and Mr Stephen Ryan, and to record the author's thanks to them too.

**Note**   The legislation resulting from the vote of General Synod in favour of the ordination of women to the priesthood is not covered by this revision.

# Opening Prayers

PCC members meet together to do God's work. For this reason, we seek his will and guidance for our daily lives and all the items on the PCC agenda. Prayer also helps to provide a spiritual setting and a Christian atmosphere for the meeting. It is helpful if PCC members as a group can grow together in the faith. Dr Donald Coggan (former Archbishop of Canterbury) wrote, 'The most important part of your PCC meetings is that unhurried period of quiet thought and prayer which precedes the time you give to consideration of the agenda — when you wait on God to discover His mind and will for the parish.'

**Three suggestions**  One of the following is suggested to achieve this 'unhurried period of quiet thought and prayer' before the meeting, and to help the PCC to be the Body of Christ in the parish:

(1) Eucharist
(2) Evensong (from 'O Lord, open our lips')
(3) A simple form of prayer as below, taken by a lay person:

| | |
|---|---|
| *Leader* | In the name of the Father, and of the Son, and of the Holy Spirit. |
| *All* | Amen. |
| *Leader* | O Lord, come to our aid and hear our prayer. |
| *All* | Give us grace to draw near with praise, and to bless your holy name. |
| *Leader* | Glory be to the Father, and to the Son, and to the Holy Spirit, |
| *All* | As it was in the beginning, is now, and ever shall be, world without end. Amen. |
| *Leader* | *(If prayer books are available)* |

You are invited to say the even verses of Psalm number
_____ making a pause at each colon.
(*When no prayer books are available*)
John Smith will say alternate verses of Psalm number
_____ with me.
*Or*: I will read from Psalm number _____.

Suggested psalms (or the psalms appointed for Evensong – or choose your own).

|  | Even years | Odd years |
|---|---|---|
| April | 23 and 32 | 89, verses 1–18 |
| May | 37, verses 1–11, 40–41 | 91 |
| June | 39 | 92 |
| July | 40, verses 1–13 | 95 and 96 |
| September | 45 | 97 and 99 |
| October | 47 and 48 | 103 |
| November | 62 and 63 | 116 |
| December | 67 | 119, verses 1–16 |
| January | 75 | 121 and 124 |
| February | 84 and 85 | 133 and 138 |
| March | 16 and 20 | 86 |

**Suggested Scripture readings** An alternative: you could choose your own, for there are many other suitable readings. Another suggestion: use the Evensong readings from the lectionary, or the readings for next Sunday's Service.

| March | Exodus 18.13–23 | Ephesians 4.1–16 |
|---|---|---|
| April | Joshua 1.1–9 | Ephesians 6.10–20 |
| May | Isaiah 6.1–8 | Philippians 2.1–11 |
| June | Isaiah 40.1–8 | Colossians 1.3–14 |
| July | Ezekiel 2.1–10 | Colossians 3.12–17 |
| September | Ezekiel 34.1–10 | 2 Timothy 2.1–13 |
| October | Hosea 11.1–11 | Hebrews 10.19–25 |
| November | Joel 2.12–17 | James 1.19–27 |
| December | St Matthew 9.35–38 | 1 Peter 2.1–10 |
| January | St Luke 14.15–24 | 1 John 1.1–10 |
| February | St John 13.1–17 | 1 John 4.7–16 |

*Leader either* We share five minutes' silence thinking about the meaning of the Scripture reading.
*or* We now have a short exposition by John Smith to draw out the meaning for us.
*This will be followed by a short silence.*

*One of the canticles can be used here.*

*Leader* Lord, have mercy upon us.
*All* Christ, have mercy upon us.
*Leader* Lord, have mercy upon us.

| | |
|---|---|
| *Leader* | Let us pray for the coming of the Kingdom, here, and throughout the world.<br>As our Saviour taught us, so we pray,<br>Our Father . . . |
| *Leader* | Let us ask for God's forgiveness for our sins,<br>for any lack of loyalty and commitment,<br>for our failures to share his love with others,<br>and for any lack of love and the presence of jealousy in our meetings. |
| | *Pause* |
| | Lord, in your mercy, hear our prayer. |
| *All* | Forgive our sins and give us your healing love. |
| *Leader* | We ask God to bless and prosper the work and witness of the Church in this parish and this deanery.<br>We ask for the help and guidance of the Holy Spirit for each item on the agenda.<br>We pray for ourselves, and for all other church councils meeting this evening. |
| *All say* | Eternal God and Father, you sent your Spirit to the Church at Pentecost:<br>renew your gift of the same Spirit in your servants gathered here in this place;<br>help us faithfully to seek your will in all things,<br>and to show your love by our words and actions,<br>through Jesus Christ our Lord, Amen. |

*One or more of the following prayers*

| | |
|---|---|
| *Leader* | Gracious God and Father, you have gathered us together for the praise of your glory;<br>pour out your grace on the Church and help us by the power of your Spirit to share in the ministry of your Son.<br>We ask this in the name of our Lord and Saviour Jesus Christ. |
| *All* | Amen. |
| *Leader* | God our Father, you have called us all to serve you in the family of your Church on earth:<br>help us by your Spirit to fulfil the work to which you have called us all, through Jesus Christ our Lord, |
| *All* | Amen. |
| *Leader* | Go before us, O Lord, in all our doings with thy most gracious favour, and further us with thy continual help; that in all our works, begun, continued, and ended in thee, we may glorify thy holy name, and finally by thy mercy obtain everlasting life; through Jesus Christ our Lord, |
| *All* | Amen. |
| *Leader* | Remember, O Lord, what thou hast wrought in us, and not what we deserve, and as thou hast called us to thy service, make us worthy of our calling, through Jesus Christ our Lord, |
| *All* | Amen. |
| *Leader* | Teach us, good Lord, to serve thee as thou deservest; to give and not to count the cost; to fight and not to heed the wounds; |

to toil and not to seek for rest; to labour and not to ask for any reward, save that of knowing that we do thy will; through Jesus Christ our Lord,

*All*     Amen.

**Prayers after the meeting**  Many prayers are suitable. The closing prayers may be taken by a lay person (using the Grace instead of the Blessing).

*Priest*     God our Father, you sent your Son to bring us new life in your love:

*All say*     O Lord God, when thou givest to thy servants to endeavour any great matter, grant us also to know that it is not the beginning, but the continuing of the same, until it be thoroughly finished, which yieldeth the true glory, through him who for the finishing of thy work laid down his life for us, our Redeemer, Jesus Christ,

*All*     Amen.

*Priest*     The Lord be with you,

*All*     and also with you.

*Priest*     The Blessing. (*or* The Grace.)

# A

**About this ABC**  This book gives, in easy-to-read language, the legal duties and responsibilities of PCC members and the priest (*see* pages 136–40). It offers practical and spiritual suggestions, and a variety of ways in which PCC members can help with the work of the Church.

Can you improve any of the things you are doing already? Are there any new ideas and challenges for your parish? Every parish is unique in its own needs and expectations and membership. What will work in one parish will not work in the next.

Every parish differs in size, churchmanship, and in the stage of development it has reached. Practical suggestions are given to help 'ordinary' parishes with the life and work of the local church.

Serving on a PCC ideally requires a high degree of commitment, and also a willingness to learn about the work. It involves trying to work out what God wants for his Church. Above all, it involves acting and speaking in a Christian way at all times, and particularly at PCC meetings.

The *ABC* is not a perfect blueprint for every circumstance, but it offers a starting point from which to consider the situation in your parish. When contemplating action or change, the starting point should always be prayer.

The *ABC* contains ideas for what has been called 'pastoral evangelism' to build up the life and work of the Church.

*Question for discussion*
What is the Spirit saying to the Church in your parish?

**Action**  Most churches seem to collect at least a few people who are good at talking. Some will 'talk the hind leg off a

1

donkey' if given half a chance. We must of course be kind and loving to them, particularly if they are lonely. But a priest should ration the time spent in listening to these people, and it is far better to spend time in a more productive way, particularly with those who do not know the love of God. The Church certainly needs people who are capable of expressing their ideas at a meeting, but the Church also needs people who are willing to get on with the job. 'Only be sure that you act on the message and do not merely listen' (James 1.22). Also 'A man may think he is religious, but if he has no control over his tongue, he is deceiving himself' (James 1.26 NEB). 'Not everyone who says, Lord, Lord, shall enter the Kingdom of God, but only he who does the will of my Father, who is in heaven.'

Empty vessels make the most sound, and actions speak louder than words. When discussing who should be invited to join the catering committee, one lady once said, 'We want a mover – not a talker'. God calls us to go out and work in his vineyard. A faith without good works is a dead faith. In the last prayer of the ASB Eucharist, we ask God to send us out in the power of his Spirit to live and work to his praise and glory. Then, at the dismissal, the priest exhorts us to go in peace to love and serve the Lord.

On their spiritual journey, many people respond to God's love for us in three main stages. First of all, we are usually attracted to Jesus Christ as a person. Then we discover the Church, and how we are all involved in the life of God's Church through our Baptism. Finally we realize that God wants all members of his Church to share in the work of extending his kingdom in the world.

God so loved the world that he gave his only Son to die on the cross. Part of our response to his love can be to offer back a proportion of our time and skills to do his work (*see Stewardship of time* and *Stewardship of skills* on page 38).

*Food for thought*
When someone really is extremely talkative, perhaps two questions might be asked: (1) Is this important? (2) Is it urgent?

**Additional Curates Society**  ACS is an important agent for mission and evangelism in England and Wales, in a number of ways. ACS pays and prays for curates in parishes which are not able to provide the money for this purpose. ACS encourages and fosters vocations to the sacred ministry, and organizes conferences for those who believe they may have a vocation. ACS arranges 'parish placements' in various parishes around the country where those who feel they might have a vocation can spend time in a parish (from three months to three years) to explore their call to the priesthood, to help in parish work, and to receive whatever academic or other help they need.

Although of Tractarian (High Church) foundation, ACS has always supported parishes of all shades of churchmanship. There are only three conditions: (1) there is a financial need; (2) the curate must be licensed by the bishop; (3) the curate lives and works full time in the parish. Most dioceses in England and Wales have an honorary ACS secretary but the backbone of the work is done by the ACS parish secretaries. Many parishes and individuals give regular financial support, and receive the ACS magazine twice a year. ACS publishes a wide variety of liturgical and devotional material and undertakes printing for PCCs and individuals. Send for details and a free catalogue and magazine from The Additional Curates Society, Gordon Browning House, 8 Spitfire Road, Birmingham B24 9PB. Tel: 021-382 5533.

**Addresses – useful**   *See* pages 208-10.

**Administration**   Every parish is a highly complex community which has to be administered. Unfortunately, not everyone is a born organizer. The church, the church hall, possibly a school and numerous church organizations all have to be looked after. Volunteers with appropriate skills have to be found and guided to the right place. Efficient administration is important in every aspect of parish life, and it can save much time and money and prevent chaos and aggravation. Administration is not the main job of the priest, and it takes up time which can be used in better ways. The Church exists to worship God and to extend his kingdom in the world. Administration is not an end in itself, but only a means to achieve these ends. But administration has to be done by someone, so that the mission and pastoral care and worship are not surrounded by inefficiency (*see* **Delegation** on page 66 and **Secretary for the priest** on page 173).

*Questions for discussion*
Some parishes (an increasing number of parishes?) now have a

paid administrator. Would that be possible in your church? If much of the administration falls to the lot of the priest, how can the standing committee or PCC help to share more of this work-load?

**Agenda** for the Annual Parochial Church Meeting is given on pages 4–8. The agenda for the PCC is given on pages 145–6.

**Annual meetings** The Vestry Meeting is usually held immediately before the Annual Parochial Church Meeting, but it can be held at another time (*see* **Vestry Meeting**, page 199, and **Churchwardens**, pages 52–3).

**Annual Parochial Church Meeting** A notice, signed by the minister to convene the meeting, must be displayed on the notice board for two Sundays before the meeting.

Who may attend? All on the electoral roll, and all licensed clergy. If the parish is part of a team or group ministry, the clergy from the other parishes may also attend. It is desirable to encourage as many as possible to come and hear about church activities and plans for the future, but only those on the roll may vote. It is a good idea, but not a legal requirement, to send a letter, inviting all on the electoral roll (and anyone else who might be encouraged to come) and giving the agenda (and perhaps last year's minutes, accounts and reports). If a contentious matter is on the agenda, it is obviously wise to invite only those who are legally entitled to be there, i.e. those with their names on the electoral roll.

The APCM is not a meeting which can make decisions. It can only make recommendations, and it elects PCC members to make decisions for the church. The APCM can, however, make certain decisions about the form of the elections and the number of people to serve on the PCC.

*Agenda for the APCM* Schedule 3 of the Synodical Government Measure 1969, para. 8.

(1) Opening prayers (Scripture reading and a hymn): *see* pages xi–xiv.
(2) Apologies for absence.
(3) Any Other Business. Many parishes ask for any items for this heading to be sent in writing to the PCC secretary three days before the APCM. These items are announced

at the beginning, and appropriate time can be allocated for them later on the agenda (see Item 18 below).

(4) Minutes of the previous year's APCM.

(5) Matters arising from the minutes.

(6) The Vicar's Report. It can be given at this point of the agenda or as the last item on the agenda (see Item 19 below). There is no legal requirement for a report to be given, but it is an opportunity which priests use to good advantage for three purposes: (a) to review the last year; (b) to thank those who have served in various ways; and (c) to present a plan or vision for the coming year. It might include a review of attendance at worship, and comparison with the numbers of the electoral roll etc. One of the church-wardens usually proposes a vote of thanks afterwards.

(7) Report on the electoral roll (see pages 69–70 about when the roll is displayed on the notice board). The electoral roll officer reports on: (a) the number of names on the roll; (b) the number of names added; (c) the number of names removed. The meeting can discuss the roll, and make recommendations to the PCC, but the APCM cannot add or remove a name from the roll.

(8) Report on the proceedings of the PCC (usually done by the PCC secretary).

(9) Report on the financial affairs of the parish. The Steward-ship Report can be presented here (with average donation per person, the number of covenants, and those not cove-nanted). Missionary giving can be included, remem-bering that each PCC is asked to practise stewardship by giving 10 per cent of its gross income to the Church overseas (*see Donations made by the PCC* under **Finance** on page 77). It is a good idea to show this figure and the gross income of the PCC for former years to measure progress.

(10) Audited PCC Accounts. The meeting can discuss the accounts, ask questions and make recommendations to the PCC, but it cannot alter them. When adopted by the meeting, the accounts are signed by the chairman and displayed on the notice board for a further fourteen days. A vote of thanks is usually proposed for the treasurer and the two auditors.

(11) Audited statement of the funds and property in the hands of the PCC (if any).

(12) Report on the fabric, goods and ornaments of the church. The churchwardens present the annual fabric report. *See*

**Buildings** on pages 22–30, and also **Churchwardens** on page 49.

Those at the meeting will be much involved in raising the money for repairs and they will want to be assured that the buildings have been properly looked after during the past year, and that full inspections were carried out with due care and attention. *See* the recommendations under **Buildings** on pages 23–4.

The annual fabric report should show the following:

(a) The inspections in the official checklist on the log book have all been carried out, and each item initialled and the date entered in the log. This includes inspection of all gutters, downpipes, gullies and drains; a check for beetle activity in roof timbers, organ chamber and elsewhere; inspection of electrical installations, wiring, plumbing and the heating system.

(b) The quinquennial report recommendations dated . . . are now completed (or will be completed by . . .).

(c) All repair work done last year has been recorded in the log book, signed and dated. A faculty was obtained for this (*see Faculties* under **Buildings** on pages 29–30).

(d) Goods and ornaments are correct and as recorded in the inventory and terrier. The following repairs/replacements are needed (*see* page 25).

(e) The church has a full comprehensive insurance policy for £. . . . If not, state the position. Is it index-linked? When was it last revised? Permission to rebuild after a fire is not given automatically, especially if the PCC did not have adequate insurance cover. Any financial help from diocesan funds may be withheld if the church is not properly insured (*see* **Insurance** on pages 100–2).

(f) Report on the church hall and future repairs.

(13) Deanery Synod report, given by a lay representative.

(14) Deanery Synod election – every third year only. Those elected are *ex-officio* members of the PCC. What is involved? Attend all Synod meetings – there are usually between three and five per year. (If you are unable to attend, arrange for someone else to go in your place as an observer if this is the system in your deanery.) Report back to the next PCC about the proceedings of the Deanery Synod, and also any future Synod business. Occasionally

it happens that a PCC will pass a resolution and ask that it be debated at Deanery Synod, and this would involve the Deanery Synod representatives of the parish.

(15) Election of the PCC. It is helpful to ask for nomination forms to be completed well before the meeting. In this way, the names for the election can be photocopied or duplicated on a list before the meeting. But it should be noted that nominations can be accepted at the meeting. Two tellers are appointed, whose job it is to count the votes cast for each candidate. The results are obviously announced as soon as possible during the meeting, and the list of elected and *ex-officio* members of the PCC must also be put on the church notice board for fourteen days by the PCC secretary.

Some parishes have a time of prayer and silence before the election and after the results are announced.

Announce date of ceremony to welcome the new PCC and churchwardens (usually done during the main Sunday service). *See* pages 53–4. *See* also *What is expected of me if I become a member of the PCC?* on pages 9–11.

How many PCC members should there be? There is no legal advice given on this, and some feel that a small number of committed PCC members is far better than a larger PCC which does not take its responsibilities seriously. On the other hand, those who are not so committed could be influenced and encouraged by those who are more committed to the work of the Church.

The actual number of members to be elected must be the same as in the previous year. The number can be altered by a resolution at the APCM, but this cannot take effect until the next APCM twelve months later. It is most unwise for the PCC at its first meeting to co-opt those who were not elected at the APCM. That would defeat the whole purpose of having an election, and go against the wishes of those at the meeting. Surely the Holy Spirit is at work in church elections?

The APCM may pass a resolution that one-third of the members of the PCC shall retire each year. In this case, the longest serving members shall retire first. The meeting may decide that no lay-person may serve continuously on the PCC for more than a certain number of years, and also the number of years before those concerned can stand for re-election. New blood can often work wonders on a PCC which is in a parochial rut!

(16) Election of sidesmen and sideswomen. *See* **Sidesmen** on pages 178–81. They are elected every year, and anyone whose name is on the electoral roll is eligible to be elected.

Some people like to cling on to a job when they are elderly. Indeed, it is good for elderly people to be able to have a job in the Church. However, some elderly sidesmen who are regular worshippers may think it is important for them to stand down, so that younger men and women can take their place – provided always that there are younger people available.

(17) Appointment of two auditors. They must not be members of the PCC. *See Auditors* on page 73.

(18) Any Other Business. This item is part of the legal agenda at the APCM (but not at a PCC meeting). Church Representation Rules state: 'Any person entitled to attend the annual meeting may ask any question about parochial church matters, or bring about a discussion of any matter of parochial or general church interest, by moving a general resolution or by moving to give any particular recommendation to the Council in relation to its duties.'

Some parishes ask for written notice about any matter to be raised at the APCM to be given a few days before the meeting. Other parishes ask at the beginning of the APCM if there are any matters to be raised at the end of the meeting under this section. They can then be listed, and time provided for them at the end.

After the legal agenda has been duly completed, the opportunity may be made to discuss a particular subject, perhaps inviting a diocesan or other speaker to the meeting.

(19) The Vicar's Report. There is no legal requirement for a report to be given by the vicar, but it is a good opportunity which most use to advantage. There are usually three parts: (a) to review the past year (including perhaps comparison of numbers at worship with the numbers on the electoral roll); (b) to thank those who have served in various ways; and (c) to present a plan or vision for the coming year.

The churchwardens usually propose a vote of thanks afterwards for the vicar – and the curates and NSM or semi-retired priests.

*Unpleasant meetings* These do happen when one or two unpleasant people use the APCM to cause trouble and stir up strife. This is not good for the Church, and if any new people or fringe members are present, they could well be put off the Church for the rest of their lives! 'How these Christians love one another!'

Three thoughts to help in this situation: (1) A member of the PCC or a warden could say firmly, 'This is rather an un-Christian note to bring into our meeting. I suggest that it should be considered at the next PCC meeting, or by the vicar and wardens'. Then ask the meeting if they agree with this suggestion; (2) Praying about the meeting for two or three weeks before the APCM. Also ask individuals to pray silently during the actual meeting. If the meeting does turn unpleasant, someone might say 'We need to remember that this is a meeting of God's Church, and we are called by on God to act in a Christian way'. The chairman could ask the warden to read 1 Corinthians 13, to be followed by a short silence and prayer; (3) *See* **Trouble-maker** on page 197.

*What is expected of me if I become a member of the PCC?* Much indeed is expected of each and every PCC member. No one should stand for election unless he or she clearly understands what is required of them. The PCC is unlike any secular committee because it has a mixture of pastoral, missionary, spiritual, financial and legal responsibilities. Membership of the PCC involves:

(a) Acceptance of the responsibilities laid down in the Synodical Government Measure 1969 relating to PCCs, and the other legal responsibilities involved. *See* pages 135–51.
(b) Attend all PCC meetings, and make sure that these meetings have first claim on your time before any secular meeting or social function. Most PCCs meet on a set day every month, e.g. the first Tuesday of the month, except August (see Hebrews 10.24–25).
(c) The PCC has a duty to discuss all matters which affect the life of the parish. Take part in the discussions at the actual meeting, rather than in the car-park afterwards. Ask yourself, 'What does God want us (me) to do in this situation?' Then be willing to vote accordingly. Be open to the leading of the Holy Spirit.
(d) After the vote, action is usually required by PCC members.

Be willing to offer your help. If you voted against the resolution which is passed by the majority, where do you stand as a result? Even if you voted against the resolution, are you big enough and thus able to support the views of the majority? Do you join the others for the sake of unity and corporate loyalty, and for the good of the Church? Or do you sit back and take no action? (Or do you resign?) Obviously, much will depend on the circumstances.

(e) The function of the PCC includes 'co-operation with the incumbent . . .'. The Church is not helped unless there is a genuine desire and commitment for each PCC member to work together with the priest for the good of the Church.

(f) PCC members are asked to co-operate with the incumbent 'in the whole mission of the Church, pastoral, evangelistic, social and ecumenical'. This is clearly the responsibility of all who allow their names to be put forward for election to the PCC, and not simply those who like that kind of thing (*see* **Mission – Evangelism – Renewal** on pages 113–19).

(g) Courage is sometimes needed to speak the truth boldly at a meeting, but always with love. Loyalty to the Church, to the priest and to the other members of the PCC are all highly desirable qualities in PCC members. Where does your loyalty really lie?

(h) Love is required of every PCC member, both for God and for your neighbour in its widest meaning. This includes learning to love those who have been difficult at PCC meetings.

(i) Take your spiritual life seriously, and adopt a rule of life which is appropriate for one who is to be a lay representative on the PCC. Priority to prayer is vital for every PCC member. No one can act and speak as a member of the Body of Christ unless they take prayer and Bible reading seriously, and receive Holy Communion at least every Sunday. PCC members should regard Sunday worship as a 'day of obligation' and not even unexpected visitors should keep them from coming to worship on Sunday morning (*see* **Spiritual life**, pages 182–94).

(j) The PCC is responsible for the repair, upkeep and insurance of the Church and other parish buildings. *See* **Insurance**, pages 100–2.

(k) The PCC must ensure that the church has an adequate income. Legally speaking, the debts of the PCC are not the personal responsibility of individual PCC members beyond the funds belonging to the church. They obviously have a responsibility to do what they can to ensure that the morale of the congregation is good, and that the money comes in regularly. *See* **Christian stewardship** on pages 37–42.

The PCC members are 'jointly responsible' with the incumbent for the expenditure of PCC funds. *See* **Finance**, pages 72–83.

(l) Take seriously the words of St Paul, 'Know the reason for the faith within you'. Read a Church newspaper or magazine every week, e.g. the *Church Times* or *Church of England Newspaper*. When did you last read a religious book?

(m) The most important part of every PCC member's job is to follow our Lord's command: 'Seek ye first the kingdom of God'.

In some parishes, the PCC secretary reads out these thirteen recommendations for PCC members before the election each year.

**'Any Questions?'**   An enjoyable evening with three or four carefully selected speakers for the panel, perhaps including an atheist/agnostic/humanist, a trade union official or local government councillor. A good chairman is needed. The event is an ideal opportunity to invite fringe members and people not connected with the Church. All present will no doubt be exposed to some Christian reasoning. Refreshments make a welcome end to the evening.

**Archdeacon**   The archdeacon is appointed to carry out legal and administrative functions in a large area called an archdeaconary, on behalf of the bishop and the diocese. The duties of an archdeacon include (1) Seeing that each parish looks after its buildings and the parsonage house; (2) The general discipline of the clergy; (3) Inducting a new priest to a parish – to show that the priest legally has control and possession of the church and the parish; (4) Carrying out parish visitations (inspections), which are often delegated to the rural (area) dean; (5) Admitting the churchwardens to their office every year; (6) Organizing the Quinquennial Inspection of Churches to be carried out by the appropriate architect; (7) Carrying out various legal and financial duties, and sitting on the Diocesan Advisory Committee, which deals with faculties.

**Archives** The Church includes those who are alive at this present time and also those who have worshipped and served God in former generations. Every parish has its own story and there is usually a sense of community and continuity with those who have gone before. Thus it is a good idea to keep relevant documents, newspaper cuttings, cassettes and photographs. It is a good reminder to those who see photographs of former priests in the vestry (or wherever they are displayed) to pray for the former shepherds of the parish.

There is all the difference in the world between a systematic collection and a mass of clutter and junk on top of a dusty cupboard in the vestry!

**Area dean** *See* **Rural dean** on pages 169–70.

**Arrive early** It is discourteous and distracting to others to arrive late for a meeting or service, and you certainly cannot be properly prepared for worship if you arrive in a hurry. It is good to be early so that you can settle down before the meeting or service begins.

**Arrow prayers** *See* **Spiritual life of PCC members** on page 186.

**Association of Church Fellowships** The ACF exists throughout the Anglican Communion, and the Archbishops of Canterbury and York are the patrons. Membership is not confined to church members, and it is open to all who wish to join, men, women and young people.

ACF offers friendship, and its programmes include some teaching of the Christian faith. ACF seeks to make the worshipping community into a fellowship of friends, and through this, to bring others into the family of the Church. ACF seeks to foster Christian fellowship, and to strengthen the lives of its members through prayer and study, and this is designed to lead on to Christian action, witness and service in the community. Each ACF group develops to suit its own needs in the parish. ACF is linked by deanery and diocesan groups. The headquarters of ACF is at Bickenhill House, 154 Lode Lane, Solihull, West Midlands B91 2HP. Tel: 021–704 9281.

ACF can supply stationery and publicity material, and an attractive range of its goods are available for sale, which help local groups with publicity and finance. There is a link association with a regular newsletter for members who are local, single and isolated. Each year, ACF chooses a 'charitable project' and all ACF branches are asked to support this appeal.

To start an ACF group, consult the General Secretary at the above address.

**Baptism**  A request for Baptism presents every church with a wonderful opportunity for evangelization. It is an opportunity because the request comes from the parents, and not from the Church. Obviously, the family has been inspired by God (through someone) to ask for Baptism, and this inspiration needs to be encouraged, in order to draw the family into the Church community. (Perhaps the art of fishing comes to mind?) A request for Baptism is not an opportunity to raise barriers, but to show them the love of God, for this is what attracts people to the Church.

Every priest and parish will have their own method of dealing with a request for Baptism. It is an area where lay-people can help, either in the preparation, or the follow-up afterwards (or both).

One method is to have a Baptism Preparation Group. It will need careful selection and training. A video/sound cassette with slides can be useful in the preparation of the parents. Appropriate literature, whether bought or home-produced, is needed to give to the parents. Various short films and booklets are available on Baptism, or perhaps the parish could produce its own video.

The rubric in the ASB states: 'Holy Baptism is normally administered by the parish priest in the course of public worship on Sunday.' In this way, the newly baptized can be welcomed by the whole congregation into the fellowship of the church. When a godparent cannot get to the service in time because they are coming from a distance, then it is possible for someone to stand in as proxy in their absence. Afternoon baptisms have been described as secretive and hole-in-the-corner affairs. Most parishes seem to avoid them, and obey the rules by having baptisms in the main Sunday service.

It is a good investment for the PCC to give to the family a Baptism candle and candle-holder (which will not collapse if the baby sits on it). This is a reminder of an important event in the life of their child.

Some parishes ask for sponsors from the congregation. One parish sponsor is allotted to each family as an unofficial fourth godparent. The sponsor attends the preparation, and gets to

13

know the family. It is helpful to give the godparent cards to the family at the time of the actual Baptism. But the sponsor can visit the family later in the week and deliver the Baptism card at the same time. This follow-up is a good opportunity to talk about the church and its activities.

Each sponsor follows up the baby and family in the years to come, and this can include delivering a birthday card. Perhaps the parish could produce a suitable letter to send with the card at each succeeding birthday. The parents and children can be invited to special events at the church, socials, mother and toddler group, pram services, and Sunday School. The most important thing that the sponsor can do is to be steadfast in prayer for the child and the family, day by day, continuing until confirmation, marriage and beyond. . . . 'More things are wrought by prayer than this world dreams of' (Tennyson).

**Bereavement**   The Church is in a privileged position to help the bereaved, and this is both a heavy responsibility and a unique opportunity for mission. PCC members and other Christians can help to support the bereaved, and perhaps on occasion share in the mission of the Church to the bereaved. Present-day Western society expects people to get over their grief in a short time. Neighbours and family usually rally round for three or four weeks, but this type of caring does not continue indefinitely. After a while, people simply do not want to know about grief. Sadly, there are also those who have no relatives and friends to provide this support in the first place.

The priest always visits the family before the funeral, but usually pressure of work does not allow time for a follow-up visit in most cases. The opportunity for lay-people to help is there in every parish. Lay-people can do a great deal, both for the bereaved and also for the Church. Careful selection is vital, particularly in not choosing any who have themselves suffered a bereavement in the last two years. The diocese or the deanery may be able to help with the necessary training.

Every parish will no doubt develop its own way of providing a support group. Here are a few thoughts on the subject:

(a) The initial opening comes through the vicar, who can ask the bereaved if they would like a visitor from the church to call in a few days time. The visitor can bring a copy of the Funeral Address at the same time.
(b) On the whole, the visitor is not usually asked difficult

questions about the Christian faith. It is usually a matter of listening to the bereaved talking about the one who has died. It often involves listening to the same thing more than once, and tears are not uncommon. Tears are all part of the healing process. Tremendous patience is required, but in course of time the bereaved will work through the grief, and trust and friendship can be built up.

(c) Each visitor must be sensitive and aware of the different stages of grief. These frequently include guilt, anger, fear, resentment, and a feeling of hopelessness and deep grief itself.

(d) A number of visits may be needed over the coming weeks. The visitor has a double aim. The first is to help and comfort the bereaved; the second is to try to bring the bereaved into the Church, but this should never be hurried, particularly if the bereaved has no previous connection with the Church. Never try to jump in with Christian answers to death, but wait until the appropriate moment presents itself.

(e) Training is needed for the visitors, and this could be done on a parish basis – or perhaps by sharing with the next parish – or on a deanery basis.

(f) Those who have died are remembered each year in the Church Calendar on All Souls' Day – 2 November. This is an opportunity to invite all who have been bereaved to a special service, by either letter or personal visit, or both. Many bereaved people do find it helpful to share in this type of service. (Refreshments afterwards?)

(g) Above all, regular prayer is needed by the visitors (and every PCC member) on a long-term basis. 'Heavenly Father, you sent your Son to be our Redeemer: send your Holy Spirit to comfort all who are bereaved, and especially to _____ that he/she may come to know you and your love in your Son, Jesus Christ our Lord. Amen.'

*Letter to the bereaved*   This letter can be printed on the back of the Funeral Address. It can be kept on the word processor file. Usually only the name and date need altering each time it is used:

## Bereavement

From                                          Address

Phone                                         date

Dear

May I share with you some thoughts about the Christian faith? At a time of sadness, many find it helps to try to 'draw near to God'. Some people ask for a traditional Memorial Service (at the 10 a.m. Sunday service). We announce that it is a Memorial Service at the beginning, and appropriate prayers are offered later. If you would like a Memorial Service, please telephone, so that we can arrange a date.

Some psalms and Scripture readings you may find helpful:

| | |
|---|---|
| Psalm 23 | Isaiah 25, verses 8 and 9 |
| Psalm 121 | 1 Peter 1, verses 3–9 |
| Psalm 130 | St John 20, verses 1–9 |
| Psalm 27 | St John 14, verses 1–6 |
| Psalm 42, verses 1–7 | 1 Corinthians 15, 20–end |
| Psalm 118, verses 14–21 and 28–29 | St John 11, verses 25–26 |
| Psalm 139, verses 1–11 and 17–18 | |

You may wish to turn to God in a quiet time of prayer.
It is easier to pray after you have read from the Bible. Here are some suggestions:

(1) God our Father in heaven,
    you sent your Son to open the gate of eternal life:
        forgive us all our sins;
        send your Holy Spirit to comfort those who mourn;
        and, in your mercy, bring us at the last,
        together with our loved one _____
        and all our departed relatives,
        to the fullness of eternal life,
        through Jesus Christ our Lord. Amen.

(2) Our Father, who art in heaven . . . (written out in full)

(3) The prayer on the reverse side of this paper.

(4) The Grace of our Lord Jesus Christ, the love of God, and the fellowship of the Holy Spirit, be with us and with those we love, now and always. Amen.

It does help to read the Bible regularly. If you decide to do this, may I suggest a chapter a day (or less), starting at St Matthew, chapter 1, verse 18? A book-marker/postcard is useful to find the place. As you read, ask yourself two questions: 'Who is Jesus Christ?' and 'How can he help me now?'

On All Souls' Day, 2 November, the Church through the centuries has remembered the departed. We have a service at 7.30 p.m. on 2 November each year, and you are welcome to join us.

Many people go through different stages of bereavement including anger, guilt, and painful memories. If you would like to talk things over, please telephone me and we can arrange to meet again.

With best wishes.

***The Funeral Address***   This is kept on the word processor for people who have no connection with the Church. It can easily be altered as appropriate:

## JOHN SMITH
## RIP

Details of his or her life, work, hobbies, clubs, etc. are included here. The following ending occasionally needs altering:

We cannot see God. He does not show himself to us on the television screen. It is easy to forget God, with so many attractions competing for our attention. But the death of a loved one often prompts us to think deeply about the mysteries of life and death. And to help us, God sent his Son Jesus Christ to save us from our sins, and to open the way to eternal life. He created the Church to help us to know God in our earthly life, so that we don't meet him as an unknown stranger in the next life.

May you respond to God's love in Jesus Christ through his Church. May you find hope, comfort and strength in the risen Jesus Christ. May you come to know him, who is 'the Way, the Truth and the Life', and know him as Friend and Saviour.

We end with a prayer:

Heavenly Father,
in your Son Jesus Christ
you have given us a true faith and a sure hope.
Strengthen this faith and hope in us all our days,
that we may live as those who believe in
    the communion of saints,
    the forgiveness of sins,
    and the resurrection to eternal life,
through your Son Jesus Christ our Lord, Amen.

**Bible**  We need to work out the proper relationship between the Scriptures and the Church, and also between the Scriptures and mission and the social problems of modern society. The Holy Bible is a vital resource book for every PCC member, but there are problems and difficulties connected with it. How much is fact, how much myth or poetic writing? How accurate is it? In addition, many people outside the Church believe that science has disproved the Bible, and inside the Church, Christians hold at least two completely different views about it.

Some believe that the whole Bible is completely true and divinely inspired from beginning to end. It is for them the unerring word of God, correct to the last comma and full stop. Those who hold this view are called fundamentalists, and their faith in the Bible is absolute. They do not accept the discoveries and teachings of science, nor the work of biblical scholars, whenever these discoveries contradict what is actually written in the Bible.

The alternative view accepts the findings of science and scholarship, but at the same time firmly believes that the Bible contains the living word of God which is so vital for this present time. They hold that some parts of the Bible are more inspired and valuable than others, and that the Bible contains contradictions and inaccurate statements. (The author holds this latter view.)

Whichever view is held, it is vital that every PCC member should read the Bible regularly and systematically.

***Why do Christians read the Bible regularly?*** Life and conditions have changed very much since those primitive times when the Bible was written. So why is it vital for Christians today?

One answer is in the Epistle to the Hebrews: 'For the word of God is alive and active. It cuts more keenly than any two-edged sword, piercing as far as the place where life and spirit, joints and marrow, divide. It sifts the purposes and thoughts of the heart. There is nothing in creation that can hide from him; everything lies naked and exposed to the eyes of the One with whom we have to reckon' (Hebrews 4.12–13 NEB).

Another reason why the Bible is so vital is given by Saint Jerome. He said 'To be ignorant of the Bible is to be ignorant of Christ'.

The Bible strengthens faith, and gives a deeper knowledge of God's ways and purposes. It gives comfort and encouragement, and helps us to respond to the love of God. It educates the conscience. To achieve spiritual wholeness, Christians have to read the Bible and also to receive Holy Communion regularly.

***Individuals and the Bible*** The collect for Advent 2 is a prayer that we may 'read, mark, learn and inwardly digest' the Scriptures. Learn your way around your Bible, and have two or three book-markers in it. Get to know the contents of the Gospels and the New Testament letters (and also the great books of the Old Testament, such as Isaiah, Jeremiah and Ezekiel). If you spend ten or fifteen minutes regularly each day, it will still be the task of your lifetime even to know the contents of the New Testament. But it is a worthy objective for every PCC member (*see* **Spiritual life**, page 184).

Bible reading is not just a question of reading a passage. The Bible has so much more to give, but it will produce its riches only if you read it slowly. Read the passage again, thinking carefully about its meaning for you. This is one of life's most rewarding tasks – far more so than many other pursuits.

***Lent Bible Study Course*** It is helpful to hear other people's views and comments about a particular passage, and also to compare a passage of Scripture with a similar one. Much can be gained when a group of people meet regularly to study and to share each other's understanding, e.g. for a Lent Course.

Experience has shown that groups of eight work well. More than one group can always be formed. A leader is needed, whose task is to keep the discussions on the subject. The leader should have some understanding of the passage before the session starts. Everyone must be allowed to speak. Encourage some, and discourage others! Starting and finishing times should be prompt, incorporating a prayer.

The Bible Reading Fellowship and the Scripture Union both suggest questions for discussion in their booklets. The first meeting of the group(s) could take place in the church hall, or in church, after the Eucharist. Later, people may find it possible and desirable to meet in each other's homes in turn. Have refreshments (if any) after, and not during the discussion.

***Help in Bible reading*** The Bible is a book for adults. In other words, it is not easy to understand. There are two main organizations for guidance, and it is wise to select the one which fits in with your understanding of the Bible.

***The Scripture Union*** The policy of the SU clearly states, 'We believe in the divine inspiration and entire trustworthiness of Holy Scripture, and its supreme authority in all matters of faith and conduct.' It produces various daily readings and notes. Details from: Scripture Union House, 130 City Road, London EC1V 2NJ. Tel: 071–250 1966.

***The Bible Reading Fellowship*** The BRF also produces small booklets of daily readings with comment and a prayer, all on one page for each day. Appropriate notes are produced for different age groups, as is the case with the SU.

When he was Archbishop of Canterbury, Dr Donald Coggan wrote a commentary for the BRF film strip called *The People of the Book*. He said, 'I believe there are few things – if any – of more vital importance to the life and work of the Church than that its members should have an intelligent grasp of their faith, such a grasp as will enable them to pass it on with confidence and joy. This means a steady and careful study of the Bible by clergy and laity alike. It is for this that our BRF exists, and I would like to think that every parish had a branch actively at work.'

Further details from: The Bible Reading Fellowship, Peter's Way, Sandy Lane West, Oxford OX4 5HG. Tel: 0865–748227.

***The parish BRF or SU secretary***   The tasks of the secretary include:

1. Order the booklets and deliver them to the individuals concerned every three or four months;
2. Order a few spare copies for the bookstall or table in church;
3. Encourage new people to use the daily notes;
4. Pray for all who use the booklets.

*Questions for discussion*
1. Would it help the church in the parish if the PCC met for a Bible study – forming three or four groups – meeting in Lent, or monthly?
2. Is it better for the BRF/SU secretary to set up Bible study groups, or could this be done more effectively through the PCC?
3. Some basic understanding of group leadership is desirable – could this be provided by the diocesan education team?

**Bishop**   Two functions distinguish a bishop from an ordinary priest – the bishop administers the sacraments of Ordination and Confirmation.

Every bishop is consecrated by the Metropolitan Bishop of the province (i.e. an archbishop) together with two other bishops, who have themselves been duly consecrated in the same way.

A bishop is consecrated either to take charge of a diocese, or to be an area bishop, assistant bishop or suffragan bishop.

*Food for thought*
Do you pray for your bishop and the clergy of your deanery every day?

**Blessing a house**   *See* **Home** on page 97.

**Body of Christ**   The whole question of learning how to work together is being forced more and more on people in the secular world and in the Church. The crisis facing the Church has partly led to the rediscovery of the New Testament concept of the body of Christ. The Church – the whole people of God – forms the body of Christ, and it is a continuation and extension of the work of Christ himself, who said 'As the Father has sent me, even so send I you.' He also said 'Receive the Holy Spirit.' (St John 20.21, 22)

Every Christian is made a member of the mystical body of Christ by Baptism, but membership is not a reward for services rendered, nor for virtue. Christ took this kind of body because he has work for it to do. He had finished his part of God's work of salvation, perfectly completed in itself, and then he was taken into heaven. Salvation still has to be applied to the world in each succeeding generation. That is why Jesus needed another body to continue his work.

When a limb or organ stops working, the whole body then only limps through life, and other parts of the body have to work harder to compensate for dead areas which no longer function properly. The human body has many parts which function in different ways, and likewise in the body of Christ there is a diversity of function and ministry. Men and women are called within the total work of Christ, according to their abilities and temperaments, to serve in different ways in the mission of the Church and in the situation in which they work and pursue their leisure activities. Christians are always a part of the body of Christ, and the Holy Spirit equips the members with different gifts for the life and work of the whole body.

No single Christian has all the gifts, and no gift can function without the other gifts. God's work is carried on only by the harmonious co-operation of all members working together, with love (the greatest gift) binding all together in one body.

Read St Paul's words on the body of Christ in his letter to the Ephesians – 4.11–16.

*Question for discussion*
Is the body of Christ discernible in the parish?

**Bookstall**   In addition to a library, many parishes have a bookstall, whether books are sold only on Sunday after the main service, or throughout the week.

The church can apply to the Publishers Association,

21

19 Bedford Square, London W1B 3HJ to be registered as a
book agency. One or two bookshops have to be nominated on
the application form, and when the licence has been granted,
the books can be purchased at a discount – which is usually 10
per cent. This is not to raise money for church funds, but to help
the bookstall cover its costs. A wide range of attractive books
and booklets are available from various Christian publishers.

Two thoughts. What about an annual Book Fair or Book
Party? Good publicity and individual invitations are needed.

Useful addresses:

Christian Bookstall Managers Association, 17 Rowan Walk,
Crawley Down, Crawley, West Sussex RH10 4JP. Tel:
0342–715 889.

Bookstalls Newsletter, 11 Thorpe Chase, Ripon, North
Yorkshire HG4 1UA. Tel: 0765–602 907.

**Buildings**   Vast sums of money are spent each year to repair
and maintain church buildings. No PCC wants to be faced with
an enormous repair bill.

### Prevention is better than cure

Unfortunately, many problems with buildings usually creep up
on the PCC unnoticed until the costly damage has been done.
Constant vigilance is required. The PCC has been entrusted
with the care of these buildings which former generations of
Christians worked hard to provide and maintain. The careful
stewardship of buildings belongs to each successive generation
of PCC members.

The best way to avoid costly repair bills is to inspect the
buildings regularly. If this is done carefully and thoroughly by
the churchwardens – or by someone formally acting on their
behalf (as is required by the Care of Churches and Ecclesiastical
Jurisdiction Measure 1991) – it can save the PCC a great deal
of work and money. *See* **Churchwardens** on page 49.

### The fabric committee   Some parishes find it helpful to appoint
a small fabric committee (or building committee). If there are
any building experts in the parish, e.g. surveyors or architects,
it can be invaluable to have their advice. A free second opinion
is always useful.

Whether it is the churchwardens or the fabric committee who
look after the building, the key words are vigilance and prompt
action (via the due legal channels).

*Regular inspections and work*   Much needs to be done to look after a large building, especially if the church is an old one. A full, careful and detailed inspection of the entire church is required 'at least once every year'. The wording of the 1991 Measure implies that one inspection is the legal minimum. Much more than one inspection is needed, if proper care is to be taken of the building. The people responsible for finding the money would no doubt be much happier if regular inspections were carried out. The following suggestions are offered:

*Early in the year*
> Check the outside of the roof and make sure that no slates or tiles have slipped. Check on the inside of the roof to see that no water has been seeping through, particularly in the tower/spire.
> Check *all* gutters, valleys, hopper heads, down-spouts and drains. The best time to do this is during a heavy rainstorm! In this way, you can see where the problems exist. Dripping gutters can cause much damage.

*Spring*
> Carry out a full inspection of the whole church and prepare a report for the Annual Parochial Church Meeting.
> Check that the gutters, valleys, hopper heads, down-spouts and drains are all right after the frost. Check the roofs for any form of damage, whether from wind, frost, snow or other cause. Check the stonework and brickwork for damage after frost.
> Arrange for someone to clean out the gutters, hopper heads, down-spouts and drains. Also all ventilation holes. Cut down all vegetation on the walls of the church, and apply weed-killer as required until it is completely dead. Clean out the tower/spire, and check the birdproofing mesh. Arrange for a thorough spring clean of the church, including a washing of the windows.
> Carefully inspect all woodwork, and particularly on the inside of the organ, and the roof timbers, to see if someone has been having a nibble! All exposed timber, both inside and outside, should be painted with a wood preservative every fifth year, including the eaves and the woodwork in the tower/spire. Death-watch beetle, woodworm, wet and

23

dry rot, all need professional advice and prompt action through the church architect.

*Summer*

Arrange for annual service of central heating system.
Check for leaks and bleed the radiators.
Check for any signs of dry rot, fungus, or signs of damp on the walls or ceilings, and particularly for any swelling in the plaster.
Make sure that there is good lagging to protect all pipes and tanks from the frost.

*Autumn*

Leaves will need removing from the gutters, drains, etc. in the late autumn.
Check all gutters and the entire rainwater system. A few buckets of water and some ladders is one way of finding the problems – but an easier way is to inspect during a storm!
Clear out and check all drains, and rod them if necessary.
Check that the froststat is working properly.
Check all snowboards and creosote them.

*Winter*

Inspect the log book to see that the details of alterations carried out during the last twelve months were all fully recorded.

When there is a fall of snow, check in the tower/spire and any roof space to see if the snow has blown into the church. Remove all snow as soon as possible before it melts and causes damage. Only use a wood or plastic snow scraper – this avoids causing damage to the roof etc.
The lightning conductor needs checking every year.
All windows need washing, inside and out, every year. Not an easy task, except for giraffes!
All ventilators must be carefully checked.
Check and look after all boundary walls, fences and gates. Oil hinges and clean all locks each year.
Leaves, branches and roots from trees can cause problems. Extra vigilance is needed if there is a tree near the church. Should it be removed?
All electrical wiring and electrical equipment, the froststat

and the public address system should be professionally tested every fifth year, and each written report should be kept in the fabric committee files. Fires are usually caused by faulty wiring, particularly in the organ.

The above is a basic outline of the jobs which need to be done – whether by volunteers from the parish or by paying someone to do them for the church. Further information and help can be found in the book *How to Look After Your Church* published by Church House Publishing.

It is good to keep the PCC informed with a very brief fabric committee report at each meeting, and a fuller report when necessary. When detailed consideration is needed, the standing committee could be involved.

The fabric committee can work out how much money will be required for repairs and maintenance for the coming year, and provide an estimate for those who are preparing the annual budget in the late autumn each year.

**The duty of the churchwardens to record information**   Under the Care of Churches and Ecclesiastical Jurisdiction Measure 1991, it is the duty of the churchwardens, in consultation with the minister, to maintain a terrier, an inventory and a log book in accordance with the recommendations of the Council for the Care of Churches.

**The terrier and inventory**   A terrier is a list of lands belonging to the church. An inventory is a record of all the goods and possessions of the parish church and any chapels.

The churchwardens must send a copy of the inventory to the person chosen by the bishop as soon as practicable after it is compiled. They must notify this person of any alterations.

**The log book**   All alterations, additions and repairs to the church, the lands, and articles belonging to them, must be recorded in the log book. Also 'any other events' affecting them. The location of any documents must be given which relate to the alterations, additions, repairs and events – if they are not kept with the log book.

The churchwardens must deliver to the PCC, at the first meeting each year, the inventory and the log book which relate to the previous year, and any other records which will assist the PCC in its duties. They must be accompanied by a statement, signed by the two churchwardens, that the contents of the terrier, inventory and log book are accurate.

### The duty of the churchwardens in respect of the buildings

At least once every year, the wardens must inspect the buildings, and all articles belonging to the church. Alternatively, they must ask someone to do this on their behalf. The churchwardens must act in consultation with the minister in this inspection.

The churchwardens must give the annual fabric report, on the fabric and contents of the church, to the PCC meeting held before the Annual Parochial Church Meeting. The report must include all action taken during the year, and any proposed action for the future. In particular, it must include any recommendation made in the quinquennial report. The churchwardens must give the annual fabric report to the Annual Parochial Church Meeting on behalf of the PCC, and with any amendments made by the PCC.

*Maintenance and mission*   Looking after the church buildings can take up much of the PCC's time, unless the work is delegated to an effective and hard-working fabric committee. Maintaining the building properly is vital, but the question needs asking – Does maintenance hinder the mission of the local church? Maintenance could certainly hinder mission, unless it is delegated. But, on the other hand, the building is a symbol of worship and mission to those who do not belong. For church members, it is the place where they worship and receive inspiration for mission. For outsiders, the building is a silent spiritual witness to the living faith which has endured through the centuries. The building can be a powerful tool in evangelism in various ways, and it can be a focus and symbol for the local community. It is a shrine or sacred place which many seem to want or need, even though they may never come to worship there. Many feel that 'something' is enshrined in the building that is 'life' and which has a sense of eternal changelessness. Security, of course, comes not from the building, but from what it contains – ultimately the benefits of our Lord's death and resurrection. Much goodwill often exists towards the building, and the PCC has to try to channel this interest towards our Creator.

There is a saying: people matter more than buildings. There is truth in this, but buildings are also important, particularly for mission. What really matters is to have the correct relationship between buildings and people, and to encourage enough people to worship and to maintain the church for the future.

*State aid*   The ancient parish churches are a major part of our national heritage, and many things of artistic or historic interest have been gathered in them through the centuries. Parliament has acknowledged (1978) the historic value of ancient churches and the problems of maintaining them. State aid is available for certain categories of historic churches, and details about it and other grants are available from the archdeacon.

*Can more use be made of your church building?*   Many churches are only used for a limited time each week – and on one day only in some parishes. Are there other ways in which the building could be used to help the work of the Church? In thinking about this, we have to get our theology correct. Life is not divided into two separate compartments – sacred and secular. The whole of life is created by God, belongs to God and will one day return to God. It is wrong to think that only part of life (e.g. an hour on Sunday) belongs to God and that the rest has nothing to do with God. This may give new ideas about what can and cannot be done in a church building. Any event which will bring outsiders or fringe members in through the church doors is important. Music and drama, a competition for children speaking well-known passages of the Bible, a singing competition, appropriate films, a debate, exhibitions, a wave of prayer, conducted tours of the church?

*The fabric fund*   Most parishes make provision in the annual budget to put away a realistic sum of money into a fabric fund, over and above what is needed for the current maintenance and repairs. The Central Board of Finance has facilities for investing PCC funds at special rates, whether in equities or on deposit, and interest/dividends are paid without deduction of income tax. Details from the Central Board of Finance (*see* pages 74–5).

*Friends of the Church*   Many people are willing to contribute towards the cost of preserving and improving the church building, even though they have no wish to be involved in its life and worship. Some parishes have set up a 'body of friends' to attract financial support.

## Buildings

The friends have a separate constitution, bank account, annual meeting, annual church service, and perhaps a reception, lunch or tea. The constitution usually provides for a majority of church members on the committee. For example, on a committee of seven, three are elected by the AGM of the friends, one is elected by the PCC (or APCM) and three are *ex officio* – the incumbent and churchwardens. Advice can be obtained from The Council for the Care of Churches (address on page 31).

**Survey of churches (Canon F18)** Every three years, the archdeacon – or the area/rural dean acting on his behalf – inspects the church, the chancel and the churchyard. The archdeacon gives directions for any repair work which is needed on the fabric, ornaments or furniture of the church.

**Appointment of the church architect** The architect is chosen by the incumbent and PCC. If a new architect is to be appointed, always consult the archdeacon about the architects who are approved by the diocese to work on church buildings.

**The quinquennial inspection and report** All parish churches have to be inspected every five years by the church architect. The initial inspection and the quinquennial report are paid for by the diocese (or through a diocesan scheme). However, the PCC pays the architect's fees for any work done as a result of the quinquennial report, e.g. drawing up specifications, obtaining estimates, supervising, and inspecting the work at the end.

It is the archdeacon who instructs the architect to carry out the quinquennial inspection every five years. Well before this inspection, it is wise to ask the architect whether he requires a ladder or any other help. It is always a good idea for someone from the PCC to meet the architect. A copy of the quinquennial report is sent both to the PCC and to the archdeacon. The PCC should make a start on the recommendations in the report as soon as possible. A faculty will be required and the archdeacon will give advice about the matter. The PCC instructs the architect to prepare specifications and to obtain estimates from builders. Sometimes, immediate action is required, and in such a case, the archdeacon should be consulted as soon as possible.

The church hall and other property do not have to be inspected as a legal requirement under the Quinquennial Inspection of Churches Measure. But the PCC would be wise to instruct the architect to carry out a proper inspection on the hall and other property belonging to the parish at the same time as the quinquennial inspection is carried out on the church. (The vicarage is inspected every five years under a separate scheme.) It is also wise to have an inspection and written report on the electrical system for the hall every five years.

*Faculties* Church buildings are exempt from local government control. The Church exercises its own control through the faculty system. The diocesan bishop exercises control of all churches and their contents, and churchyards, through the diocesan chancellor, with the assistance of the archdeacon.

The chancellor delegates uncontended applications to the archdeacon, provided there is unanimous agreement and the Diocesan Advisory Committee has approved the application.

No work can be carried out on a church without a legal faculty, whether in connection with the quinquennial report or any interim repairs. No changes can be made to the fabric or contents of the church without a faculty. The 'Visitation Questionaire', which is signed by the churchwardens each year, usually has a question about any work carried out on the church, and whether legal authority was obtained for it.

PCCs are sometimes irritated by this strict faculty procedure. The reason for having a faculty procedure is to keep the control of church buildings in the hands of church members. The alternative would be for people who are not members of the church (e.g. the local planning authority) to make decisions about what we can or cannot do in our church buildings. The faculty system protects the churches and their contents for future generations. It protects PCC members and the incumbent from criticism and legal action, as well as protecting the rights of individuals and parishioners.

*How to apply for a faculty* It is wise to seek the advice of the archdeacon at an early stage, and certainly before any action is taken. The Diocesan Advisory Committee usually has to be consulted, and the archdeacon is always a member of the DAC. The archdeacon also has considerable legal responsibilities in connection with church property. It may be helpful to invite the archdeacon to come to a PCC meeting. The archdeacon will usually have a good idea about how the DAC is likely to react to the proposals. The next step is to consult the DAC, which often sends a delegation to inspect the proposals at the church.

All correspondence and advice from the DAC has to be submitted with the faculty application to the chancellor (made through the diocesan registrar).

The chancellor does not have to accept the views of the DAC, but he will normally treat the expert advice of the DAC with great respect. The DAC can commend – or decline to commend – an application, but it cannot approve or turn it down. The chancellor is the person who makes the decision on the basis of the evidence which is produced with the application. The chancellor uses his discretion on a judicial basis, and personal likes and dislikes do not come into it.

When there is opposition to a faculty application, the chancellor always consults the DAC.

Who may apply for a faculty? Normally the incumbent and churchwardens are the petitioners, and they sign the form when the PCC is applying for a faculty. The numbers voting for and against the application, and abstentions, have to be recorded on the form.

Any individual with an interest is legally entitled to apply for a faculty without permission from anyone else.

An official notice, called the Citation, must be displayed on the notice board for a period of ten days, including two Sundays. The Citation comes from the registrar, and it gives details of the proposed works or changes. An address is given on the Citation, and anyone can send in a formal objection to the proposals within a period of ten days. When there are no objections, the faculty will be issued soon afterwards. When an objection is made, a Consistory Court is convened by the chancellor to deal with the matter. Legal costs are usually heavy, especially when barristers are involved, and thus it is wise to consider who will most probably have to pay the costs when an objection is made.

When work is undertaken without a faculty or written approval from the archdeacon, then the PCC has to apply for a confirmatory faculty. Full statutory fees are payable by the PCC, and also a written explanation is required about the circumstances. If any work is done without legal authority and a faculty would have been turned down if an application had been made, then the chancellor can give an order for the work to be undone. In this case, the cost of the work, and all legal expenses and fees, have to be paid for by those who were responsible for the illegal work being done in the first place.

**Council for the Care of Churches**   The CCC publishes books and information about looking after church buildings and their contents. Details from: The Council for the Care of Churches, 83 London Wall, London EC2M 5NA. Tel: 071-638 0971.

*Food for thought*

1. Does the PCC have a contract with a builder to clean out the gutters and drains for the church and the church hall (and the vicarage?) each spring and autumn?
2. Have the church buildings deteriorated – or improved – during the period for which you were a member of the PCC?

**Cassettes**   *See* **Videos** on page 201.

**Catering**   *See* **Hospitality** on pages 99–100.

**Changes in the parish**   God created the Church to bring the gospel to the world. In some ways, the Church has to change, but in other ways the gospel and the cross, the discipline of prayer, and many other things, are just the same as always. The PCC is usually dealing with the things which can and do change, without affecting those things which are eternal and unchanging.

To change or not to change is often a problem in a parish. It is natural to try to preserve those things which were successful in the past, but some things can outlive their usefulness, and now serve only to hinder the work of the Church. A job may have been done in the same way for many years, because no one has worked out a better way. The PCC – or the priest – may be in a rut with parochial blinkers. People often see changes from their own point of view, rather than ask the question 'What is best for God's Church? What would our Lord want in this situation?' No one in their right mind would want to change for change's sake. However, it is very desirable to change if that change will help God's work in the parish.

Some PCC members can cope quite well with change, and see changes as an opportunity for growth. PCC members are elected 'to co-operate with the incumbent in the whole mission of the Church' and this requires them to be forward-looking, and sometimes to take calculated risks. Did not God take an enormous risk by entrusting the gospel of eternal salvation into the hands of the local church?

How often do people say, 'But we have never done it that

way before!'? Why not give it a try, upheld by prayer and careful planning?

Christianity is a process of listening to what God has done for us in Jesus Christ, and what he is doing today. We need to listen carefully, and then to respond. The PCC has to work out how to apply Christian beliefs and insights to each item on the agenda at the PCC meeting. It involves sharing thoughts, reflecting on them, making decisions and then acting on them. Sometimes, the first thing that the PCC has to do is to become aware of the need for change. For example, if the PCC is satisfied with the number of people in the parish who belong to the Church, then there will be no need for change. Every PCC needs a vision, and this gives us a sense of purpose and encouragement.

Changes sometimes lead to discontent and problems, but change can also lead to growth. How much better when changes and new ideas are welcomed and encouraged with helpful and constructive comments. In all the changes in the Church, remember that the toughest and most precious commodity is love. Cardinal Newman said 'To live is to change'.

Whatever the situation in the parish, it is helpful to remember that we all belong to the same Body of Christ, even though some will want to move on, and others will prefer to remain where they are at present. Tension and hurt are often involved when decisions have to be made, but PCC members are elected to make decisions. Careful communication and explanations by PCC members can do much to help forward God's work in the parish.

*Food for thought*

1. Are any changes needed in your own life? Should any of your priorities be changed?
2. Should any of the weekly activities of the church be changed?

**Children and toddlers of the Church** Children are an important group in terms of mission and evangelization. If the Church fails to win the children at an early age, the task is so much harder at a later age. If the opportunity is not grasped when they are young, the Church may not have a second chance to win them.

One parish will have a completely different approach from the next one. It is helpful if the PCC is clear about what it is trying to achieve in its work with children. It is a good idea to have a written parish policy on the subject, worked on and accepted at a parish meeting.

*Problems and some suggested answers* There are many problems connected with children's work, but it is possible to find a solution to most of them.

1. How do we find Sunday School teachers? Parents are often willing to help on a rota system, doing their turn, say, once a month, but not every Sunday. Parents wishing to have their children taught the Christian faith may well be pleased to be asked for help. It can be very rewarding to work with children and to see them grow in the faith.

2. Not everyone can teach. Some training and help is essential. The diocesan education team will usually visit a Sunday School teachers' gathering or PCC meeting – or both combined — to give help and advice, and describe the resources which are available.

3. It can be difficult to keep the interest of children, especially with so many other interests powerfully competing for their attention. Boredom is the great enemy. But the Church does have many resources to counteract this. Apart from short, interesting lessons, there is the opportunity of belonging to the Church as a large worldwide organization. The children can meet other children. The hall and the church building itself are resources which can be used to advantage.

4. Some children are lost when they finish their time at Sunday School and are confirmed. One solution is to make sure that they are integrated with the congregation right from the beginning. In this way, they become friends with adults in the congregation. Children are an important part of the Church at the present time, as well as being part of the Church in the future. It is vital that they offer their worship to God with the adults, as well as in a short service in the Sunday School. 'A branch cut off from the vine will not bear fruit.'

5. Maybe some members of the congregation are disturbed by the very young. Some compromise has to be reached. It may be necessary to have an alternative service for the adults if there is not an 8 a.m. service. Much Christian love and understanding is needed. PCC members can explain that work with children is an important area of mission and

evangelization. Adults in the congregation and PCC members can help with this work by praying for the children if they are noisy. A disapproving look can drive children and families from the Church – perhaps for ever. A friendly smile and a kind word (and prayer too) can work wonders. Jesus rebuked the disciples when they tried to keep the children away from him. 'The kingdom of God belongs to such as these.' Many people do want the children in church with the adults, because they are just as much sons and daughters of God as the adults. They want the children to feel at home in God's house from an early age, and they feel that God's family is not complete without them.

*What are the aims of the Sunday School?* The whole question of Christian formation at an early age is not easy. It is tempting to try to feed the children with as many facts as possible while they still belong to the Church. There are dangers in this approach. Our work with young children is perhaps much more about leading them to a trusting friendship and relationship with the living God. 'Give me a child until he is seven, and you can keep the man.' What do you think those words mean? Can we learn from those words? Are we teaching the children in the right way, and with the right lessons?

Here are some suggestions about our aims. Would you agree with them, and with the order of priority?

1. To help the children to worship God.
2. To integrate the children into the Church from an early age.
3. To teach the children how to pray (a) at Sunday School, (b) with the adults in church, and (c) each night at home.
4. To bear in mind that the faith is 'caught' from adults, before it can be taught.
5. To provide interesting and imaginative teaching of the faith at the level which is appropriate for the children.
6. To try to keep all the children, and avoid losing any through boredom. ('That not one of them be lost.')
7. To try to expand the work, and to attract as many children as possible.
8. To offer our best efforts to God in all our work with the children.
9. To provide for the social needs as well as the spiritual needs of the children.

*How do the children fit into Sunday worship?* What are the main ways of approaching this subject?

1.  Many parishes have the children in church from the begin-
    ning of the service until the end of the gospel. Then they
    withdraw to the hall, vestry or nearby house for their own
    act of worship (and the toddlers go to the crèche). Usually
    this is followed by separate activities in groups. The children
    and teachers then return – the children to receive a blessing
    at the altar rails and the adults to receive communion. They
    remain for the final prayers, hymn and the blessing. Careful
    consideration is needed in choosing the hymns – how many
    hymns should be specifically for the children?

    A system is needed to tell the Sunday School when to
    return to church, giving them at least five minutes' warning.

    Most Sunday Schools follow the theme of the ASB Com-
    munion Service readings. As adults and children work on
    the same theme each Sunday, how can the results be shared
    after the service? Could the children occasionally explain to
    the adults at the end of the service what they learned in their
    lesson?

2.  Some parishes involve the whole family in the main act of
    worship every Sunday. There is no separate worship for the
    children. Perhaps a crèche area is provided for the toddlers.

3.  A monthly 'Family Service' instead of the normal Parish
    Communion is an option. It is fairly easy to attract a number
    of young families. Families seem to come while their
    children are young, but there is a problem with this type of
    watered-down service. When the children are older, they
    and their parents stop coming to church. Perhaps the short-
    term success and popularity of family services needs to be
    weighed against the long-term mission of the Church.
    Because of this, many parishes opt for the method described
    in paragraph 1 above or, as an alternative, the Family Ser-
    vice in the setting of the Eucharist. When this latter course
    is followed, all parts of the Eucharist which are not man-
    datory are left out.

4.  Another approach (much less common now?) is where the
    Sunday School meets at a different time from the main adult
    service. There are many drawbacks with this method. It
    mainly attracts children whose parents are not connected
    with the Church. This is not a bad thing, but the problem
    arises when they finish their time in Sunday School, and

efforts are made to transfer them to the main Sunday service. Many leave at that point, because they are not integrated with the congregation from an early age.

***Some suggestions*** When a child has been absent for two or three weeks, a visit to the home by a Sunday School teacher is very important.

Meetings of parents with the teachers/leaders is useful, perhaps combined with a social evening, slide/video show of the Sunday School and church activities during the year. A concert given by the children. A Sunday lunch. A Sunday School outing, or walk. Delivering a birthday card on the appropriate date, and singing 'Happy Birthday' at Sunday School on the nearest Sunday.

As children grow up, they need more challenging interests, and the Church has to provide this challenge in order to keep the children. It is not an easy task, but every opportunity to bring children nearer to the kingdom of God is a precious opportunity and a privilege.

*Questions for discussion*

1. How can the PCC fulfil its mission to the children of the parish?
2. Has your parish considered additional Sunday School activities during the week?
3. What about a junior choir?
4. What proportion of the PCC's work is concerned with people under forty years of age, and what percentage with those over sixty years of age? Is the balance correct?
5. What is the best way to recruit new teachers? How are they trained?
6. Does your parish have a written parish policy on its work with children?

**Choir** *See* **Music in worship** on pages 123–31.

**Choral speaking** Join in all parts of the service which are spoken by the congregation with a clear and firm voice. Do not get ahead or behind the others, as this can be most distracting. Listen carefully to the rhythm of the congregation and especially to the priest taking the service.

A thought – Do some people try to rush quickly through

the Lord's Prayer because they are spiritually uncomfortable with it?

**Christian stewardship** Parishes differ enormously, but most PCCs have been involved in Christian stewardship, either to find the money to pay the diocesan quota, or as part of a deliberate policy about stewardship. The principles of Christian stewardship are firmly based on the Bible, and they are a sound basis for the life of every parish. They can also help to identify a vision about the needs and opportunities of the Church.

*What is meant by stewardship?* The definition given by the Lambeth Conference (1958) is as follows:

> There can be no forward steps without a full acceptance of Christian Stewardship. By Stewardship, we mean the regarding of ourselves, our time, our talents, and our money – as a trust from God to be utilized in his service. This teaching is an urgent need in every congregation; a parish without a sense of Stewardship has within it the seeds of decay.

The Church needs both this traditional view of Christian stewardship and also a vision for the parish, which is based on the Gospel.

The fundamental principle of Christianity is 'giving'. God created us, and he gave us life. His gift of life is under our own control, and we can do what we like with our lives. Sadly, most people ignore God and forget his ways. Because of this rebellion against God, he gave his only Son, so that we may not perish but have life. Thus, there are two parts of God's giving (creation and redemption). First of all, he gives us the gift of our lives. Secondly, he gave us himself in his Son on the Cross at Calvary. It takes time for most of us to realize the full extent of God's love and total self-giving to us.

How can a Christian give thanks to God in practical ways for what he has done for us on the Cross? We can respond to God's love for us by giving back to God a proportion of our money, our time and our talents. Self-giving is perhaps one of the main aspects of the Christian life, both God's total giving to us, and our learning to give back to God what he has first given to us. It involves a certain amount of self-surrender to God. Christian stewardship invites us – and perhaps challenges us – to think about the following three areas: (1) our time, (2) our skills and talents, and (3) our money, and to make a definite decision about each of them. Stewardship is about our personal response and commitment. We ourselves are stewards (not owners) of our time, our money and our skills, and we are responsible for how we use them at each stage of our lives.

*Stewardship of time*  People today have much more spare time than in former generations. Modern technology makes our daily work-load easier. We are stewards of the time which God has given to us here on earth, and we alone are responsible to God for how we use our time. Our time is a gift from God, and it really belongs to God. We can acknowledge this by offering back a proportion of our time to God each week. How do you work out what is a responsible amount of time to give for God's work each week? It is important to work out something specific – rather than waiting for a job to turn up in the parish.

*Stewardship of skills and abilities (talents)*  Perhaps no one in your parish is a true genius, but virtually everyone has been given some natural skill or ability by God, and this can be offered back to God. We are expected to make something of the different skills, resources and energies which we've been given, and to develop them to the best of our abilities. It is so easy for our abilities to be unused or eroded by laziness, selfishness, lack of thought and courage. In a similar way, we have received a rich spiritual heritage, and it is easy to be self-satisfied simply by being a part of this spiritual heritage today. But are not all these blessings from God given to us on trust, which we can use for the work of his Church?

One approach is to produce a list of jobs which need doing in the parish. Perhaps a better approach is to identify the various talents and skills which exist among members of the congregation. Then try to work out how these talents and skills could be used. (Which comes first – the vacancy, or the individual with the talent?) For example, you may discover three musicians in the congregation – how could their musical skills be used?

*Stewardship of money*  Stewardship is not a new idea to solve the financial problems of the Church. It goes right back to the Old and New Testaments. It is interesting to note that the Bible has more references to money than to any other subject. The standard of giving set for the people of God in the Old Testament is one tenth (the 'tithe'). Genesis 14.20: 'Abraham gave him a tithe of all the booty.' Deuteronomy 14.22: 'Year by year, you shall set aside a tithe of all the produce of your seed, of everything that grows on the land.' Deuteronomy 16.16–17: 'No one shall come into the presence of the Lord empty-handed. Each of you shall bring such a gift as he can in proportion to the blessing which the Lord your God has given you' (NEB). The tithe is not put forward in the New Testament, but emphasis is given to sacrificial and thankful giving. It also stresses the blessings which will come to the giver as well as to the recipient. St Luke 6.38: 'Give, and gifts will be given you. Good measure, pressed down, shaken together, and running over, will be poured into your lap; for whatever measure you deal out to others will be dealt to you in return.' 2 Corinthians 9.6–8: 'Remember, sparse sowing, sparse reaping; sow bountifully, and you will reap bountifully. Each person should give as he has decided for himself; there should be no reluctance, no sense of compulsion; God loves a cheerful giver. And it is in God's power to provide you richly with every good gift; thus you will have ample means in yourselves to meet each and every situation, with enough and to spare for every good cause' (NEB).

Not everyone can give a tenth of their income, but a tithe is perhaps a good standard to have before us, and one which some people use to work out their giving to the Church today. Other people aim to work towards giving 5 per cent of their net income – which was the standard which General Synod recommended for giving to and through the Church.

Christian stewardship invites us to be responsible stewards of our money. What, then, is a realistic and responsible proportion of your income to give back to God through his Church? You cannot make a responsible decision without taking the trouble to work out the facts about your income. One way (after deduction of income tax) is to calculate what is 2 per cent, 3 per cent, 4 per cent, 5 per cent and 10 per cent of your weekly income. Then work out what is the right 'proportion' of your income to give back to God through the Church. It is a good idea to think about it for at least 24 hours after you have worked out the figures. Then pray about it. What does God want you to do about it?

Some people try to strike a balance between the amount which they spend on themselves and the amount they give back to God.

### Christian stewardship

Stewardship of money is learning how to give according to your means. Whatever method you decide to use, it should be realistic and responsible. Pray about it, and make a deliberate decision (each year).

*A vision for the pilgrim people of God*  It is so easy to think of Christian stewardship mainly in terms of money. But the Church is much more than money. In the PCC annual accounts, it is better to have a heading 'stewardship of money' rather than 'stewardship income'. The Church of God is a pilgrim people, and we need a Christian approach not just for our money, but for the whole of our lives. Our Christian commitment should pervade all aspects of our daily lives.

*The stewardship committee and the annual renewal*  A Christian stewardship programme is a defined opportunity. But it is only the beginning. The important part of stewardship is the challenge to maintain the teaching and impetus about giving, and stewardship principles, year after year. An efficient stewardship committee is needed to maintain and raise the level of giving, and to bring new people into the scheme when it is appropriate to do so. In this way, there should be no need to have separate, one-off campaigns, providing the stewardship committee does its job properly throughout the year. It is wise to keep in contact with the diocesan stewardship adviser each year, to see what new programmes are available for the parishes.

*A job specification for the stewardship committee*

1. To maintain and increase regular giving and to bring new members into the scheme when appropriate.
2. To communicate regularly with those in the scheme, and also to thank them.
3. To organize the annual renewal, and to recommend to the PCC when the committee would like to have another diocesan directed programme.
4. To organize the time and talents side of stewardship in the parish.
5. To develop the teaching of Christian stewardship principles, and to create a vision for the growth of the Church and its service to the community.
6. When no other group is responsible for mission audit,

perhaps the stewardship committee could include this in its work?

7. To keep the stewardship records (and electoral roll) up to date, and to remove the names of those who have died.

*A deed of covenant*  Anyone who pays income tax can make a deed of covenant with the Church. The Church simply reclaims the tax which has already been paid to the Inland Revenue. This is a valuable source of income for the Church, and it is a painless way by which individuals can increase the value of their gift to God. Your covenant secretary or treasurer will no doubt have the details of the different types of covenant (including Gift Aid) which are available for helping the parishes.

A definition of Christian stewardship by Robert Williamson (Bishop of Southwark) to General Synod in 1990:

> It is a personal conviction of mine that money is congealed life. It is my work, my talents, my personality, reduced to negotiable form. In so far as I give money to God, or anyone else, I give that which represents me. Whether my model for stewardship reflects the Creator–creature or the Redeemer–redeemed relationship or a proper combination of the two, I am faced with responding to the tremendous generosity of God. If I claim to be his child, and if, by his Spirit, I am being changed into his likeness, then I must surely expect some of his generosity to rub off on me and to see my Christian giving move from the level of obligation through the level of generosity to the level of sacrifice.

*Questions for discussion*

1. What vision does the PCC (and the parish) have for the growth of the Church and its service to the local community in the coming years? Will the financial commitment of the PCC match this vision?

2. What policy does the PCC have to develop its teaching about Christian stewardship? Is this policy regularly reviewed?

3. Does the PCC have a system for reviewing the levels of giving each year? Is this policy clear to the PCC members and to the congregation?

4. Does the parish have a policy for teaching Christian stewardship as part of Christian formation, e.g. in preparation for Confirmation?

5. How can people be inspired with a vision of the Church's

mission and ministry? How can they be inspired to make the work of the Church a high priority for their giving?

6. Does your PCC work out the cost of its mission to the parish each year, review progress, and initiate new plans?
7. How does Christian stewardship measure the extent of your trust in Christ?
8. To what extent is stewardship a barometer of the spiritual health of the parish?
9. In what direction should the stewardship committee now be concentrating its efforts?
10. Do the PCC and the stewardship committee know what help and support is available from the diocese? Does the parish make use of these resources?

**Church Army**   This is a Church of England Society founded in 1882 to proclaim the gospel by word and by action. After a three-year training course, the Captains and the Sisters of the Church Army are admitted to the office of Evangelist by the Archbishop of Canterbury. The Church Army covers a whole range of 'churchmanship' and the officers are all united by service and evangelism, and a concern for people.

*Evangelism*   The Church Army conducts missions in parishes. A mission may only last ten days, but it always involves careful preparation by the PCC beforehand. The Church Army also conducts long-term missions, such as a pioneering mission in new housing areas, say, for a three-year period, before handing it over to the local church.

One hundred and forty officers now work in parishes, and a high percentage of them work in the difficult sphere of the inner city parishes.

*Social evangelism*   The Church Army is much involved in helping single homeless young people, and the elderly. They operate eighteen hostels for this work. In addition, much work is done with HM Forces, holiday camps and seaside resorts. There is a farm adventure station at Sheldon in Devon run by the Church Army.

*Resource centre*   The Church Army undertakes teaching and training sessions in parishes, including the Christian Advance Training Scheme, which helps lay people to be involved in the work of the Church. The resource centre has a large stock of audio-visual aids and literature, and a good book centre, all at their headquarters. Details from: Church Army Headquarters, Independents Road, Blackheath, London SE3 9LG. Tel: 081–318 1226/3916.

**Church hall** Together with the church and vicarage, the hall is one of the main assets of the parish. A basic question: What is the purpose of having a church hall? To build up the fellowship of the congregation? To provide a meeting place for studying the faith, recreation and entertainment? To serve as a meeting place for community organizations, wedding and baptism receptions, and dances? The hall can be a powerful element in mission, and also generate income which can help to balance the PCC's budget in some parishes.

In order to attract people, the appearance of the hall must be appealing. It has to compete with high standards and facilities which are available elsewhere. It is a great disadvantage to have draughts, bare floor-boards with knots, dull brown or green paint which was put there sixty years ago.

Imagination and bold long-term planning can achieve a remarkable transformation, carried out in stages when the money becomes available.

*Questions for discussion*

1. Is the hall fulfilling the purposes which the PCC intends it to fulfil?
2. Are improvements desirable in the kitchen, lavatories, cloakrooms, stage, notice boards, entrance area, committee rooms? Would a new front door or extended entrance improve the facilities and appearance? Would carpets be appropriate in certain places? More comfortable chairs?
3. Is the hall adequate for the needs of the parish? Should the PCC be thinking in terms of building a new one?
4. The church has a thorough inspection every five years, and a written report is sent to the PCC. Should the PCC also ask the architect to inspect the hall? Is a report made every year to the Annual Parochial Church Meeting about the condition of the hall, the work done in the past year, and plans for the future?
5. Is a log book kept for the hall, where details are recorded of all repairs, alterations and improvements?
6. Is there room in the hall to make a parish office? If not, could one be built adjacent to the hall or church?

**Church Housing Trust**   *See* **Housing Associations** on page 100. This is a fund-raising charity which works for the needs of the homeless. It provides hostel accommodation for the single homeless, where they can stay for a maximum period of six months. During this period, CHT tries to find a place to re-settle them in the community. Some elderly residents become permanent, as it would be unkind to turn them out. CHT also owns a small number of houses which are used for homeless families.

Church Housing Trust deals with drug and alcohol addicts, ex-offenders and ex-psychiatric patients.

Church Housing Trust was originally the Church Housing Association and the Church Army Hostels (both Anglican) but it became ecumenical in 1991 when it was merged with the Baptist Housing Association. Much of the income comes from donations from PCCs, and perhaps your PCC might consider supporting CHT. Further details from: Church Housing Trust, Sutherland House, 70–78 West Hendon Broadway, London NW9 7BT. Tel: 081-203 9233.

**Church newspaper**   Many Christians read a church newspaper each week, in order to be well informed about their faith, and to see what is going on in the wider family of the Church. It is a good idea for every PCC member to read a church newspaper regularly.

The *Church Times* is central in churchmanship and has a wide circulation. The *Church of England Newspaper* has an evangelical emphasis. Both can be ordered through a newsagent or sent direct by post from: The Church Times, 7 Portugal Street, Kingsway, London WC2A 2HP; The Church of England Newspaper, 146 Queen Victoria Street, London EC4V 4EH.

**Church Pastoral Aid Society**   Founded in 1836, the object of the society is 'the salvation of souls, with a single eye to the glory of God, and in humble dependence on his blessings'. CPAS provides grants for curates and lay workers to help the clergy in parishes of both the Church of England and the Church of Wales. CPAS has a distinct protestant and evangelical position in doctrine and principles.

The society is involved in youth work and youth camps, women's action, and the administration of patronage of 'evangelical' livings. CPAS also produces leaflets, adult Christian

education material, teaching aids, videos and film strips, and mission resources. Details from: The General Secretary, Church Pastoral Aid Society, 32 Fleet Street, London EC4Y 1DB. Tel: 071-353 0751.

**Church schools** *See* **Education of Christians** on page 68, and **Confirmation** on page 58. The Church has played a leading part in the education of the country through the centuries. The monasteries were great places of learning, and later on, the Church was a pioneer with the State in making education generally available to everyone in the nineteenth century.

Many fundamental changes have taken place in education since the 1986 Education Act. School governors now have much more responsibility and work to do than in earlier years, under the Local Management of Schools (LMS). There are still two types of church schools. An 'aided school' has a majority of church-appointed governors or managers. The 'controlled school' is a church school, but the local government-appointed governors or managers have a majority over the church-appointed managers.

It is vital to keep the Christian commitment of church schools. The diocesan education officer will always give help and advice when asked.

A church school should have a Christian 'ethos'. Three questions need to be considered in this matter:

1. Is the act of worship in the school done properly?
2. Is the religious education right? The church governors must never allow this to become a second-class area, and proper resources are needed for it.
3. Are there good relationships between the school, the staff, the church and the PCC?

How can the PCC help to build up and maintain a good relationship between the church and the school? Do the PCC-appointed governors report regularly to PCC meetings? What are the connections between the PCC and the Parent–Teacher Association? Good communication between church and school is vital, particularly to avoid a clash of dates for coming events. Have the church governors attended diocesan training sessions for church managers?

**Church Union** Founded in 1859 as a result of the great catholic renewal in the Church of England which began in

Oxford in 1833, the purpose of the Church Union remains 'to uphold the catholic doctrine, worship, order and discipline of the Church of England, and to renew and extend catholic faith and practice within that Church both at home and abroad'. The main areas of work include renewal and mission, theology, literature and publishing, children and young people, social concern, liturgy and unity. Membership is open to both individual members and parishes who support the work of the Church Union by their subscriptions and by donations. They receive a journal, the *Church Observer*, three times a year; this contains general articles and news of Union activities, and details of coming events. *Living Stones* is published twice a year, and contains articles concerned with renewal in schools, colleges and parishes. It carries both theological and practical articles on liturgy and catechesis. There is a large, world-famous bookshop at the headquarters in London, supplying, in addition to books, sacristy supplies, objects of devotion and recorded music, and preparation material for Confirmation and Sunday School. Details from: The General Secretary, The Church Union, Faith House, 7 Tufton Street, Westminster, London SW1P 3QN. Tel: 071-222 6952.

**Churchwardens** Status and dignity are attached to the ancient office of churchwarden, but much more is expected of those who accept office today. The warden has a strong mixture of legal, spiritual and pastoral responsibilities, as well as looking after the church and its contents. It is a role of leadership, and it sometimes needs courage, insight, and the ability to stand up and speak up, when necessary.

It is vital to have the right people as churchwardens, because so much depends on their loyalty, leadership and hard work. Anyone who is asked to be a warden should carefully consider the responsibilities involved, long before allowing his or her name to go forward for the election. If you have just been asked to consider becoming a churchwarden, do not be put off by these thoughts. Every warden grows into the job in the course of time, and God gives us all the necessary grace to do his work. Is this what God wants you to do?

*Canon Law and the churchwardens* The duties and responsibilities are clearly set out in Canon E1, para. 4, and they are quite a tall order to fulfil properly! Presumably no one would accept office without truly intending to do his or her very best

for God's work in the parish, and each warden signs a formal declaration about faithfully and diligently performing these duties. The Canon Law has been subdivided to make it easier to comment on each section:

*'The churchwardens when admitted are the officers of the ordinary'* The ordinary is the bishop. The wardens carry their wands of office in front of the bishop when he visits the parish, because they are the representatives of the bishop in the parish. What does this mean? 'Once in a blue moon' a situation may arise where the priest persistently and wilfully neglects to carry out his duties, or commits a serious moral or criminal act. Fortunately, a major problem of this nature does not happen very often. Most clergy work hard and pray and do their utmost to fulfil the high calling of the sacred ministry.

As a lay officer of the bishop, a churchwarden has the responsibility to report to the bishop if there is a major 'neglect or default' by the priest in carrying out his duties. It is, of course, a very serious step indeed to report the priest to the bishop, and it should only be done as a very last resort, and after serious consideration and much prayer. A question to ask is – 'What would our Lord want in this situation?' The warden has to weigh the good which might result from talking to the bishop, with the harm which would come to the priest's future ministry, to the parish, and perhaps to the Church as a whole. If the action leads to a court action, or a libel case, who will pay the costs? What harm would be done to the relationships of those concerned? The warden might also ask – 'Have I neglected any of my duties as a warden?' Remember the words of our Lord, 'Let him that is without sin throw the first stone'. The priest may also appoint another churchwarden at the next vestry meeting. The bishop will probably send a photocopy of correspondence to the priest. If a difficult situation does arise, the first step is for the wardens to talk to the priest about it. After all, the wardens have a loyalty to the priest and to the parish who elected them as wardens, as well as a loyalty to the bishop. This is not a pleasant subject, especially as the first item in the Canon Law, and fortunately most churchwardens will never be called upon to act in such circumstances.

*'They shall discharge such duties and responsibilities as are by law and custom assigned to them'* What does this mean? Customs vary from parish to parish, but the law is the same

everywhere. What, then, are the duties assigned to the wardens by custom?

1. It is customary for the two wardens to sit on one side of the vicar and the PCC secretary on the other side at the Annual Parochial Church Meeting. This is not just to give them a special place, but to show that they are a united team who work together throughout the year. This aspect of working together with the priest is of great importance for the work and worship of the Church.

2. It is customary for the wardens to be the 'job masters' of the parish. They arrange special events as well as routine jobs. This includes finding the right person to take over a job when necessary. These matters can be discussed and lists of names drawn up of people who might help. It will sometimes be appropriate for the priest to approach a particular person, and at other times more appropriate for the warden.

There are many situations where the warden can be actively involved, including the following: finding and organizing group leaders for the Lent Course; someone to organize door-to-door collections for the Children's Society and Christian Aid; someone to look after the grass-cutting rota; finding a hall cleaner/verger; arranging a thorough spring-clean and polish, including a window wash; arranging sidesmen for Church festivals, weddings and funerals; recruiting new sidesmen; finding someone to deal with the heating system; routine maintenance jobs, e.g. replacing light bulbs in difficult places.

It is helpful if the wardens can visit and get to know the various groups and organizations which use the hall, including the uniformed organizations, youth club and choir. Perhaps the wardens could speak about the work of the churchwarden to some of the groups.

It is very desirable for both wardens to get to know the names of the congregation, and the fringe members. To greet someone by name shows that the Church cares about people.

The wardens should regularly attend the main service on Sunday morning (and if possible, the evening service too) and also major occasions in the Church calendar, e.g. Ascension Day, Ash Wednesday, Holy Week and Good Friday services, the Patronal Festival and the Christmas services.

To sum up, it is customary for the wardens to be actively involved in the whole life and work of the Church. This is aiming very high, and not every churchwarden will be able to give time for all of this. However, each will know how much he or she can give, and it is a good idea to talk this over with the priest and other churchwarden before accepting office.

The responsibilities assigned to the wardens by law are much easier to define than those assigned to them by custom:

1. The wardens, in consultation with the minister, must maintain a terrier, inventory and log book in the form recommended by the Council for the Care of Churches.
2. A copy of the inventory must be sent to the person nominated by the bishop at the appropriate time, and this person must be notified of all alterations.
3. The wardens must record all alterations, additions and repairs to the church and anything belonging to the church, in the log book.
4. The wardens must inspect the church buildings, and all articles belonging to them, at least once a year, or alternatively arrange for someone else to carry out the inspection for them. Again, the wardens must act in consultation with the minister in this matter.
5. The wardens must give the annual fabric report on the fabric and contents of the church to the PCC meeting held before the Annual Meeting. The wardens also present this report, together with any amendments made by the PCC, to the Annual Parochial Church Meeting.
6. During the time that they are in office, the wardens are the legal owners of the contents of the church, including all movable furniture, ornaments and plate. The wardens must ensure that the PCC fulfils its responsibility for the proper care, maintenance and insurance of these items. The priest, of course, has the right to use them as and when he feels appropriate. Neither the wardens, nor anyone else, can remove anything, nor introduce anything new, without a legal faculty or archdeacon's certificate. However, a worn-out article may be replaced by a new one (similar to the original), in consultation with the priest.
7. The wardens must present to the Annual Meeting a signed statement to certify that the contents of the terrier, inventory and log book are accurate.
8. The wardens are responsible for allocating all seats in the nave of the church. To ask someone to move to another seat

can cause great offence, and should only be done when absolutely necessary, and done in a tactful way.

9. It is the responsibility of the wardens to provide the wafers and wine for the Eucharist, but at the expense of the PCC, and on the 'advice and direction' of the priest. This duty is usually delegated to the sacristan.

10. When a priest retires, dies in office, or moves to another parish, then the benefice becomes vacant. One or both of the wardens are usually appointed as sequestrators (usually with the diocesan secretary). Much extra work is always involved. The duties and responsibilities which have to be done when there is no priest in the parish are separately described under **Interregnum** on pages 102–8. The wardens are also usually involved in the process of appointing a new priest.

11. When the PCC fails to appoint a treasurer, it is the legal duty of one or both of the wardens to take over the duties and responsibilities of the treasurer of the PCC. In the normal way, it is not a good idea for a churchwarden to hold the additional office of treasurer, because the work of churchwarden is in itself very demanding, if done properly.

12. It is the responsibility of the wardens, assisted by the sidesmen, to take the collection, and to see that it is duly counted and recorded in the Register of Services. It is a wise custom to have at least two people present when the money is counted, and those concerned both sign the book.

13. The wardens should try to ensure that the PCC pays its quota – sometimes called Common Fund or Parish Assignment. This could be seen as their duty as 'Officers of the Ordinary'. The wardens could also ensure that the working expenses of the priest are paid each year.

*'They shall be foremost in representing the laity and in co-operating with the incumbent'*   At first glance, this seems to be difficult, but in practice there should be no conflict of loyalty. The wardens have been called the 'go-between' through whom parishioners can make known their views to the priest. At the same time, the wardens must also be 'foremost in co-operating with the priest'. It is desirable to have a parish policy written down. The wardens certainly have an important leadership role at PCC meetings, particularly in the whole matter of co-operation with the incumbent. The church will only succeed

if there is this co-operation, together with mutual support, loyalty and good teamwork with 'united endeavours'. It is interesting to note that the Synodical Government Measure and Canon Law both use the same phrase of 'co-operating with the incumbent'.

*'They shall use their best endeavours by example and by precept to encourage the parishioners in the practice of true religion'*
This sentence has many implications for churchwardens and for the parish. Canon Law gives a clear and definite leadership role to every warden to encourage parishioners in the practice of true religion. 'Parishioners' includes church members and also those who live within the parish boundaries. Canon Law gives to the wardens a task which is similar to that given to every PCC member in the Synodical Government Measure – 'to co-operate with the incumbent in the whole mission of the Church, pastoral, evangelistic, social and ecumenical'.

The wardens are asked not only to set an example for other people to follow, but actively to encourage people in the practice of true religion. Not an easy task for any leader, whether lay or ordained, but a word of praise and encouragement from the warden can often do a great deal of good for the Church. Just because this is a difficult task assigned to the wardens by the makers of Canon Law, it does not mean that the warden can quietly forget about it. How the wardens fulfil their responsibilities in this matter will, to a large extent, influence and govern how the rest of the PCC carry out their responsibilities in this matter. To 'use their best endeavours' will surely require much thought and prayer, which hopefully will lead on to action.

*'And to promote peace and unity among them'*  This clearly assumes that there will be problems in every parish from time to time. Even the apostles had their quarrels, and on one occasion Paul and Barnabas quarrelled so much that they parted company and went on separate missionary journeys.

What causes problems to arise? Does the answer include tactless remarks, jealousy, fears, personality clashes, people putting their own interests before God's wishes, changes in the parish, and resistance as church membership grows (the devil getting worried by the success of the Church so he makes a counter-attack)? It is also helpful for people to know and to respect the boundaries and areas of responsibility (*see Rights and responsibilities of the incumbent*, and *of the PCC* under **Parochial Church Council**, on pages 136–40). PCCs do on occasions have an extraordinary capacity for causing division in the parish. As God's kingdom advances, so there is resistance. Unresolved tensions between individuals or groups might surface from time to time. Some people may pull in one direction while others are striving to go in the opposite direction, like a tug of war.

What a difficult job is given to the wardens to promote peace and unity among the parishioners! 'Blessed are the peacemakers.' But peace must never be appeasement, by giving in to wrong. When faced with a difficult situation, every warden would do well to consider two questions carefully: (a) What are all the facts in the matter? (b) What would our Lord want us to do in this situation? The wardens may on occasions need courage to speak out at a meeting, and perhaps to visit people in their homes to try to resolve the problem. Usually a problem will not go away on its own, and it is the responsibility of the wardens to take the appropriate action. It is, in most cases, not helpful to allow a problem to simmer, unresolved, just below the surface of parish life. Unless the PCC is able to heal its own divisions, no one outside the Church will take seriously its gospel of reconciliation and love and peace. Planning ahead and anticipating problems is an important part of the warden's work.

*'They shall maintain order and decency in the church and churchyard, especially during times of divine services'* The enemies of the Church usually ignore public worship, and it is unlikely that the vicar's sermon will cause a riot! Even so, the doors may well have to be guarded if a crowd of noisy drunks tries to invade the church for a midnight service. People sometimes use the churchyard in unfortunate ways, and children will climb on to the church or hall roof if at all possible. All these and similar matters are clearly the responsibility of the churchwardens, but it is unlikely that they will have to exercise the power of arrest which is vested in them under the Ecclesiastical Jurisdiction Act 1860.

*Selecting and appointing the churchwardens* When a churchwarden is not standing for election again, it is helpful to inform the priest as soon as possible. This gives the priest time to consult and make discreet enquiries about a successor, who in

their turn can have time to consider the duties and responsibilities involved. It avoids having to make a quick decision at
the meeting, without due thought and prayer. The ancient procedure of priest and parishioners choosing both wardens by
'joint consent' is a very sound principle. The priest gives his
consent formally, either before the motion is put, or immediately after the election result is declared. Where there is
failure to agree, the priest appoints one warden first, and then
the meeting elects the other one. During an interregnum, the
meeting elects both wardens. The newly-appointed churchwarden becomes a member of the PCC immediately after
appointment, but he or she does not take up the duties of
churchwarden until actually admitted to office at the visitation
by the archdeacon, and having signed the register. The time
between the election and the archdeacon's visitation is very
useful for the warden-elect to learn the ropes from the outgoing
warden, and to check the contents of the church before the
hand-over.

In addition to being admitted to office in a legal way at the
archdeacon's visitation, many parishes have a short ceremony
in the main act of worship on the Sunday after the visitation.

*A Form of Service to welcome the churchwardens* A Form of
Service for this purpose may have been authorized in your
diocese. If not, this Form of Service could be used at the beginning of the Eucharist, or at the Offertory, or during Morning
or Evening Prayer.

The priest gives an appropriate Introduction about how every Christian is
called to share in Christ's work and ministry, because through Baptism,
we are members of the Royal Priesthood of Christ. The churchwardens
and PCC members in particular are elected to share in the whole mission
of the Church in the parish – pastoral, evangelistic, social and
ecumenical.

The churchwardens and newly-elected PCC members are invited to
stand.

**Priest**
You have been elected by the people of this parish to serve as
churchwardens and as members of the PCC. Will you dedicate
yourself to this work and ministry, and will you carry out your
duties to the best of your ability?

**PCC members and wardens reply**
With the help of Almighty God, we will.

**Priest**
You, the Christian people of this parish, have duly elected these

people to serve on the Church Council of St . . . .'s Church. Will you also do your part by supporting them and by remembering them regularly in your prayers?

**The Congregation**
With the help of Almighty God, we will.

**Priest**
May you be strengthened and renewed by the Holy Spirit to fulfil this work and ministry for the extension of God's kingdom in this church and in this parish. Amen.

**All**
O God, for as much as without thee, we are not able to please thee. Mercifully grant that thy Holy Spirit may in this, and in all things, direct and rule our hearts, through Jesus Christ our Lord. Amen.

*Early resignation procedure*  A churchwarden can resign before the year of office is completed only by means of a complicated procedure. This is because the wardens are not just the officers of the parish, but also the officers of the bishop. Early resignation involves writing to the bishop to explain the reason for early resignation, and the bishop usually wants to see the warden in person. The written consent of the incumbent and of the co-warden is also required. If the bishop accepts the resignation, then it takes effect immediately.

*How long in office?*  It is not an appointment for life! It is usually not in the best interests of the church to have the same person continuing in office year after year. No one is indispensable, and a change of churchwardens can often release new energies in a parish. The question needs serious consideration, and it is a good idea to discuss this before accepting office. The question arises, 'What is best for God's work in the parish?'

*A deputy churchwarden*  There is no legal standing or requirement to appoint a deputy warden, but it can be a very good way to introduce someone to the job.

## Some desirable qualities in a churchwarden

1. Undivided loyalty to the church and the priest is essential, and this includes putting the church before all other meetings and social functions. It may be that a choice has to be made between social functions and God's work. A warden cannot do a good job for the church if he or she is involved in too many other things in the community.

2. The warden should be a person of prayer, and able to see things from a spiritual point of view. At the same time, it is good to have both feet firmly on the ground.
3. From a practical point of view, the wardens (and members of the fabric committee) should know the location of the stopcocks for the water mains, the electrical fuse-boxes and where to find fuse wire and screwdriver, and the mains gas tap, for the church, the hall and the vicarage.

**Churchyard** First impressions are lasting, and a well kept churchyard can create a good impression. An untidy churchyard shows no respect for the departed, and gives the impression of an uncaring and ineffective church.

Mounds and kerbs make it difficult and costly to keep the churchyard tidy. The best answer is to obtain a faculty to remove kerbs and mounds over fifty years old, and not to allow new ones.

Burial space is scarce and it is costly to purchase new ground (if available). One solution is to re-use the churchyard, which is possible seventy years after the last burial has taken place. Always consult the archdeacon about this.

The PCC applies to the Department of the Environment for the churchyard to be closed by Order in Council. Then the responsibility for maintenance can be transferred to the local authority (while the legal ownership remains with the church). Alternatively the local authority can make an annual contribution towards the upkeep of a closed churchyard. It is possible to close part of a churchyard, while using the remainder for burials.

An old churchyard can be used in various ways, while retaining the headstones on the perimeter. The archdeacon is the person to consult before any action is taken.

*Garden of Rest* A faculty is required 'to set apart a portion of the churchyard for the burial of cremated ashes'. It is desirable to make at least two rules: (1) Ashes to be buried without any casket. This is the practice followed at many crematoriums, and it prevents disturbing or cutting into the casket with a spade when further ashes are buried. It eliminates the problem of people digging up and stealing caskets, for they are usually buried fairly near the surface. (2) No cremation tablets or memorials. To sink a small stone slab into the grass can cause many problems in the future. An alternative is to have a book of remembrance inside the church – with suitable prayers nearby.

**Clergy – How to address them**   Not a vital matter, but it can be useful to know the correct procedure. Simple styles were introduced by the Lambeth Conference 1968 for letters, as follows:

| | |
|---|---|
| *Archbishop* | The Most Revd & The Right Hon. the Archbishop of . . . (In speech – Your Grace, or Archbishop) |
| *Diocesan bishop* | The Right Revd The Lord Bishop of . . . (In speech – My Lord, or Bishop) |
| *Assistant and retired bishops* | The Right Revd J. Smith (In speech – Bishop) |
| *Dean* | The Very Revd The Dean of . . . (In speech – Mr Dean, or Dean) |
| *Provost* | The Very Revd The Provost of . . . (In speech – Mr Provost, or Provost) |
| *Archdeacon* | The Venerable The Archdeacon of . . . (In speech – Mr Archdeacon, or Archdeacon) |
| *Canon* | The Revd Canon J. Smith (In speech – Canon) |
| *Prebendary* | The Revd Prebendary J. Smith (In speech – Prebendary) |
| *Other clergy* | The Revd J. Smith |
| *Clergyman and wife* | The Revd J. and Mrs Smith |

In speech, the parish clergy are addressed in different ways, partly depending on the tradition of the parish: Vicar, Rector, Father Smith, Mr Smith, Father John; and some clergy encourage use of Christian names, but never 'Reverend Smith'. (Does familiarity breed contempt?)

**Clocks**   A useful snippet of information. Local government authorities have power to pay the cost of repairing, maintaining and lighting public clocks, including clocks on church towers, even though the local authority does not own the clock.

**Coffee after the service**   The Church is more than a collection of isolated individuals and interest groups. It is a family – the family of God where different groups are built into a community by sharing and partaking in the Eucharist. But fellowship needs to be built up in other ways to express the unity of the church family. One well-tried method is to have coffee and biscuits after the service every Sunday. This is also a good opportunity to welcome and introduce new people to the congregation.

Where there is no church hall, and no possibility of building one, one answer is to serve coffee at the back of the church (obtaining permission to remove a pew or two). A rota of helpers is needed, and a practical job like this is one way of bringing in fringe members.

Having said all of this, we must recognize that not everyone is of an extrovert nature, keen to meet other people. The very idea of being introduced to a group of unknown strangers can be a very frightening prospect to some people. A thought comes to mind – how many people actually stay away from church because they are afraid of the social gatherings after the service?

**Commitment**   In days gone by, the church was the centre of life for most people, but today there are many other attractions and demands on our time. How, then, should PCC members think about their commitment to their church?

The answer will vary for each individual. Surely, no PCC member thinks of the church in terms of just another social club, to which they give their time so long as it does not interrupt anything else? Many think of commitment in terms of one hour's worship on Sunday, the responsible giving of money and attending PCC meetings. Some regard PCC meetings as a priority, which they put before any other social function. Others think also of commitment and loyalty to other PCC members, to their priest and to God.

There is a simple story about commitment. A hen and a pig were looking at a poster on a church notice board. It was inviting donations for 'Feed the Minds'. The hen said to the pig, 'You and I could help with this problem. We could supply them with bacon and eggs.' The pig thought for a moment, and then said, 'For you, that is only a token offering. For me, it is complete commitment.'

It raises the question – does the level of commitment vary among PCC members? What prevents firmer commitment in some people? What encourages commitment in others? Is there any connection between commitment and Christian steward-ship? *See* **Motivation and morale** on page 121.

**Community action**   *See* **Social responsibility and concern** on page 181.

**Community care**   *See* **Pastoral care** on page 151.

**Community lunch**   *See* **Hospitality and parish catering** on page 99.

**Community voice**   The Christian point of view is sometimes not put forward on issues of local importance. When the occasion demands, how many are ready to speak out clearly and firmly to put the Christian point of view? It must be done with humility, and not in an arrogant manner. It will not always be popular. Likewise, the PCC can send a letter to the local government council, or to the press, when the occasion demands it.

**Confirmation**   How does the Church recruit, retain, educate and motivate members? The failure rate with young people after Confirmation is alarming. What can the PCC and congregation do to help in this whole area? One answer – to become more aware of the nature and extent of the problem.

Young people are comparatively stable and mature, and have a capacity to learn, at about 11 or 12 years of age. After that it is difficult for them to make a commitment to the Church because they are going through a time of powerful emotional change, and even emotional contradictions. They examine their beliefs and many reject the faith, partly because it makes demands on their newly acquired freedom. These are generalizations, and no doubt there are many exceptions.

Another method must be mentioned, which many think is the answer (time will tell if this is so). It is that young people are formally admitted by the parish priest to receive Holy Communion after appropriate instruction, at a much earlier age – about 7 or 8 years old. Confirmation takes place later on, after the 'rebellion stage', and it is administered by the bishop as a sacrament of Christian maturity and commitment. The bishop's formal approval in writing is required before this course may be followed.

*Why do candidates lapse after Confirmation?*   Instead of trying to give an answer, further questions are raised for consideration:

(a) How much is the problem caused by lack of support and example from the parents? Would it be more helpful to concentrate more on the family as a unit? One question for discussion at a meeting of parents could be, 'What are the responsibilities of parents in connection with the Confirmation of their children?' Young people rebel as part of growing up, including rebellion against the Church. Could some form of liaison with the parents help them to live through the time of their children's rebellion?

(b) In Confirmation preparation, is more emphasis required on the feelings and experience of candidates and perhaps less on beliefs at this stage? It is so easy to make Christianity too difficult and unattractive. More important than learning, one vital issue for each candidate is the question – how do I fit into the Church? If the interest of the young can be kept, creeds and beliefs can be learned in years to come.

(c) Is there an adequate lay ministry in the parish to help to integrate into the congregation those who have been confirmed? Is there adequate follow-up by lay people?

(d) What is the expectation of the candidates and their parents about Confirmation?

(e) What is the best way for young people to find out about Church membership and to learn about the faith? Would it help if the candidates visited certain selected Church members to discuss their faith? Perhaps the families concerned could help to keep in touch with the candidates in the years to come?

(f) Are tensions created by the process of spiritual growth which has started in the candidates? Is it true that the more that Christianity is understood, the more it is rejected?

(g) There is much wastage in nature (parable of the sower, St Luke 8). Is 'wastage' inevitable with Confirmation candidates? Can the PCC do anything about this?

(h) Would a system of 'sponsors' be helpful, with one adult or mature young person being responsible for every candidate, in addition to the godparents? The sponsor would be asked to pray regularly for the candidate over the years, and help in other ways as opportunities came along.

(i) Is full use made of video and audio material? Could the parish produce its own teaching material for Confirmation?

(j) How does Confirmation preparation fit into an overall parish education policy? (*See* **Education** on page 68.)

(k) Is the Church too keen on trying to make candidates

conform and keep the rules before Confirmation?

(l) 'God is at the starting gate (Confirmation) but as the candidates go around the course, there is no one at the jumps to catch them when they fall.' How far is this true? What can be done about it?

The whole subject is not an easy one in practice, but it is surely one of the key issues which require the attention of priest and PCC members today.

***Finding Confirmation candidates*** This letter is photocopied or duplicated on A4 paper and sent to anyone who may be interested in Confirmation. This includes parents and godparents from Baptism services, the bereaved, young married couples.

From _____     Address _____

Tel: _____     Date _____

Dear

I'm writing to ask if you would think about Confirmation. In some ways, this is a strange request. May I invite you to spend a little time thinking about some of the reasons why people are confirmed?

1. Baptism is completed with Confirmation and Holy Communion. Many – but not all – are baptized as babies, and godparents make promises for them. At Confirmation, the person is old enough to make the promises for himself or herself. The promises and questions we are talking about are these:

*The candidates stand before the Bishop; he says*

You have come here to be confirmed. You stand in the presence of God and his Church. With your own mouth and from your own heart you must declare your allegiance to Christ and your rejection of all that is evil. Therefore I ask these questions:

Do you turn to Christ?
*Answer*   **I turn to Christ.**

Do you repent of your sins?
*Answer*   **I repent of my sins.**

Do you renounce evil?
*Answer*   **I renounce evil.**

*Then the Bishop says*

You must now declare before God and his Church that you accept the Christian faith into which you were baptized, and in which you will live and grow.

Do you believe and trust in God the Father, who made the world?
*Answer*   **I believe and trust in him.**

Do you believe and trust in his Son Jesus Christ, who
redeemed mankind?

*Answer* **I believe and trust in him.**

Do you believe and trust in his Holy Spirit, who gives life to
the people of God?

*Answer* **I believe and trust in him.**

*The candidates answer all together as a group.*

2. We receive the benefits which Christ won for us on the cross through
receiving Holy Communion. Confirmation is the traditional way to admit
people to full adult membership of the Church, and thus to receive
Holy Communion.

3. We can approach this through the words of Scripture. We read in the
Acts of the Apostles: 'When the Apostles at Jerusalem heard that
Samaria had received the word of God, they sent to them Peter and
John, who came down and prayed for them that they might receive the
Holy Spirit; for it had not yet fallen on any of them, but they had only
been baptized in the name of the Lord Jesus. Then they laid their
hands on them and they received the Holy Spirit' (Acts 8.14–17 RSV).

4. Another approach to Confirmation is to think about the meaning of
Jesus on the cross. There is a story of a man who was interested in
the Christian faith and what it had to offer to him. He was rather
confused, and he said, 'Vicar, what is the point of the cross today?'
The vicar explained that the cross means different things to different
people:

   – to the person who is suffering and in distress, the cross shows us
   that God knows about suffering, and that he feels it with us.
   – to the person who is burdened with guilt from some former sin, the
   cross tells us that God offers his forgiveness to all who truly repent
   (are sorry for their sins).
   – to someone who is concerned about evil in the world today, the
   cross proclaims that God has won the final victory.
   – to someone near to death, the cross means that God will not
   abandon us, and that nothing can separate us from the love of God
   in Christ Jesus.
   – to anyone who feels separated from God, the cross reminds us that
   God has bridged the gap between us and himself.
   – to the person who is unsure of life itself, the cross shows us that the
   greatest and most lasting reality in the world is Christian love.

5. Jesus Christ is the centre of Christianity. (Could we even say that
Christ is Christianity?) Who is this person Jesus Christ? Both the
enemies of the Christian faith, and countless disciples, have all
carefully studied the four gospels to find an answer to the question –
'What think ye of Christ? Whose son is he?' Much indeed depends
upon your own answer to that question.

If you are interested in thinking about this subject, some people like
yourself will be meeting on. . . . at. . . . and you are welcome to join us.
     Yours sincerely.

P.S. Some questions to think about:

1. What is a Christian, and what is the Church?

2. Which of your hopes and ambitions for the future have you achieved
so far? Will you achieve them all one day? Have you ever thought
about God's vision and hopes for you?

3. What makes it difficult to be a Christian in our modern world? How and where can you find help to overcome these difficulties?

*Follow-up to this letter*   Obviously a personal visit is essential. Further letters can then be sent to encourage more thought. Pastoral evangelism in this way can be very effective.

*The Confirmation service*   Many parishes print an Order of Service for the Confirmation. A sentence might be included in the service on these lines:

To anyone who has not been confirmed (or baptized): is this something you might consider for yourself? Ask your priest about it.

*Sponsors for the candidates*   The sponsor is a member of the Church who agrees (1) to befriend and get to know the candidate and the candidate's family; (2) to be present at the service – and in some dioceses, to put a hand on the candidate's shoulder while he or she is actually being confirmed; (3) to give an appropriate present to the candidate – in consultation with the priest (and paid for by the PCC?); (4) to pray for the candidate during preparation, and regularly after the Confirmation service, over the years. . . .

**Congregation and conversion**   You may feel this is a strange heading, for after all, a congregation is a group of people who come and worship God week by week. So why does a congregation need to be 'converted'? One answer may be found in our Lord's words, 'Not everyone who says to me Lord, Lord, shall enter the kingdom of heaven, but only those who do the will of my Father who is in heaven.' Another answer – the members of the congregation will no doubt all be at different stages of spiritual growth. Some will have a deep love and knowledge of God, and others will be near the beginning of their spiritual pilgrimage.

Some people are 'converted' suddenly, as happened to St Paul, while for most people the process seems to be slow and gradual. However, no one is free from sin during this earthly life, and everyone needs God's forgiveness each day. Jesus said at the beginning of his ministry, 'Repent and believe the gospel'. The word conversion means a turning to God, and every Christian needs to turn to God again and again and again.

What prevents spiritual growth? Is it sin? Apathy? The doors

of heart and soul firmly closed to the influence of the Holy
Spirit?

What helps and encourages spiritual growth? A combination
of the Eucharist, personal Bible reading, and private prayer
(similar to the Benedictine triangle?).

The gospel makes us revise and change our thinking, and it
frequently contains the unexpected. It keeps us from becoming
self-centred and puts God back in the centre again. It gives us
a new awareness of his presence, and it helps to change the
hearts of both the congregation and the priest.

*Questions for discussion*

1. To what extent is the church 'a school for sinners'?
2. When new people join the congregation, is it just left to
   chance whether they come again or not? Does it depend on
   the priest? Or the friendship of the congregation? Or is there
   a Nurture and Welcome group?
3. Is it possible that some people come to church regularly, but
   are virtually untouched by the word of God?

**Consistory Court**   Ecclesiastical law is administered in each
diocese through a Consistory Court, and the judge of the court
is called the Chancellor. PCC applications for faculties are dealt
with in the Consistory Court, and when there is a dispute it is
possible to appeal to the Court of Arches. Appeals are always
costly.

**Council for the Care of Churches**   The PCC is responsible
for the care and maintenance of the church buildings, but it cannot make alterations without proper authority to do so. Each
diocese has a Diocesan Advisory Committee for the care of
churches which gives formal advice to the diocesan chancellor
about any proposed change in a church. The DAC will also give
informal advice to the PCC to help them in their difficult task
of caring for ancient buildings.

The Council for the Care of Churches is a permanent body
set up by General Synod. One of its main tasks is to co-ordinate
and guide the work of all the diocesan advisory committees. It
has a statutory duty to provide information and views on architectural and historic merits, whenever a church is considered for
redundancy or demolition.

The Council for the Care of Churches has twelve specialist

sub-committees which deal with the following subjects: bells, books and manuscripts, clocks, decorative plasterwork, metalwork, monuments, organs, paintings on canvas and wood, stained glass, structural timberwork and wooden furnishings, textiles and wallpaintings. The council has an extensive library, and will give advice to PCCs when asked to do so. Address: Council for the Care of Churches, 83 London Wall, London EC2M 5NA. Tel: 071–638 0971/2.

**Curate** The rector or vicar has 'the cure of souls' in the parish, so the curate is really the Assistant Curate. However, the assistant priest is known as the curate, who assists the vicar or rector in the parish.

The ministry of the Church is a corporate ministry, in which bishops, priests, deacons and members of the congregation all have a distinct role. A curate, whether deacon or priest, has a share in the corporate ministry of the Church, but it is important to remember that a curacy is also a time of training, and growing in confidence, spirituality and maturity. The basis for the future pattern of ministry is firmly established during the curacy years, and there is much to learn, particularly from the vicar.

**Daily offices of Morning and Evening Prayer** Every priest is under an obligation to say Morning and Evening Prayer every day (Canon C26/1) in church (1662 BCP rubric). These daily offices – or the Roman Catholic 'divine office' which some clergy use as an ecumenical gesture – are a vital part of every priest's life.

*Lay people and the offices* The shorter versions of Morning and Evening Prayer in the ASB can be used by PCC members each day. They form a solid foundation for personal prayer, and provide for the regular and systematic use of the Bible, with appropriate readings for each day and season of the year. The individual Christian using these daily offices at home is not praying alone, but is part of the worshipping community of the whole Church of God. The basic pattern of the office is:

> Quiet reflection and preparation;
> 'O Lord open our lips' etc. and the Gloria;
> the appointed psalm (see ASB lectionary);
> Old Testament reading (you may wish to leave this out?);

New Testament reading. Think about its meaning (then re-read it?);

a canticle;

Lord's Prayer, collect for the day, and the daily collect.

The Office is followed by a time of intercession and thanksgiving. (*See also Daily with God* on page 184.)

*Food for thought*

1. Could those who use the daily offices in the parish form a community of prayer, praying for each other each day, and for the clergy and the parish?
2. For those who are married, would Morning and Evening Prayer be a helpful way of praying together?

**Dancing in church**   Not 'slow, slow, quick quick, slow'. The very thought of dancing in an act of worship will horrify some people, even if they are only spectators. Early hostility by more traditionally minded people can be modified, or even disappear, after they have experienced liturgical dance.

There are different types of dance. In some churches, the congregation regularly sways from side to side, and people raise their hands as they sing. This is part of charismatic worship, and the author has no experience of this type of dance.

A more cautious approach is to have a group of people performing for the rest of the congregation. This type of liturgical dance can be used with powerful effect during the Eucharist at the Gloria, Sanctus, Benedictus and Agnus Dei. Biblical passages and themes can also be portrayed in a powerful way through dance.

Christianity is about the whole of life and not just worship and spiritual matters. 'Here we offer and present our souls and bodies to be a living sacrifice.'

Young people or adults can be involved, but proper training is required. The training itself is useful, as those involved have to think carefully about the meaning of the words they will express in actions with their bodies.

A service with liturgical dance can only be done very occasionally, and even so, it will not appeal to everyone.

**Dates for the year**   It is helpful if the Standing Committee does some forward planning and works out dates of the main events for the coming year. These can be discussed by the PCC and published at the New Year, with a request that everyone enters them in their new diary. (Patronal Festival, Harvest, the fête, carol services, barbecue, outings, PCC meetings, social evenings, parish conference, retreat.)

**Deanery Synod** *See* **Synods of the Church** on page 195.

**Delegation** The priest is not a one-man band, and a great deal of delegation takes place in every church. We are all called by God to share in Christ's ministry and work. Everyone, if willing, has something to offer, no matter how small. Talent spotting is a very important part of the work of the priest and the churchwardens. Acorns must be given the chance to grow into oak trees.

The initial explanation of the task involved is of considerable importance. A clear vision of the ultimate goal and of the work involved before arrival must be imparted. It is a good idea to write down the job specification – for private use. The following points need to be covered:

1. How much authority is being given?
2. How much time is needed to do the job?
3. Will anyone else be involved in this work?
4. Who is available to help when a problem arises?
5. What are the arrangements for a progress report?
6. Is any preparation or training needed to do this work properly?
7. When the above points have been worked out, a detailed description of the job can then be given.

It may be appropriate to discuss how long the person will do the job: one year, five, or. . . .?

**Diocesan Board of Finance** *See* **Finance** on pages 72–83.

**Diocesan Synod** *See* **Synods of the Church** on page 195.

**Donations book** A well-bound 'gifts and donations' book placed on display on a table at the back of the church is useful to record recent donations (e.g. a new Bible) to the parish church.

**Drama in church** Life was hard and often violent in the Middle Ages. The Church used religious drama to brighten up the

lives of ordinary people when there was virtually no other entertainment. Religious drama was also a very effective way of
teaching people about the life of Jesus. Religious drama began
with the mystery (miracle) plays, and later on came the morality
plays.

All religious drama was forbidden during the Reformation.
But since the end of the nineteenth century, there has been a
revival of the use of drama in churches and cathedrals,
presented by both professional and amateur companies.

Religious drama is still a very effective and also an enjoyable
way of furthering the Christian cause. It provides an opportunity for young and old to work together and to use their skills
and talents on a project which can be spiritually enriching.
Non-believers will sometimes come to a play in church, while
they would not come to a religious service.

The leading professional companies include Theatre Round-
about, Riding Lights, Cornerstones, and the Aldersgate
Theatre Company. They will usually come and perform in any
parish. For further information, apply to the Administrative
Secretary, RADIUS (Religious Drama Society of Great
Britain), Christ Church and Upton Chapel, Kennington Road,
London SE1 7QP. Tel: 071–401 2422.

There is now a wide range of religious plays which are
suitable for use in church. A short dramatic sketch might occasionally be used instead of a sermon.

**Drawing pins**   A small point which needs stressing – drawing
pins and nails leave a nasty hole in church furniture and doors.
No member of the congregation would put a drawing pin in a
valuable piece of antique furniture in his own home. One solution, apart from buying or making a notice board, is to use
Blu-Tac (similar to putty) which does not leave any woodworm-
like holes in the furniture.

**Easter offering**   *See* **Finance** on page 78.

**Ecumenical thoughts**   A divided Church is a sin, and it is one
factor which prevents the spread of the gospel. God wants his
Church to be one. Surely different Churches should no longer
do separately those things which it is possible for them to do
together.

Special situations exist where it is desirable to elect one or
more people to the PCC who are not members of the Church

of England. The prior permission of the bishop is required for this. The person concerned must be baptized, a communicant member of a Church which believes in the Holy Trinity, and also in good standing with that Church. The person must be a regular communicant at the parish church, and be 17 years of age or above. How many non-Anglicans can be elected to the PCC in this way? The answer is that at least two-thirds of the lay members of the PCC must be members of the Church of England.

**Education of Christians**   *See* **Confirmation** on page 58 and **Church schools** on page 45. Christian education is often assumed to be for children only. If this is so, the Church should not be surprised when children discard their faith when they grow up.

*Questions for discussion*

1. Is the weekly sermon the only form of ongoing adult Christian education in the parish? If so, what is needed to provide additional educational facilities for the congregation and interested fringe members?
2. The question needs to be considered briefly – Education for what?
3. Is the PCC aware of the training opportunities provided by the diocesan education team for adults, for those who work with adults as group leaders, and for those who work with young people?
4. How can the PCC help to link the work done by the Sunday School with the adult worship of the congregation?
5. Does the PCC have a copy of the magazine for Church teachers and Sunday School leaders, published by CIO and called *Together*?
6. Is there any project, or holiday scheme, which the PCC could organize for children *and* parents together?
7. Has the PCC discussed and written down a parish education policy for people of all ages in the parish? And with the help of the diocesan education team?
8. Do PCC members as individuals take responsibility for their own Christian growth and learning?
9. Is the PCC's ministry to children weak or strong?
10. Is the PCC aware of the needs of the children of one-parent families, broken homes, and those who are mentally and physically handicapped?

**Electoral roll**   Not to be confused with the list of parliamentary voters. The PCC appoints an electoral roll officer, who has charge of the electoral roll.

The electoral roll is the foundation of the whole structure of synodical government in the Church. The people on the electoral roll:

1.  Elect the new PCC every year;
2.  Elect the new Deanery Synod representatives every three years.

The Deanery Synod representatives:

1.  Elect the Diocesan Synod representatives every three years;
2.  Elect the General Synod representatives every five years.

*Qualifications for the electoral roll*   To qualify to be on the roll, a person has to be:

   (a)  a member of the Church of England (or a Church 'in communion' with the Church of England),
   (b)  baptized,
   (c)  16 years of age or over,
   (d)  a resident of the parish (or if not a resident, has 'habitually attended public worship in the church' for six months),
   (e)  has signed an electoral roll application form.

*The annual revision of the electoral roll*   This is done by the electoral roll officer before the Annual Parochial Church Meeting every year, with the following timetable:

Notice of Revision – displayed on the notice board for a period of 14 days; after this the revision is made – not more than 28 days, and not less than 15 days, before the Annual Meeting.

The revised roll is then displayed for 14 days before the Annual Meeting, and also a list of the names removed since the last revision.

*Preparation of a new electoral roll*   The old roll is destroyed and a new electoral roll has to be made every sixth year from 1972 – namely 1996, 2002 etc. The timetable is as follows:

   (a)  Notice of preparation of a new roll is displayed two months before the Annual Meeting for a period of 14 days on the notice board. It must also be announced in church on the two Sundays.

(b) Preparation of the roll is done not more than 28 days, and not less than 15 days, before the Annual Meeting.

(c) The new roll is then displayed for 14 days before the Annual Meeting.

***Informing those on the old roll*** Church Representation Rules (Rule 2(5)) state: 'The PCC shall take reasonable steps to inform every person whose name is entered on the previous roll that a new roll is being prepared, and that if he wishes to have his name entered on the new roll, he must apply for enrolment.'

An obvious method of doing this is a friendly letter from the electoral roll officer. It is a good opportunity to use – so consult the vicar to ask if he would like to include anything in or with the letter. Take care not to miss anyone, nor to write to someone who has died.

An alternative to writing is for the PCC to visit every member on the electoral roll. This is valuable in terms of pastoral care and keeping in touch especially with those who are not regular worshippers. Visiting the electoral roll members is the easiest kind of visiting, and no one need be afraid of doing it, as all on the electoral roll are members of the Church. If the PCC decides to undertake a visitation, a briefing session will be needed for those involved. In addition, a letter from the electoral roll officer is useful, delivered two or three days before the visit.

In some rural parishes, it might be wise to visit every home. (Could this also be done in other parishes too?) Again, a letter before the visit is a good idea.

The forms needed for the revision of the electoral roll are available from church bookshops. *See* pages 205–7.

***Annual Parochial Church Meeting*** Invite everyone on the electoral roll to the Annual Meeting (with duplicated minutes of last year's meeting, the agenda, accounts and written reports).

***When someone moves*** It is possible to be on two electoral rolls. When someone is moving, ask whether they want their names removed from the present roll; and it is helpful to write to the new parish to inform them of the arrival of the new church family, so that they can be welcomed.

*Active electoral roll officer*   How many people know the names
of all the members of the congregation? The electoral roll officer
should be one of them, to make sure that all in the congregation
are on the roll. Approach the youth club leaders and older
members, the uniformed organization leaders, their members
and parents, the flower rota, and the various groups and
organizations connected with the church. It is not wise to
include what might be called 'dead wood'. On the other hand,
any opportunities to bring people to the kingdom should not be
dismissed too lightly.

**Employment**   PCCs often employ paid staff. There is a great
deal of legislation which affects the employer–employee relationship. The PCC has wide statutory responsibilities and
obligations which should not be taken lightly. Some dioceses
have a Lay Employee Agency which will give advice and
encourage 'good employment practice'. Otherwise, consult
your archdeacon for advice, particularly when problems arise.

**Enquiry Centre**   Either write or telephone, if you have a
query, to: The Church of England Enquiry Centre, Church
House, Great Smith Street, Westminster, London SW1P 3NZ.
Tel: 071-222 9011 (ask the switchboard for Enquiry Centre).

**Eucharist**   *See* **Holy Communion** on pages 92–7.

**Evangelization**   *See* **Mission – Evangelism – Renewal** on
pages 113–19.

**Expenses of clergy**   *See* **Finance** on page 79.

**Fête**   Many parishes organize an annual church fête, some to
make money for their own funds, and others to support the
Church overseas or some specifically Christian charity. Many
people will support a charity, but it is usually only Christians
who support the Church overseas and specifically Christian
charities.
   A fête can generate much interest and good will towards the
Church, and many fringe and non-church members are willing
to lend a hand at the fête. Who knows – perhaps even a church
fête may lead someone into the kingdom of God!
   The date of the fête should be arranged at the beginning of
the year when the other church events are planned for the coming year. The fête committee could well include non-church and

fringe members, and it is wise to start planning for the fête about six months before the event.

It is useful to keep brief records in a notebook for the following year. Careful planning, good publicity, imagination, and new attractions every year, are a good recipe for success – if you are lucky with the main uncertain factor in arranging a fête – the British weather!

**Finance**  The finances of the Church are a complete mystery to some people. The relationship between policy and finance is important, and hopefully policy drives finance. Thus it is helpful if every PCC has a good understanding of church finance, and the governing rules. Here is a summary of the main aspects:

*Accounts*  The *Parochial Church Accounts Book* is highly recommended for all PCCs (obtainable from Church House Bookshop, 31 Great Smith Street, Westminster, London SW1P 3BN. Tel: 071–222 9011). This book is helpful for preparing the accounts, and the annual statistical returns. It contains useful information about the budget and the accounts.

PCC accounts have to be kept for a period of not less than six years after the end of the relevant financial year (Charities Act 1992). Many parishes keep them for future reference.

### The timetable for the accounts

1. Early in January, prepare the accounts (ending 31 December).
2. Arrange for the accounts to be audited, with the books, documents, vouchers and receipts.
3. Present the audited accounts to the PCC early in February. After discussion (and possible amendment), the resolution is proposed 'that the PCC accepts the accounts for presentation to the Annual Parochial Church Meeting'.
4. Fix a copy of the audited accounts on the church notice board seven days before the Annual Parochial Church Meeting.
5. At the APCM, the resolution is proposed 'that the accounts be adopted'. The accounts are then signed at the meeting by the chairman (or vice-chairman in an interregnum). The accounts can be rejected (in extreme situations) but they cannot be amended by the APCM.
6. After the meeting, the treasurer puts the accounts back on the notice board for a further fourteen days.

The PCC is responsible for the accounts, even though the work is delegated to the treasurer. After the accounts are accepted by the PCC for presentation to the Annual Parochial Church Meeting, they become the PCC's accounts and the treasurer will expect full support from PCC members at the APCM.

*Auditors*   The accounts must be audited each year, and certified as correct by two people. The auditors are elected at the Annual Meeting and they must not be members of the PCC. (It is possible that the Charities Act 1992 may bring in stricter rules about who can be an auditor.)

*Budget*   A budget is a plan of action using figures. It is wise for the finance committee (or standing committee) to plan ahead for the coming year in November (or earlier) and then to work out the costs of the plans. It should be noted that the treasurer does not make policy decisions, e.g. the treasurer does not say, 'We cannot do this because we do not have the money'. The correct procedure is for the treasurer to say, 'The PCC has £x available, and this means that the PCC will have to raise £y to do this'. But the PCC makes the decision. It is a good idea to get the principle right first, and then to work towards the principle. It is always desirable to involve as many people as possible in formulating the policy and plans of the church. Once the plan has been accepted by the PCC, it is (in many cases) a good idea to present it for discussion at the APCM or a Parish Meeting. The aim is to obtain support and commitment from as many people as possible.

The budget is brought to the PCC at the first meeting in the New Year, usually at the same time as the annual accounts.

What are the most important items in the budget? To put it another way, how should the money be used if there is a shortfall of income? Should the PCC borrow from reserves? Each PCC must work out its own order of priority about making payments from PCC income, after payment of urgent bills. How far would you agree with this suggested order?

1. Diocesan quota (sometimes called Common Fund or Apportionment) – this has first claim on parish income. Otherwise the life of the Church in the parish and in the diocese would grind to a halt.
2. Missionary giving for the Church overseas – at 10 per cent of the gross income of the PCC. *See Donations made by the PCC* on pages 77–8.

3. Full cover for all aspects of insurance.
4. Parochial expenses (i.e. expenses of the clergy).
5. The church roof (assuming careful stewardship and regular inspections of the buildings).
6. Missionary work in the parish (e.g. a free magazine delivered to every home in the parish).
7. Vicarage improvements and redecorations.

***Central Board of Finance of the Church of England (CBF)*** The CBF is the financial executive body of the Church of England. Among many other duties, it prepares and administers the budget of the General Synod. The income of the General Synod is from the free will apportionment of the dioceses. Each of the 44 dioceses has a representative on the Board, and they ensure that the CBF is kept fully informed of opinion in the dioceses. The CBF operates three funds which are very useful for PCC money.

1. *The CBF deposit fund* This offers a very good rate of interest for PCCs (generally higher than the clearing banks). Money can be withdrawn from the fund on demand, and it can be used for small or large amounts of money. Gross interest (i.e. with no income tax deducted) is paid into a bank account every quarter, or it can be reinvested.
2. *The CBF investment fund* This is invested mainly in equities on the Stock Market and property, and it is thus suitable for long-term investment. The aim of this fund is to provide a steady growth of income and capital. Gross dividends (i.e. with no tax deducted) can be paid direct into a bank or reinvested to purchase further units in the fund if the income is not required.
3. *The fixed interest and securities fund* This invests only in 'fixed income' stock, and thus it offers a higher income than the investment fund. However, it gives no protection of the capital against inflation! Shares in this fund are available only on monthly valuation dates. Gross dividends can be paid each quarter into a bank account, or reinvested to purchase further units.

The interest rate of the deposit fund, the offer price (at which the units are sold to the PCC or Parish Trust), the bid price (at which the units are bought back by the CBF), the yield of the investment fund and the fixed interest and securities fund, are published daily in *The Times*, the *Daily Telegraph* and the

*Financial Times* under 'Central Board of Finance of the Church
of England'. They are also published weekly in the *Church
Times*. The telephone number of the CBF Investment Office is
071-588 1815. The administrative office of the CBF (not the
same as the Investment Office) is: The Central Board of
Finance of the Church of England, Church House, Great Smith
Street, Westminster, London SW1P 3NZ. Tel: 071-222 9011.

*Church Commissioners*   They were created in 1948 when the
Ecclesiastical Commissioners (formed in 1836) were united
with the Queen Anne's Bounty (formed in 1704).

The main functions of the Commissioners are to look after
the ancient endowments, to act as the central stipend authority
of the Church to pay the clergy, to approve redundancy
schemes, and to make pastoral orders. The capital assets are
held in trust, and legally this means that only the income and
not the capital itself can be used. The income is mainly used:

1. To provide part of the clergy stipends, and housing costs.
2. To pay the pensions of retired clergy and clergy widows.

The income of the Commissioners is large, but not nearly
large enough to meet all its demands. Once the Commissioners
paid the lion's share of clergy stipends. Now, a greater
proportion of the Commissioners' income goes to pay clergy
pensions. Thus a larger amount of money from the parishes
through the quotas makes up a growing proportion of the clergy
stipends.

The wealth of the Church Commissioners has been a great
blessing. It has enabled the Church to pay the clergy through
difficult times, and to keep clergy working in areas which could
not otherwise afford a priest. But in some ways, the Commissioners' wealth has been a mixed blessing. Present-day Christians have depended to a considerable extent on the generous
giving of Christians in former times. As the resources of the
Commissioners are not sufficient to meet the needs of the
Church, so PCCs are asked to provide more money. This
challenge usually brings new spiritual life and commitment in
a parish, and often a response which includes the principles of
Christian stewardship. *See* pages 37-42.

*The address*   The Church Commissioners, 1 Millbank,
Westminster, London SW1P 3JZ. Tel: 071-222 7010.

***Church hall accounts*** The rent from the hire of the hall is a significant part of the income in many parishes, and there is certainly great potential there which is not always fully realized. Does the PCC charge a realistic amount per hour for hall lettings? What charge is made by neighbouring churches? Does the PCC charge church organizations for the use of the hall? Does the PCC measure how much electricity and gas are used per hour in the hall for annual calculation purposes?

***Churchwardens*** When it is not possible to find a PCC treasurer, then it becomes the legal duty of the wardens to take over the work of the treasurer. *See* **Churchwardens** on page 50, para. 11.

***Collections and stewardship envelopes*** Two sidesmen or women should always be present when envelopes are opened and cash collections are counted. The amount contained in each envelope must always be written on the outside by the sidesmen to prove that the money has actually been paid to the Church by the donor (under Inland Revenue Rules). The total cash collections and the stewardship of money totals are entered in the Register of Services, and it is then signed by both sidesmen. All money should be kept in the church safe, and banked on Monday morning by the treasurer, or someone acting for the treasurer. A paying-in book is useful, and the source of the money should always be recorded.

***Covenants*** Income tax certificates are prepared either by the PCC treasurer or by the covenant secretary to relieve the workload of the treasurer. Details about current regulations for covenants and Gift Aid can be obtained from the diocesan secretary, or direct from: HM Inspector of Taxes, The Inland Revenue, Claims Branch for Trusts and Charities, St John's House, Merton Road, Bootle, Merseyside L69 9BB. Tel: 051–922 6363. The Inland Revenue will provide a charity pack on request.

***Diocesan Board of Finance (DBF)*** The DBF recommends to the Diocesan Synod how much money needs to be raised from the parishes each year through the quota. The income of the DBF comes from five main sources:

(a) Quota payments from the parishes. This is the DBF's main source of income.

(b) The Church Commissioners' grant, which is mainly for clergy stipends (salaries). The proportion from the Commissioners has decreased, while the proportion from the parishes has increased over the years.

(c) Income from any investments and trusts held by the DBF.

(d) Bequests from wills, and donations to the DBF. *See Will and Testament* on pages 82–3.

(e) Fees from weddings, funerals, and any part-time chaplaincy work done by parish clergy. The vicar's 'fees' are either deducted from the stipend, or alternatively they are 'assigned' and paid to the DBF.

The main diocesan expenditure is the payment of the clergy, which is done through the Church Commissioners. The diocese is also responsible for the upkeep of all vicarages and other diocesan property, and for paying diocesan staff, the education team, Christian stewardship advisers, etc.

***Disagreement about how PCC money is to be used***   The priest and the PCC have an equal voice in deciding how PCC money is to be used. If there is a disagreement, for example, about how much money is to be given to a particular missionary society, the matter is referred to the bishop, and he gives directions about how it is to be settled. This does not happen very often, of course, but it is a safeguard for difficult situations.

***Donations – 'Gift Aid'***   When someone makes a 'one-off' donation to the Church of £400 or more, the Church can reclaim the tax paid on this gift, under a scheme with the Inland Revenue called Gift Aid. This also applies to donations of £400 or more on a Gift Day.

***Donations made by the PCC***   Individual Christians are asked to give in a realistic and responsible way for God's work through the Church. Individuals expect the PCC in its turn to exercise the same stewardship principles when the PCC is giving money to missionary societies and the Church overseas. What percentage of its income did the PCC give away last year? It is useful to compare this figure each year with the previous years. In this way, the PCC can see how much progress has been made in this area.

Christians give for different reasons. Some give generously

because they want to use the church building, and to keep it in good repair. Others give generously because they want to give money away through the Church to help in its worldwide mission.

The PCC should not be 'tight-fisted' when it comes to giving away money: 'Cast your bread on the waters, and it will return to you'. God is very bounteous and generous, and the PCC too should aim to be generous. Some PCCs give as much money to the Church overseas as they spend on themselves. Others give away any surplus balance at the end of each year (after paying the quota, all bills, and giving 10 per cent to the Church overseas).

The need for financial support is still urgent in many overseas churches. Priests will be withdrawn and the gospel will not be heard in some areas, unless money is sent from this country for some years to come. (There is also a need for people – ordained and lay – to work for the Church overseas. This need is particularly urgent in countries where Christians are heavily outnumbered by members of other faiths.)

Many PCCs give 10 per cent of their income to the Church overseas, as recommended by the General Synod. Others give more than 10 per cent. Some PCCs have their own problems, but the call from overseas is urgent. Does your PCC have the Church overseas high on its list of priorities when the annual budget is discussed?

One PCC treasurer was concerned about the production costs of a large and glossy magazine. Thus he wrote to all the missionary societies and asked:

(a) What percentage of your total income was spent on administration last year?
(b) How much was spent on publicity and magazines?

*Food for thought*

1. Does the PCC have an active overseas mission committee?
2. Does the parish use the diocesan intercessions list regularly?
3. Does the PCC give 10 per cent of its income to the Church overseas?

*Easter offering* In former years, all collections on Easter Day were presented to the vicar to thank him for his work and ministry during the past year. Likewise, the collections at Pentecost (Whit-Sunday) were given to the assistant curates.

The Easter offering is no longer presented to the priest (in most parishes), because if it is, it is usually deducted from the stipend by the diocese. Parishioners now normally find other ways of thanking their priest.

*Expenses of the clergy*   Clergy cannot produce their best work if there is a constant worry about money. *See* **Motivation and morale** on page 121. The more a priest works, the more it costs in 'parochial expenses'. In most parishes, the PCC treasurer repays in full all expenses which the priest incurs in carrying out normal parish work. The following are generally recognized as parochial expenses, accepted as such by the Inland Revenue and reimbursed by PCC treasurers:

(a) Car road tax, insurance, depreciation, maintenance, repairs and servicing, petrol and oil.
(b) Public transport expenses.
(c) Telephone.
(d) Purchase of modern office equipment.
(e) Secretarial help, to free the priest for the work for which he was ordained. A secretary can help with typing/word processing, general administration, filing, registers, returns, minutes, weekly notice sheets, answer the phone and doorbell, and carry out routine tasks for which a priest is not needed.
(f) Postage and stationery.
(g) Maintenance of robes.
(h) Payment of fees of locum tenens (visiting clergy) and their travelling expenses.
(i) 'In-service' training.
(j) Hospitality. This includes meals for visiting preachers, committee meetings, parish party, numerous cups of tea and coffee during the year (and snacks for tramps?).

When a priest looks after more than one parish, it is helpful for the wardens or group council to work out what proportion each parish pays towards the whole (one method is to base this on the diocesan quota).

It is of more help financially to the priest if the PCC treasurer pays certain bills direct, rather than reimbursing the priest afterwards, e.g. the priest's secretary, and the telephone bill. Concerning the use of car and telephone, the proportion for private use is worked out and agreed with the Inland Revenue, e.g. one-fifth for private use.

*Finance*

**Fabric fund**   It is desirable that the finance or standing committee work out what percentage of the PCC's income should be transferred to the fabric fund each year, and recommend this to the PCC in the budget.

**Faculties**   All alterations, additions and removals regarding the church require legal authorization. When work is done without a faculty, the PCC may be ordered by a Consistory Court to pay the costs of putting the work back to its original state, and also reimbursing the legal costs. *See Faculties* under **Buildings** on page 29.

**Fees**   The Official Table of Parochial Fees (weddings, funerals, etc.) is usually displayed in a prominent place on the notice board, or in the vestry. It shows the current fees payable to the incumbent, the PCC, and (if there is one) to the clerk or sexton. The table does not include charges for organist, organ fund, flowers, photographs/video, sweeping up confetti, choir, bell fund and bell-ringers, or heating. These charges are set by the incumbent or PCC. The incumbent's fee always goes to the incumbent, even when the assistant curate takes the service. The rule applies when another priest is invited (with the incumbent's permission) to conduct a wedding or funeral: the fee goes to the incumbent. The same applies to a visiting organist – the organist's fees must be paid to the regular organist.

**Insurance**   The PCC is legally responsible for insuring the church buildings, the hall, the contents and those who use them. *See* **Insurance** on page 100.

**Interregnum**   Special financial arrangements have to be made about PCC finances when there is a vacancy in the living (i.e. the priest has moved, died or resigned). *See The sequestration account* under **Interregnum** on page 105.

**Shares**   It is possible to make a gift to the Church of shares, unit or investment trust units, money, property or land. This can be done as a gift, or under the terms of a will. Neither the donor, nor the Church, has to pay any form of capital gains tax, inheritance tax or any other tax on such a gift.

**Stewardship**   *See* **Christian stewardship** on pages 37–42.

***Treasurer of the PCC*** The treasurer is elected by the PCC at the first meeting after the APCM from among its membership. If this is not possible, someone may be co-opted to full membership of the PCC. If no one is willing to take over the treasurer's job, then it is the legal responsibility of the churchwardens jointly to discharge the office of treasurer. No payment can be made for the work done by the treasurer.

Obviously the treasurer is a prime candidate for election to the standing committee each year. The treasurer's job is to look after the money, to report to the PCC on the financial situation, and to advise the PCC on the financial implications of any decision it is about to make. When the treasurer gives advice, not only the liabilities and resources must be taken into account but also the order of priority which the PCC attaches to the expenditure of its money.

It is wise to make as many payments as possible by cheque. This protects the treasurer, and it ensures that a record is kept of all transactions. All petty cash payments should be recorded, and vouchers and receipts kept safely.

Some parishes have a team of treasurers, or an assistant treasurer. Whatever the situation, it is helpful if a new treasurer and the existing treasurer can work together (if possible for a whole year?) before the handover.

The treasurer is responsible for paying the organist, choirmaster, choir, cleaner, verger, hall caretaker, the parish/vicar's secretary, and the expenses of the vicar and assistant curates.

Prompt payment of the diocesan quota via a monthly standing order with the bank is to be highly recommended. Long discussions and grumbles about the quota are not helpful. Most deaneries and dioceses have by now produced a system which is as fair as possible for every parish. The money has to be found – otherwise the Church in the whole diocese would simply grind to a halt. It is wrong (and un-Christian?) to withhold payment of the quota until the very end of the financial year. The diocese then has to borrow money, at commercial rates of interest, and this causes an increase in the quota for every parish in the future. (Some dioceses publish each year a list of parishes which pay late – or do not pay in full – in the diocesan accounts.)

Proper records should be kept of all financial transactions, and the books kept up to date and checked with the monthly bank statement.

Obviously, it is not good stewardship to keep too much

money in the current account. *See* entry about CBF deposit and other accounts on page 74.

Bills should always be paid promptly. It gives the church a bad name if they are settled late.

***Will and testament*** Not an easy subject, but one which should not be neglected. The rubric in the visitation of the sick states: 'and if he hath not before disposed of his goods, let him then be admonished to make his Will'. This is good advice from the 1662 Book of Common Prayer.

Christians usually leave most of their money and possessions to their nearest and dearest when they die. But, in addition, many leave a proportion of their estate to the Church. Presumably you would only leave a small proportion of your money to the Church if you have a family. But if you have no relatives, then you might consider leaving the whole of your estate to the Church.

Money or property can be left to the Diocesan Board of Finance, the Clergy Pensions Board, the Church Commissioners, a missionary society (which your church supports?), or to your own parish church. All of these are charitable bodies. This means that they are exempt from inheritance tax or gift tax, thus allowing your gift to go that much further in helping the Church. Non-Christians frequently leave *all* their money to a particular charity, but it is only Church members who leave money to the Church. Should not every Christian think seriously about including a bequest for the Church in his or her will?

Many people do not want flowers at their funeral, and they specify 'Family flowers only. Donations invited for St John's Church'. This can be included in the will, and also that you want a requiem Communion (if that is your wish). It can help your relatives if you choose the hymns for the service.

Here are some suggested clauses for a will:

1. *When you wish to leave a percentage of your estate to your parish church (or to the diocese):* 'I give _____ per cent of my residuary estate to the Parochial Church Council of the parish of _____ in the diocese of _____ free of duty to be applied as to both capital and income by them for such of the purposes specified in Section 5 of the Parochial Church (Powers) Measure 1956 as are charitable and I declare that the receipt of the PCC treasurer or other proper

officer of the Council shall be a sufficient discharge to my Trustees.'

In order to carry out your exact wishes, and to avoid the effects of inflation, it is wise to leave a 'percentage' of your estate in this way, rather than a fixed sum of money.

A bequest can of course be made for a specific purpose in the church, e.g. for the roof or fabric fund, for the restoration of the bells etc., or to set up a trust fund, e.g. to pay the choir. In many cases, it can be more helpful to the PCC if no conditions are placed upon the bequest.

2. *When you wish to leave a fixed sum to your parish church*: 'I give to the Parochial Church Council of the parish of _____ in the diocese of _____ the sum of £ _____ free of duty to be applied as to both capital and income by them for such of the purposes specified in Section 5 of the Parochial Church (Powers) Measure 1956 as are charitable and I declare that the receipt of the PCC treasurer or other proper officer of the Council shall be a sufficient discharge to my Trustees.'

Making a will avoids problems concerning the disposal of your property. It also provides you with an opportunity to help with the work of the Church in the future.

If you have already made your will, it is a simple matter to add a codicil, in order to include a bequest to the Church. It is always wise to do this through a solicitor, and to tell your family about your wishes.

**Flag** The proper flag to be flown on a church is the St George's cross, with the arms of the see in the first quarter. (Earl Marshal's regulation 1938.)

**Flowers in church** A church is an ideal place for flower arrangements, and in recent years there has been an enormous growth of interest in this subject. Happily the Church has gained from this and the standard of floral decoration in many churches is quite stunning. Often, only the simplest and humblest things are needed. Imagination is cheaper than hothouse flowers.

A flower guild or church flower club can be helpful, even if it meets only once a year to watch a demonstration.

Those who belong are of course asked to do one flower arrangement in church during the year, and if possible to help at festivals. Outsiders can be asked to help at festivals, and perhaps brought on to the flower rota.

People often like to give flowers on the Sunday nearest to the anniversary of the death of a loved one. They can be invited to do this through a magazine distributed to every house in the parish.

If flowers are kept in the church throughout the week the water will need checking, as dead flowers give the impression of an uncaring church. If the church is locked during the week, the flowers can be sent out while still fresh on Monday morning to someone who is ill or housebound. A notebook for names, addresses and dates will be required for this purpose. A rota of four people (one for the first Monday, another for the second, etc.) can prepare and deliver the flowers, together with a card 'With best wishes from St Peter's Church', and signed by the vicar.

There are no flowers in church in Lent and Advent, as these are penitential seasons of preparation for Easter and Christmas. Also flowers are very costly during those periods.

Church buildings are large, and flower arrangements need to be bold and large. Plenty of long stalks and green foliage can be effective. Proportions need to look right from a distance, as well as close at hand. A flower stand at the side of the altar is better than thin vases on the altar. A large flat container is most suitable for the flower stand, with a deep layer of sand, flower arranging 'oasis', or crumpled wire mesh, to keep the flowers in position.

As a general suggestion, deeper and darker coloured flowers are better in the centre with the softer colours around the edges of the arrangement. The most suitable colours are red, orange and yellow, but others can be used with great effect.

Flowers and candles look good together. Two ideas – a paschal candle (in the sanctuary from Easter Eve until Ascension – the Great Forty Days) can be effectively decorated with flowers, and secondly, the four Advent candles.

The author is not skilled at flower arranging, and recommends more reliable sources, such as *Flowers in Church* by Jean Taylor (Mowbray).

*Food for thought*

1. Could more fringe people be included on your flower rota (and hence be slowly drawn into your church)?
2. When did your church last have a flower festival?

**Friendship**   How often is Christianity accepted or rejected by watching and hearing the behaviour and manner of a professed Christian? '*Oh*, I'm not going to church. I can't stand the vicar.' Or 'How that group of tea makers argue and squabble! I'm keeping out of their way.' This can be an absolute barrier, and many people never look beyond, for Christ. This is our fault and our tragedy.

The friendliness of church members to each other and to outsiders is vital. A friendly contact built up at general times can then be expanded and deepened in a time of need, such as illness, trouble or bereavement.

New friendship is valuable in itself for the people concerned, and a friendly church community has a powerful influence to attract outsiders.

**Funerals**   *See* **Bereavement** on page 14.

**General Synod**   *See* **Synods of the Church** on page 196.

**Going overseas?**   The Christian Church is a very large worldwide family, which cares for its members wherever they may go. If you know of any Christian who is going abroad, the Church can provide advice before he goes, arrange a welcome on arrival, and ensure that he ends up among friends.

For those going overseas permanently or for a period of months, write to The Secretary, Overseas Settlement, Board for Social Responsibility, Church House, Dean's Yard, Westminster, London SW1P 3NZ.

For those going to work in the developing countries, write to Christians Abroad, 1 Stockwell Green, London SW9 9HP. Tel: 071–737 7811.

**Group Council**   A council with lay representatives and clergy from all the PCCs in the group of parishes, who consult together on matters of common concern. Much work can be coordinated and things can be done together which in the past have been done separately by the individual parishes.

**Group and team ministries** (*See* also **Pastoral reorganization** on page 152.) A team ministry is usually more formally defined in legal terms, while a group ministry is more open-ended and informal. What are the differences between groups and teams?

In a team ministry, one or more parishes form a single benefice or unit. It has a team rector, and other clergy who are called team vicars (usually two or more). The team vicars normally have a five- or seven-year leasehold agreement, and they work under the leadership of the team rector.

In a group ministry, each parish has its own incumbent and its own separate legal existence, but the clergy and lay people work together and co-operate in all the parishes of the group. The clergy of the group are entitled to attend PCC meetings and the annual meetings of all parishes within the group.

Whether a team or a group, great benefits can undoubtedly be found when clergy work together. What are these benefits? The clergy worshipping together during the week is helpful to the clergy themselves and to the laity, and it also provides a spiritual base or power-house for the area. (The strength and enthusiasm of the early Church perhaps came partly from their united daily worship, and also some of the ideals of the monasteries come to mind.)

No priest working in isolation can be good at all aspects of parochial ministry. There can be a division of labour and skills when clergy work together, and this is a benefit to the parishes and to the individual concerned. One magazine for all the parishes is another important benefit, particularly if it is delivered free to every home in the area.

Working together provides support and encouragement for the clergy, and an opportunity for studying the Scriptures and theology together. The clergy can find fellowship in this way, and parish problems (and perhaps personal problems?) can be shared and discussed. It is much easier to provide 'cover' for services for holiday periods and illness.

Curates, non-stipendiary priests, readers and licensed lay workers can all share in the corporate ministry, together with the churchwardens and lay people from the different parishes. Roman Catholic clergy often work together, and over the years the results have been a steady advance for the Roman Catholic faith. Perhaps we are learning from their experience?

What then are the problems? Many of the difficulties can be summed up in two words – human nature. Another difficulty can arise if a small number of priests are asked to look after too large (and increasing) a number of churches. In that situation, unless there is an increase in the number of non-stipendiary priests, the question has to be asked – should any of the churches in the area be closed?

It is easier for the clergy if there is only one PCC. However, it is far better if each parish has its own PCC and its own accounts (and perhaps with a lay chairman in some situations?). The reason for retaining PCCs is simple – there is a strong loyalty to the local parish church, but not so strong towards the 'main' church some four or eight miles away. The parish is the bedrock of our pastoral and missionary work, even in a group or team situation. However, policy and major decisions have to be made by the group committee or group council at the centre, with lay representatives from each parish putting forward the views of their own PCC.

Unless there is a considerable increase in the number of ordination candidates for the full-time ministry, it seems probable that there will be an increase in the number of large pastoral units such as teams and groups (and with an increase in non-stipendiary priests helping to work the system?). Whatever the details of the system, exciting possibilities exist for teams and groups, with much lay involvement, and this could well be one of the main areas of growth and advance for the Christian faith.

This *ABC* does not cover all the rules relating to group ministries and team ministries, and the reader is advised to consult the Synodical Government Rules for further details.

**Groups – discussion groups and the PCC**   The Church has been involved in groups ever since Jesus called twelve men to follow him. Groups exist to carry out specific tasks and also to meet certain needs. Meeting as a group can create problems and personality clashes but it can also release energy for good, and give support and encouragement.

Those involved in leading groups are well advised to learn fully about the subject. Most diocesan education teams run courses, and may even be able to offer help in the parish. Here are some basic thoughts.

Well in advance of setting up groups, certain questions need to be asked. Will an existing group – or groups – be used? If not, how will the groups be formed, and by whom?

Careful selection and training of leaders is essential. How

many leaders will be needed? Who will train them? How much time is needed for training?

If the group is ongoing, what will be required to monitor its progress? At what stage will it have outlived its usefulness?

For the smooth running of any group – including a PCC – there are three subjects which require careful attention.

1. *The task of the group* When people meet together for a specific purpose, the task is obviously clear. But in some circumstances, it is not clear – such as for a particular item of the PCC agenda. It is vital that people understand the task, and that all agree with it.

2. *The needs of individuals* Some people are anxious, embarrassed or afraid to speak in a group situation, in case they appear foolish. For this reason, they sit and listen, while others have a field day and say far too much! A good leader can help people to feel at ease, and the members of the group can help to do the same. The individuals who make up a group often have questions for which they are subconsciously searching for answers. These questions may include such thoughts as – How safe do I feel in this group? How close will I be able to get to others in it? How important am I? Who is the most important person here? What is actually going on here? Where do I fit into this situation? Who am I?

   The individual 'needs' of each person do in fact play a large part in determining how well the meeting will go. Thus it is important that people should feel at ease, and a short time at the beginning for people to relax and have a chat is time well spent.

3. *Maintaining the life of the group* People come together, but what keeps them there? Is it enough to say that they are there to do God's work, and hope that this will keep them together? More than this is needed, and people's efforts need harmonizing, encouraging, correcting and guiding. The situation in a group needs careful and constant observation. The situation reached sometimes needs to be clarified, and a consensus of opinion needs testing from time to time.

The task of the group, the needs of the individuals, and the maintenance of the life of the group are not three separate compartments. Each area overlaps the other two, and a breakdown in any one will affect the working of the group and prevent the task being carried out effectively. *See* **Motivation and morale** on page 121.

**Growth**   Some people feel that going to church is what Christianity is all about, while others try to console themselves that if they are actively doing things for the church, this is all that is required of them. But unless each Christian thinks in terms of bringing others to a knowledge and love of Christ, then they are not fulfilling the command of our Lord.

Growth of the local church starts with the spiritual awakening and renewal of individual PCC members. Renewal is not external but internal. It must be growth in the likeness of our Lord, and this involves individuals (and the PCC as a whole?) having a look at their own prayer life, and their openness to the Holy Spirit. Perhaps there is something in ourselves which needs to be put right first, before growth can take place. But it is not enough to have a deeper spirituality. Knowledge is also needed, because you cannot love a person unless you know that person. There is no growth without spiritual renewal in the lives of individuals, and all growth comes from God.

Our Lord's parables contain many thoughts about growth: the vine, the barren fig tree, the seed growing secretly, the mustard seed, the wheat and the tares, the sower, to name but a few.

*Stages of planning for growth*   A basic weakness of the Church is that there is too much talking, and not enough praying, leading to action. The PCC can approach the subject of growth in different ways, e.g. a day given to the subject, and involving the whole congregation; or two or three evening sessions, again with the members of the congregation present. Here are some thoughts which may be useful:

1. How is the Holy Spirit working in the parish, and in what ways can the members of the church share in this work?
2. What are two of the main problems which hinder growth in the local church? (Do not include buildings and money problems.)
3. How can a process of growth be set in motion in the parish?
4. How is the PCC organized for growth?
5. How do PCC members relate to each other? And how does this help or hinder the growth of the church?
6. Are the plans for growth being made in a spirit of prayer,

and with an openness to the workings of the Holy Spirit, without whom no growth is possible?

***Reasons for failure to grow***   Would the PCC feel that any of the following things prevent growth in the parish?

1. The attitude that 'nothing changes here – we've always done things this way before'. A failure to move with the Holy Spirit?
2. The PCC is too busy maintaining buildings and organizations. Discussion about growth is perhaps not welcome by PCC members?
3. 'We have tried many projects before, and they have made little difference.' (Why?)
4. The age-old conflict between good and evil?

**Guest services**   Members of the congregation are asked to invite one family to a special guest service. A verbal invitation and explanation is best, and this can be supplemented with a written invitation. How true is the saying, 'The medium is the message'?

It is a good idea to have something after the service, where the guests can meet the members of the congregation – e.g. coffee, or sherry – or a meal, e.g. harvest lunch, or a Christmas lunch. Perhaps each PCC member could undertake to invite two families to the guest service.

Could these invitations be done in a systematic way? Prayer for the families concerned is important, not simply at the time of the guest service, but on a regular long-term basis over the years.

**Guild of St Barnabas**   It was founded in 1876, and it is mainly a 'postal' fellowship of prayer for nurses and members of the caring professions. Its aim is to strengthen Christian faith and witness of members in carrying out their demanding work.

Members of the Guild undertake (1) to pray daily for other members of the Guild, (2) to read the Bible regularly, (3) examination of conscience, (4) attend divine service on Sunday, except when hindered by duty or other unavoidable cause, and (5) frequent reception of Holy Communion. There is an annual meeting, an annual Quiet Day and an annual Retreat for those who are able to attend. The *Guild* magazine is sent to all members in May and November. If there are any nurses or members of the caring professions in the congregation, please tell them about the Guild, as it is important to encourage and strengthen them in this way.

The Guild Prayer for daily use is

Lord God Almighty,
inspire, we beseech you, in us your servants,
love for you, and compassion for all who suffer.
At all times, be our guide,
in weakness our strength,
in weariness our rest,
that we may so grow in holiness
that at the last we may enter
into the eternal joy and peace of your Kingdom,
through Jesus Christ our Saviour and Lord. Amen.

Further details from:
The Organizing Secretary, 16 Copperwood, Ashford, Kent TN24 8PZ. Tel: 0233-635 334.

**Guild of St Raphael** The Guild was founded in 1915 to restore the ministry of healing in the Church. Members of the Guild undertake to pray each day as a regular intercession for all who suffer in mind or body. Members are also asked to pray at each Eucharist for God's blessing on the work of the Guild.

To pray for the sick and the dying is an important part of the work of the whole church in every parish. To have a branch of the Guild of St Raphael in the parish can be a great help in this work.

The members usually gather together in church (in the Lady Chapel) once a month. Before the Guild Office (short service), a brief meeting is held to sort out any changes on the sick list. Each member undertakes to pray for certain people who are sick. Then the Guild Office is said and the sick are prayed for by name. Sometimes Evensong is said before the Guild Office. The Guild Office can, of course, be taken by a lay person.

The Guild publishes a quarterly magazine, available to all members of the Guild.

Details from:
The Secretary, The Guild of St Raphael, St Cyprian's Church, Clarence Gate, Glentworth Street, London NW1 6AX. Tel: 071-724 7352.

**Healing** There is new interest in the healing ministry of the Church, and of course all healing comes from God. Sometimes individuals and groups are channels used by God in the healing process, and prayer and the sacraments of the Church can have a powerful effect. Is it possible that human channels can sometimes be blocked through sin, or neglect of daily prayer?

St James 5.13–15 describes anointing the sick with oil. On Maundy Thursday, the bishop blesses the three oils used for anointing. The three oils are (1) for Baptism, (2) for Confirmation and (3) for the sick.

**Holiday club**   Children are often at a loose end during holidays, especially in summer. Here is an opportunity for the church to provide a holiday club each day for a week or fortnight. Parents and others can work together to plan programmes, rotas and menus. Many things are possible, including drama, music, and painting. Also a variety of games, expeditions, picnics, hikes, competitions, concerts and a short daily act of worship.

What about a 'holiday at home for the elderly' – with outings and eating together for a week?

**Holidays**   Holidays are part of God's plan for mankind. When you are away from home on a Sunday, try to attend the nearest parish church. We don't need holidays away from God! (You may come home with new ideas.)

**Holy Communion**   It is said that the Church of England has 'found religion in its old age' through the spread of the Parish Communion movement in the twentieth century. A vast amount of literature exists on Holy Communion – or whatever name you use for this special service. The Mass comes from the Latin 'Ite missa est', which means 'You are sent out', i.e. to do God's work in the world. The Eucharist means the thanksgiving. The Lord's Supper reminds us of the meal in the upper room. The word Communion means sharing. Christians share together in the life of Christ because of their new birth at Holy Baptism. The Eucharist is a celebration – not in any rowdy sense – but a celebration of joy and thanksgiving. The Church lives and grows through the celebration of the Eucharist, done in response to our Lord's invitation and command, 'Do this in remembrance of me'.

*Participation in the Eucharist*   Much more is required of PCC members and the congregation than to be mere spectators of something done for them by the priest and the choir. It involves preparation by everyone before the service. It involves putting a special effort into singing, and concentration during the sermon, prayers and readings. 'You shall love the Lord your God with all your heart, and mind and soul and strength.' When everyone takes part in a full and active way, then the worship is enriched and the congregation grows in worship. People learn to co-operate with the grace of God, and this gives a feeling of life and love, of joy and fellowship, as well as awe and wonder. These things can be noticed and felt by visitors and occasional worshippers, and they have a powerful effect in drawing people into the life of the Church.

*Lay involvement in leading the worship*   Certain parts of the service can only be taken by a duly ordained priest. However, the priest may invite suitable people to lead other parts of the service. Providing the selection is done carefully, and there is proper preparation, then the worship can be greatly enriched by lay participation. People participate in worship in a number of ways, by praying and singing and by sharing and receiving the precious gift of our Lord himself in the consecrated bread and wine, listening carefully, shared silence, exchanging greetings at the peace, and sometimes by movement. Worship lives in and through the members of the Church, and in their fellowship and relationship with each other and with God.

*Reading a lesson*   First, some basic thoughts on preparation.

1. Read it until you have a good understanding of its meaning. The congregation can tell very quickly whether or not you have prepared the passage. This is God's work, and you should offer only of your best to God.
2. Work out what is the common theme between the Old Testament and the New Testament readings and the gospel.
3. Work out which words to stress, and where to pause. Remember that the verb is always an important word in every sentence.
4. Beware of dropping your voice in the middle of the reading, so that people have extreme difficulty in hearing. Try to listen to your own voice, and work out if people can hear you. It is far better to be too loud, than for people to miss much of what you are reading. It would be wrong to ask any

reader to bellow, but reading does require much extra effort and volume in a large building. The words have to be pushed out and projected with force and firmness, in order for them to travel.

5. Practise your delivery and make sure that everyone in the church can hear each word you speak. Aim your voice slightly above the congregation, at an imaginary deaf person on the back seat. Never hold your head low when reading, as the words will be lost in the book. Make sure your voice comes out slowly and distinctly, without anything coming between you and the congregation. Sound is easily absorbed by a congregation. Extra effort is always needed in these circumstances. Deep breathing and filling the lungs before reading is helpful. Careful preparation is all wasted unless the people can actually hear what you are saying.

6. When using a microphone, practice is vital. The reader always has to listen to the sound of his or her voice coming through the loudspeakers. Are you too near or too far away from the microphone? Most microphones are good at picking up a voice, but it is always wise to speak towards them.

7. When you have 'competition' from a baby or a road-digger outside, speak more loudly to compensate for it, so that people can still hear each word you say.

8. Do not read in a dull and stodgy way. Make the reading come alive.

9. Come out and be ready to read as soon as the congregation has settled down quietly. Silent pauses are good, but not when waiting for the reader to start reading.

*General thoughts about reading a lesson* The Eucharist is divided into two main parts – the Ministry of the Word, and the Ministry of the Sacrament. The reading of the Scriptures is the basis of the Ministry of the Word, and the congregation is fed from the table of God's living word by the reading of the Scriptures. This table needs very careful preparation by the reader.

Most people can read the words printed on the page. But much more is involved than simply reading the words in front of you. Lesson reading is an art, and the secret is to understand the spiritual meaning of the passage before you come out in front of the congregation to read.

No one should accept an invitation to read, unless he or she is willing to commit themselves to prepare it thoroughly. It is an awesome responsibility, because no less than God himself is speaking to the congregation through the words which are being read out. The reader will perhaps share the thoughts of Patrick Brontë, rector of Haworth, who felt 'power and humility when you fill the whole place with the sound of God's own voice'.

Here is a prayer to use silently before you start reading:

Cleanse me, O Lord, from all my sins.
Send your Holy Spirit,
and help me worthily to proclaim your holy Word
to all who are here today, through Jesus Christ our Lord. Amen.

In some parishes, those who are reading on the next Sunday meet (with the priest) and share thoughts and insights about the collect and three readings. This can be a great help to the priest to start his thoughts for his next sermon, and it can be a great help to those who are reading to start their preparation early. If this is not possible, each reader should do his or her preparation carefully and thoroughly by themselves. Then the Word can be proclaimed with authority on Sunday.

Much is expected from all who read, and of course it is a great privilege to read from the Sacred Scriptures in this way.

A prayer for use by PCC members and others for the person who is about to read:

Heavenly Father,
you make yourself known to us in the Scriptures:
give understanding and guidance to N (or this person)
and open all our hearts to receive your living Word. Amen.

*Reading at special services*   This is an opportunity to invite outside or fringe members, instead of using regular church members. It is also a good way of finding new readers.

*Prayers and intercessions*   Another ideal place for lay participation. The priest may decide to write the prayers himself.

Prayers should be addressed directly to God, and the phrase 'let us pray for' should not be used in each section. Intercessions are not a time for a spiritual current affairs chat with God, nor an opportunity to tell God what you think is the solution to the problem. A simple phrase is all that is needed – such as 'We pray for Africa'. This can be followed by silence.

One lay person can lead the prayers. Alternatively, a different person can read each section of the prayers. Prayers should not be too long. The temptation to give the congregation its 'money's worth' with unnecessary verbiage should be avoided at all costs. A short time of silence can be most effective. A useful book is *Intercessions at Worship* by Colin Semper, published by Mowbray.

*Altar servers*   Young boys or girls, or adults, can be of great help to the priest during the service. In addition, using the young people in this way helps to keep them in church during a difficult period of their lives. *See* **Servers** on page 177.

*Administration of the chalice*   Lay people (two or three?) can be duly authorized by the Bishop, on the recommendation of the priest, and with the agreement of the PCC, to administer the chalice. Authorization usually has to be renewed every three years.

*Offertory procession*   There is symbolic meaning in carrying the bread and wine in procession to the altar. Man's work is symbolized in the making of the bread, and his leisure activities in the wine, and these are offered to God. The offertory reminds us of our dependence on God – 'All things come from thee, O Lord, and of thine own do we give thee.'

Dignity is added to the procession if it is led by the crucifer and two processional candles – yet another way of involving young people.

*Silence in worship*   The Quakers took the use of silence with them when they left the Church. Shared silence has officially returned to liturgical worship with the Alternative Service Book. Silence is much more than absence of noise, and in moderate use, it helps us to be more aware of God's presence.

*Midnight services*   These are popular in many parishes, but there can be problems. If most of the regular worshippers attend the midnight service, there can be a thin congregation to welcome the occasional worshippers who usually flock into church on Christmas morning. The young and the elderly cannot get to the midnight service. One solution is to encourage people to try to come to the main Christmas day service, even if they have already been to the midnight service.

*The Peace*   This is a very ancient and meaningful sign, mentioned by St Paul. It is easy to say that you 'love your neighbour as yourself', but actually to turn to your neighbour during the service and shake hands reminds us of the saying, 'Actions speak louder than words'. The Peace is a positive way in which Christians can show that they do mean what they say in words.

Peace be with you. This is a prayer that Christ himself will be with your neighbour. It is also a sign of friendship and Christian love. It is a sign of unity in Christ, and an expression of the love that exists amongst God's people. The Peace often has a powerful effect on occasional worshippers and visitors, and helps to draw them into the congregation.

*The time of the early services* Is 8 a.m. the best time for the early service? Would more people be involved if it were held at 9 a.m., and the main service at 10.30 a.m.? If Evensong is not flourishing, what about an occasional evening Communion service? Would Sunday evening be a good time to hold (monthly?) discussions after a shortened service?

*Questions for discussion*

1. How are new adult members integrated into the congregation? How much is left to chance as to whether or not they pick up the faith ('some seed fell on the stony path and died . . .')? Can the PCC help in any way?
2. How can the congregation be helped to grow in faith and love as a worshipping community?
3. Is it in any way necessary for the congregation to be 'converted' again and again (a term used by the Roman Catholics)?

**Home**  Something of a person's personality is reflected in their home. A good and stable home life is a great blessing and strength to the individual and also to the Church. Some people may be willing and able to lend their home to the Church occasionally, for a discussion or prayer group, a meeting or a social evening. A good home can be a powerful tool for evangelism.

*Food for thought*

1. Could you think of your home as an outpost for mission in the parish?
2. Has your home been blessed by a priest?

**Home Communion** Parishioners usually receive Communion every Sunday in church in most parishes. When they can no longer come to church through age or illness, it is right that they should keep in communion with the Church by receiving Communion at their home.

With the large (and growing) numbers involved, the priest is not able to conduct the whole service at each home. The usual method is to take bread and wine which have been consecrated in a service in church.

It is not wise for a priest to spend too much time administering Communion to the elderly. This is an area where lay people can exercise a valuable ministry after the main Sunday service – or during the week. Careful training is needed, and the appropriate written permission of the bishop. Lay involvement in this way can free the priest for mission and other tasks.

Those who receive Communion at home need to think about their own preparation. The aim of the visit is to receive the sacrament of Holy Communion. It is good practice not to chat before the service. Suggestions for preparation: read the Scripture readings for the day, and a psalm. Pray for the person who is bringing the sacrament; for the local church; for all who receive Communion at home; for the priest and bishop; and, of course, relatives, friends and neighbours. Work out those things for which you will ask for God's forgiveness. (The priest is always available to hear a private confession if this is requested.)

Christians who can no longer go to church can still play an active part in the mission of the Church through their regular prayers. A community and fellowship of prayer can be provided during the week in this way, and it is vital for the mission of the Church. A useful prayer book, written by the author, is ideal for people who can no longer come to church: *Daily with God* (Canterbury Press, Norwich). (*See* page 184.)

**Hospital visiting** Lay people can, after some basic training, supplement the work of the priest by visiting parishioners in hospital, and paying a follow-up visit after they are discharged. This is never instead of the priest, but in addition to the priest's visit.

One difficulty can be how to find out when parishioners are in hospital. Efficient street wardens can often pass on information in this connection.

Pray in church for those who are being visited. (*See* **Guild of**

**St Raphael** on page 91.)

Leave a parish magazine and a parish card with some prayers etc. when you visit a patient. The British and Foreign Bible Society produces colourful pamphlets suitable for use in hospital. (Address: 146 Queen Victoria Street, London EC4V 4BX.)

**Hospitality and parish catering**   St Paul said 'Be hospitable to one another'. His words are relevant today. To have a meal together is an act of Christian friendship, in addition to sharing the consecrated bread and wine at the altar. Hospitality was a common practice in the early Church and it is valuable and enjoyable today. It has mission potential. 'The way to a man's heart is through his stomach', and this is a way to get nearer to his soul. With the local church as host, there are many opportunities to invite outsiders and fringe members into the warm and friendly hospitality of the church community.

There are two kinds of parish catering. Regular events – a light buffet lunch, or a more substantial monthly lunch – both open to anyone in the community who cares to come. It is helpful but not essential to know numbers beforehand, and it is unwise to turn anyone away.

Occasional events include harvest supper or harvest lunch on Sunday, Shrove Tuesday party, a parish Christmas lunch or dinner, a dinner dance, a Sunday lunch for the congregation, or a Christmas lunch for those living on their own. A buffet lunch for those involved in different forms of community work is useful for doctors, social workers, probation officers, midwives and clergy. Lunchtime lectures and discussions, when people bring sandwiches, and soup and coffee are provided by the church. Obviously no parish would undertake catering for all these events, but they are suggestions.

Five points need consideration:

1. The payment of bills should not fall on members of the catering team (even when repaid later). The best method is to open a church catering committee bank account; and the audited accounts are presented to the Annual Parochial Church Meeting.
2. The work should be shared out so that the same group does not shoulder it all. Extra helpers can be brought in for large functions. A busy parish needs two or three catering teams.

3. Imagination and variety are desirable when planning menus, while at the same time keeping costs within sensible limits. Attractive presentation is helpful, and need not cost extra money.
4. A large hard-backed note book is needed to record date and occasion, numbers served, quantities and cost of all food and wine purchased, profit or loss, and the names of those who did the work. Comments for the next time the menu is used might be helpful.
5. Most churches have a long-term interest in providing food for large parish functions. It is wise initially to use profits from catering events to buy modern catering equipment, including a catering oven, for the church hall.

*Food for thought*

1. If one does not already exist, would it be a good idea to form a catering team in the parish?
2. When did you last invite someone from the church community for a meal in your own home? (Someone who is elderly or lives alone?)

**Housing Associations**   (*See* **Church Housing Trust** on page 44.) Land not required in the future for a new hall, car park, curate's house or vicarage could be used for houses or flats for elderly or homeless people. A Housing Association can be formed by the PCC, or by the Deanery Synod, or by the local Council of Churches. Generous government grants are available to help to build and maintain these homes. Land can be leased (rather than sold) to the newly formed Housing Association.

The PCC is advised to contact the archdeacon at the initial stage, and before any money is spent on architect's fees. Selling or leasing the land to form a Housing Association is usually better than selling or leasing it to a local builder.

Useful address: National Federation of Housing Associations, 30/32 Southampton Street, London WC2E 7HE. Tel: 071–240 2771.

**Insurance**   The PCC is responsible for providing adequate insurance cover for all aspects of church life and buildings. 'Can we afford the premium?' could be put another way – 'Can we afford not to provide proper insurance cover?' The answer is surely No, as PCC members are elected as trustees in this respect for the parishioners. What happens if there is a fire, and the PCC has not fulfilled its responsibilities in respect of insurance? There is no financial fairy godmother at the diocesan office who will automatically provide the money for rebuilding the church.

Fire is always a great risk and proper cover is essential. Each PCC has to work out whether or not it wants insurance cover to provide an exact replica of the existing building. That, with fees, could be expensive. Is restoration the right answer, or would a modern building be more suitable for the circumstances? The PCC has to be quite clear about the level of insurance it has obtained.

The Ecclesiastical Insurance Group specializes in all forms of church insurance. Founded by the Church for this purpose, the company gives profits back to dioceses (in proportion to the amount of business done with each diocese).

The EIG will send a surveyor to the parish without charge or obligation. The surveyor gives advice and suggestions, but the responsibility for the final decision rests with the PCC alone.

Fire policies are at present subject to the 75 per cent 'condition of average'. This means that the total sum insured must not be less than 75 per cent of the full replacement value – otherwise the local church has to pay a proportion of the loss incurred.

Another thought – would the church be rebuilt, or would a fire solve the problem of having too many churches in the area? If the PCC has not obtained proper insurance cover, that could be the decisive factor in any decision about rebuilding.

Storm damage, lightning, burst water pipes, overflow problems, malicious damage, theft, all need consideration, and the policy should be agreed by the full PCC (on the recommendation of the standing committee).

Employers liability cover is a legal requirement. Full cover against public liability is wise, particularly in view of the vast sums awarded by the courts. All risks cover is desirable on church silver, the organ and other valuable items.

The terms of the policy should be checked, and a report given to the Annual Parochial Church Meeting every year. One method of keeping it up to date is to make it 'index-linked' – so that premiums are automatically increased in the ratio recommended by the Royal Institute of Chartered Surveyors.

The EIG has a 'No Claim' discount scheme, which reduces

the premium by 20 per cent after three years without a claim. Premiums can be paid by instalments.

The EIG also provides insurance for the homes of individuals, for cars, all other forms of insurance, and life assurance, pension schemes and an ethical unit trust. It is a friendly company, and quotations are given without obligation or charge. The address: The Ecclesiastical Insurance Group, Beaufort House, Brunswick Road, Gloucester GL1 1JZ. Tel: 0452–28533.

*Food for thought*
The majority of church fires are caused by electrical faults – particularly in the organ. Is your electricity supply for the organ on an independent system? Is it switched off at the mains every time after use? How safe is your church from someone deliberately trying to set it on fire?

The police are willing to help with the prevention of theft and vandalism. Has the local crime prevention officer inspected church property and reported to the PCC?

**Integrity**   What is absolute integrity?

**Interregnum**   (*See* **Churchwardens** on page 50, para. 10.)
The interregnum is the period between the departure of the outgoing vicar and the institution and induction of the new one. Sequestrators are appointed by the diocese, and they usually include one or both churchwardens, the rural dean (and also the diocesan secretary if the living is suspended). Their task is to maintain the life and worship of the church, and look after all church property during the interregnum. The PCC will want to be certain that everything is being done that should be done in the parish.

The rural dean may call a meeting of the churchwardens and the outgoing vicar to plan the arrangements for the interregnum. Careful preparation before the vicar leaves the parish is the best way of ensuring a smooth interregnum.

*Length of interregnum*   Some PCCs expect the new vicar to arrive within days of the previous one leaving the parish. In practice, this does not happen, and an interregnum is often a matter of months rather than weeks.

*Diocesan Pastoral Committee*   In these days of rapid change, the Diocesan Pastoral Committee usually considers the future of every parish whenever a vacancy occurs. They consider such questions as, What is the geographical position of the parish in relation to the centres of population in the deanery? Is the parish a financially viable unit – or does it depend heavily on the support of other parishes (through the quota)? Does the PCC repay the expenses of office of the priest? Is the quota paid in full each year? Does the PCC have a good record in supporting the Church overseas? What is the condition of the church building, the hall and the vicarage?

*Church services*   No priest can conduct a service unless he holds the bishop's licence, or has permission to officiate. The services may be reduced to one per Sunday and one during the week, and the times may have to be altered.

Provision has to be made for funerals, baptisms, weddings, calling of banns, home communions, and the pastoral care of the sick and elderly. Visits will have to be done for some of these services (by one of the churchwardens?). Where Holy Communion is 'reserved' in the church for use with the sick, then arrangements have to be made for its proper care.

*PCC meetings and the Annual Meeting*   When a curate is appointed as minister in charge during the interregnum, he takes the chair at meetings. Otherwise, the vice-chairman of the PCC is the chairman.

The churchwardens should make sure that no changes are made during the interregnum. Many bishops write to the churchwardens to this effect.

*The Diocesan Handbook and Canon Law*   Every parish has a loose-leaf folder with diocesan instructions on various matters, and a copy of Canon Law. These belong to the parish, and should be left with the other papers and documents for the incoming vicar. It is helpful for the sequestrators and the incoming priest if there is an extra page in the folder with details of the house, drainage, electrical or plumbing systems and their oddities and idiosyncrasies.

*The congregation*   It frequently happens that numbers drop off during an interregnum, and it is always hard work to get them back again. The best course is for the PCC to keep a close eye on the situation and see what action can be taken when

103

necessary. The curate, and the non-stipendiary priest if there is one, cannot be expected to take over the work-load of the outgoing vicar.

*Care of the vicarage*   There may be diocesan instructions on this, but here are some suggestions:

1. The churchwardens – or someone else by arrangement – should check that all is well in the house each day.
2. If squatters occupy the house, immediately notify the archdeacon, the rural dean and the police. To prevent such occupation and to prevent vandalism, it may be possible to find someone willing to live in the vicarage during the inter-regnum – but the written permission of the archdeacon must always be obtained by the sequestrators.
3. If any immediate repair work is needed, it must be reported to the archdeacon as soon as possible.
4. The house should be properly ventilated, and the heating system put on for regular periods during winter months.
5. Security needs special attention. The risk of vandalism can be lessened by the following (assuming the locks and catches are working properly and are duly fastened):

   > one or more lights on an automatic timing switch,
   > curtains hung in all windows,
   > grass and hedges cut regularly,
   > mail, milk bottles and newspapers removed from the door.

6. The telephone should not be disconnected. The rental charge is paid from the sequestration account.
7. When a priest is offered the living, he (and his wife) visit the parish and vicarage. Before he accepts the living, he and his wife will again inspect the house with the archdeacon, rural dean and churchwardens to discuss what repairs, alterations and decorations will be done before the priest moves into the house. The PCC will no doubt be asked to help with the cost, and a healthy vicarage improvement fund is useful for such occasions. Hopefully, the smell of paint will have vanished and the house will have been spring-cleaned days (not hours) before the furniture van arrives at the vicarage.
8. Any unofficial tenants living in the vicarage must leave on or before the day of departure of the vicar. The house is the responsibility of the sequestrators in all respects during the interregnum.

9. When a priest dies in office, his widow is entitled to stay on in the vicarage for at least three months. The Pensions Board normally find accommodation for her and her family. Her late husband has given loving pastoral care to so many during his ministry, and now it is his wife who will need love and care and help and prayer.

*The sequestration account*   A new account must always be opened at the bank, so that sequestration money can be kept separate from PCC money, and properly accounted for on the sequestration account balance sheet. Two sequestrators sign the cheques, and usually the rural dean signs with either of the other two. The income comes from the minister's fees (as distinct from the PCC fees) for weddings and funerals. Current fees are laid down on the Table of Ecclesiastical Fees (displayed on the church notice board). A loan from the PCC to the sequestration account is useful as a float, and it is repaid when the account is closed. Any rent from letting the vicarage garage is paid into the sequestration account.

Fees and expenses are paid from this account to visiting clergy. Never ask 'What do we owe you?' Find out the current diocesan rate for fees and expenses, and hand the money over in an envelope after the service.

The cost of heating the vicarage (or part of it – check diocesan regulations) is paid from this account. A balance sheet is prepared at the end of the interregnum, after all expenses have been paid, and it is duly signed by all three sequestrators. The bank account is of course then closed.

*The institution and induction service*   If there is no newsletter from the church delivered free to every home in the parish, the arrival of a new vicar is an opportunity to send one out, together with an invitation to the service and reception, and other news of the parish can be included.

An official parish invitation list is drawn up by the standing committee or wardens. Include the Mayor and Lady Mayoress, Member of Parliament, trade union leaders, doctors, local government councillors, and representatives from local schools, hospitals and factories, the deanery clergy and clergy of the other denominations in the area. The rural dean should be consulted about the list, and the new incumbent will want to invite friends and relatives. Most parishes print formal invitation cards, and they should be sent out in plenty of time.

A rehearsal is arranged by the rural dean, and it is important that all concerned are present, including the organist, servers and sidesmen. Most institutions now take place within the setting of the Eucharist.

A copy of the Diocesan Service of Institution and Induction – or Service of Licensing – is sent by the bishop to the new priest. When the readings and hymns have been approved, a copy of the printed service is sent by the wardens to the patron(s) and the bishop, the archdeacon and the area dean, and the service should be in their hands at least ten days before the actual service.

The cost of printing this service is normally a charge on PCC funds, and must not be taken from the sequestration account, nor from the collection at the service.

The entire collection at the Induction Service is, in most dioceses, for the bishop's discretionary fund. A notice is usually printed in the Order of Service to this effect: 'The collection will be taken in the next hymn for the bishop's discretionary fund. You are invited to support this generously, as it is used to help clergy in special need and in emergencies.' In some dioceses, the collection is given to the Church overseas (the diocesan 'link').

*Appointment of the new priest*   When the patron is the Crown, the Duchy of Lancaster or Cornwall, or the Lord Chancellor, these rules do not apply. Nor do they apply in the case of a team vicar.

A copy of the Patronage (Benefices) Measure 1986 can be obtained from HMSO (1992 price £4.90), but the diocese usually provides very clear information about this matter.

The bishop writes to the PCC secretary giving formal notice to the parish about the vacancy. The PCC must hold one or more meetings within four weeks of receiving this notice. The outgoing incumbent and spouse, and the patron and his representative, if any, are excluded from this meeting.

The PCC meeting has to make five decisions:

1. To prepare a statement describing the conditions, needs and traditions of the parish. This must be sent by the PCC secretary to the patron and the bishop within four weeks of receiving the bishop's notice about the vacancy. Unless this time limit is observed, the PCC representatives lose their right to veto any choice of incumbent.

2. To appoint two lay members to act as the PCC's representatives in connection with the selection of an incumbent. The patron and his representative, the outgoing priest and spouse, all clerks in Holy Orders, deaconesses and licensed lay workers are excluded from this. If no representatives are appointed, the two churchwardens act for the PCC. The names and addresses of the two representatives must be sent by the PCC secretary to the patron and the bishop as soon as practicable.

3. To decide whether to request the patron to consider advertising the vacancy. The final decision about advertising rests with the patron.

4. To decide whether to request a joint meeting with the patron and the bishop, which the PCC secretary must then convene. The patron or the bishop may also request a joint meeting, which the PCC secretary must convene. The bishop and/or the patron may send a representative if he is unable to attend. At least one-third of the members of the PCC must attend this meeting, and the outgoing priest and spouse are again excluded. The area/rural dean and the lay chairman of the Deanery Synod must also be invited to the meeting.

5. The meeting must decide whether to request a statement in writing from the bishop about the needs of the diocese and the wider interests of the Church, in relation to the parish.

In the case of a multi-parish benefice which does not have a team council or Joint PCC, the meeting must be a joint meeting of all the PCCs. The PCCs may make a joint statement about conditions, needs and traditions of the parishes, and each PCC may make a separate statement dealing with the parish concerned. The other decisions must be joint decisions. Four or more representatives must be appointed to act as PCC representatives, so that each parish PCC has at least one representative.

Where there is a team council or joint PCC, it carries out the functions of the PCCs in this matter.

When the patron has chosen a priest to whom he wishes to offer the benefice, he must give notice of this to the PCC representatives, who must approve the offer before it is made. They will be deemed to have approved it unless any of the PCC representatives give notice of refusal within two weeks. In the event of a refusal, the patron may refer the matter to the archbishop, who may decide to override the refusal.

If no priest has accepted appointment within nine months of the date when the benefice became vacant, the right to select the new incumbent lapses to the archbishop. He must consult the bishop and the PCC representatives as well as anyone else he thinks fit, but he does not normally need their approval before offering the benefice to a priest.

The bishop must give at least three weeks' written notice of his intention to institute or collate the priest to the PCC secretary, who must ensure that it is displayed on the notice board for two weeks.

**Inventory**   *See The terrier and inventory* under **Buildings** on page 25.

**Jealousy**   Jealousy and envy are the two curses of the ministry in the local church. Jealousy is a sign of immaturity and it has evil consequences for the individual and the church community. Pray regularly each day over a long period (years if necessary) for someone you dislike. This is strictly between you and God (unless you try to make a friendly approach to the person concerned). 'More things are wrought by prayer than this world dreams of.'

**Job in the parish**   If your priest asks you to do a job in the parish, he has thought and prayed about it beforehand. Do not undertake the situation unless you are prepared to accept the responsibility involved, and are willing to put your best efforts into doing a good job. Consider all aspects carefully, and pray about it. Do not refuse unless there is a valid reason for doing so, as your priest obviously trusts you and thinks you are the right person.

There is another side to this question. Sometimes one individual has three or four jobs in the parish. Should one person accept all this responsibility? Would the results be better if the work were shared? The answers are obvious.

**Journey**   When travelling through another parish, the sight of a church spire or tower can be a reminder to offer a silent arrow prayer: 'O Lord, bless the congregation, the PCC and the priest in this parish. Amen.'

**Kneeling in church**   In those places where the congregation kneels to pray, actually kneel down, rather than pretending to kneel by leaning forward. There is surely a good reason for kneeling, and our joints will work just as well as those of our forefathers.

**Lay Reader**   *See* **Readers** on pages 163–5.

**Learning by heart**   Former generations of Christians learned the collects, famous prayers, and well-known passages from the Bible. These passages became, as it were, an intimate part of the person's life, and they could be recalled and used whenever necessary. PCC members might find this a worthwhile idea for themselves.

**Lesson reading**   *See* **Holy Communion** on pages 93–5.

**Library**   St Paul wrote, 'Know the reason for the faith that is within you'. People often become experts with their hobbies. Christianity is more than a hobby, and it is useful if the parish can build up a library of Christian books. A notebook is required to show the borrower's name, and the date when the book is taken out, and later returned. It may not be used every week, but it is a useful resource for every parish.

**Lunchtime services and meetings**   Churches in the centre of towns and cities have a good opportunity to minister to people who are regularly away from home at lunchtime. Various ideas are possible – worship, a series of addresses, discussions, music, hospitality, a place to sit and eat sandwiches, and cloakroom facilities.

What levels of support can PCC members give to organize these events?

**Magazine**   The magazine can play an important part in the work of the church, as it goes regularly through the doors where priest and church members could not possibly go each month. There are three levels of communication through the written word:

1. *The weekly newsletter and notices*   This is given every Sunday to all the people at church, who are encouraged to take extra copies to other people who might be interested. A news-sheet avoids interrupting the worship with the notices.

2. *The traditional magazine*   Two problems constantly arise with the traditional magazine. First, how to increase the circulation. People die, move to another town, or simply do not wish to continue subscribing. Sending out a letter and free sample copies can help, but the best method to increase the circulation is by an organized sales drive with church members visiting every home in the parish.

   The second problem concerns the question of increasing costs. If the price is too high, the number of subscribers will fall. People will not buy the magazine if there are too many advertisements. The time may come when the PCC has to ask, Is it too expensive a luxury for such a limited circulation? Is there any alternative to the traditional type of magazine?

3. *Free magazine delivered to every home*   This removes all problems of how to increase the circulation! The local church has a mission to everyone who lives within the parish boundaries. A free magazine delivered every month to every home is in financial terms an important part of the Church's mission to the parish. It requires ingenuity, planning and hard work – but everything worthwhile requires effort. To keep the costs to a minimum, most parishes will produce their own magazine – whatever copying or duplicating method is used. A traditional ink duplicator is still the cheapest method. But it must never be shoddy, nor badly produced, nor badly folded. Second best is not good enough for God.

   One method used by the author is to have three pages of A4 paper, duplicated on both sides, folded and stapled with an electric stapler to form a twelve-page magazine. When there are several thousand homes in the parish, the task needs careful planning and many distributors, and a team of 'assemblers'. No advertisements are included, and the cost is seen as part of the Church's mission to the parish.

*The contents*   What is the aim of the magazine? Are the contents relevant for that purpose? Drawings, sketches, cartoons and plenty of blank spaces are helpful. Lists of sidesmen, servers, coffee and cake rotas, flower arrangers, brass cleaners, lesson and intercession readers – these are all irrelevant, irritating and of no interest to fringe members and those not connected with the church. If the contents are too 'churchy' people may not read it. How relevant are the contents for someone working in a factory, hospital, local school or shop? A different approach is needed when there is a general circulation to every home and place of work.

The cover is vital. If this is not appealing, the magazine will receive only a quick glance. For the traditional magazine, attractive covers can be bought from The Sign or Home Words, and the name of the parish and the price can be overprinted on the cover. The same picture month after month, whether a view of the church, or worse still, rows of empty pews inside, will not whet the appetite of any reader! Many parishes have the diocesan newsletter, as well as a ready printed national inset like *The Sign*, *Home Words* and *Church News*. Insets and picture covers can be obtained from The Sign, St Mary's Works, St Mary's Plain, Norwich NR3 3BM (Tel: 0603-616563), and Home Words Ltd, PO Box 44, Guildford, Surrey GU1 1XL (Tel: 0483-33944). One of the aims of the magazine is to attract people to come to church. As many people probably do not read the New Testament, there is value in printing passages of Scripture (two pages every month?) without comment. This can be one of the channels through which the Holy Spirit may work. Society today has been cut off from the Church for so long, we have to argue the case for the existence of God frequently and in very simple terms. Nothing can be taken for granted.

*The distributors*   They are a vital link between the church and the homes of the parish. It is important to deliver the magazine carefully, and if possible without folding. Get them out as soon as possible, otherwise the events will be part of history before people read about them. When a new family moves into the parish, it is important to welcome them on behalf of the church, and to leave a magazine with them.

*Editorial team*   Are there people with appropriate skills in the congregation or the community at large - e.g. journalists or artists?

*Questions for discussion*

1. Are magazines delivered free of charge to the local hospitals, schools, factories, police station, doctors' and dentists' surgeries, museum, libraries, hotels, etc.?

2. Does the PCC see the magazine in terms of its continuous mission to every home in the parish?
3. Is any diocesan material, e.g. the bishop's letter, included in the magazine?
4. If the magazine is delivered free to every home, is this a priority item on the annual budget?

**Marriage**   Marriage is an agreement between a man and a woman about love, money, a home and children, and it is a partnership of equals, which involves sharing. A Christian marriage includes all these, but has three things in addition. First, Christianity brings a deep understanding of love, shown in its most powerful way on the cross. God is the source of all love, and it is love which leads us back to God. Christian marriage is a sign which reflects something of Christ's love for the Church. It is a sacrament and a holy mystery, through which the Holy Spirit is given to the couple. Secondly, the Christian has a different understanding of forgiveness, again because of the cross. St Paul said, 'Do not let the sun go down on your wrath' (Ephesians 4.26). Thirdly, a Christian couple have the added spiritual dimension in their marriage. Jesus did not say that Christian marriage would be perfect, without tensions and rows, but there is much truth in the saying, 'A couple who pray together stay together'. Obviously, effort is needed every day to develop the marriage relationship.

*Questions for discussion for married couples*

1. Marriage has been described as the art of sustaining a relationship of love. What is your definition of love? What are the best ways of improving your marriage relationship?
2. How effectively do you communicate with each other?

**Media Awareness Project**   MAP was founded by the Mothers' Union and a charitable trust from J. Sainsbury PLC. MAP is now an ecumenical project which looks at the media from a Christian point of view. Its aims are (1) to increase awareness of the effects of the media in our lives; (2) to improve our understanding of how the media work; (3) to encourage praise and constructive criticism; and (4) to provide information, resource material and support for branches. Each MU deanery representative will come and speak to the PCC or a parish meeting about the project. Further details from: The

Media Awareness Project, 24 Tufton Street, London SW1P 3RB. Tel: 071–222 5533.

**Mission – Evangelism – Renewal** Far from feeling any strong desire or motivation in these areas, many PCC members will no doubt feel embarrassed, unsuited for that kind of thing, or even afraid. You might even wish that this section had not been written, but whatever your feelings, please read on to the end. (The author might add that it was one of the most difficult sections to write.)

There are other problems connected with mission – apart from a reluctance by some Christians to be involved. These include the divisions between the different Christian Churches. The Bible is vital, but it is also a problem for the mission of the Church, because many people believe that the Bible has been 'disproved' by science.

The Church is faced with a desperate missionary situation of enormous proportions. Who is doing anything about it in your parish? Whose responsibility is it? Jesus created his Church so that his work would be continued by his followers after the Ascension. Whose ministry it it? It is Christ's apostolic and priestly ministry, which is being continued by and through the whole Church, bishops, priests and lay people together. Many believe that mission and evangelism are the work of the vicar alone. According to the New Testament that is simply not true. All the gifts of the Spirit are not given to the priest alone. The Holy Spirit draws people together with different gifts and skills, so that the whole baptized membership of the local church can work together effectively as a single body – the body of Christ in the parish.

St Paul reminds us that some are called to be apostles, some evangelists, some prophets, some teachers, and perhaps we can add – some who make cups of tea, some to address envelopes, some to knock on doors, some to lead discussion groups or help to run the Sunday School, etc. The body does not say to the feet, 'I do not need you', nor does the hand say to the shoulder, 'I do not need you'. All parts of the body are needed for it to function properly, and they have to be co-ordinated under the head, who is Christ. Individuals are incorporated into the body of Christ by Baptism, not just to receive privileges from God, but also to serve him. The work of the local church is thus not a one-man band. It is a corporate ministry, involving the total membership of the church in one way or another, each

113

according to the gifts and abilities he has received.

Jesus himself clearly intended it to be a corporate ministry, and he gave authority for every Christian to be involved in this work. It is helpful to think carefully about what the Bible actually says, particularly in passages such as Exodus 19.4-6; Isaiah 6.1-8; Romans 12.4-8; 1 Corinthians 12; 1 Peter 2.1-10; Revelation 1.6; 5.10; 20.6.

The Church clearly endorses this authority in its legislation about PCCs, and the Synodical Government Measure defines the function of the PCC - 'to co-operate with the incumbent in the whole mission of the Church, pastoral, evangelistic, social and ecumenical'. If we love and worship God, he in turn requires us to love our neighbour as ourselves. Some people believe that it is a spiritual matter, to take the Christian gospel to all people in the parish and beyond its boundaries. Others see this love in terms of caring and action to meet the needs of society, but without any attempt to proclaim the gospel. The Church must never lose the quest for social justice in all spheres of life. Surely both these elements are needed, but in this book we concentrate on the spiritual mission of the Church. (The social gospel and mission of the Church requires another book on its own.)

Emil Brunner wrote the well-known words, 'The Church exists by mission as fire exists by burning'. The Church is not a closed club for the benefit of its members. Archbishop William Temple put it like this: 'The Church is the only society which exists for those who do not belong to it'. Mission involves 'crossing the boundaries' between the Church membership and those who have no faith in Christ and his Church. PCC members certainly have many opportunities which are not open to the clergy.

Large crowds attend football matches, but even larger numbers worship God in church every Sunday. Spectators enter the football stadium not in large groups but as individuals, one by one. This is the way in which people become members of the Church, one by one. At the beginning of his ministry, Jesus found Andrew. Andrew then went and found his brother and said, 'We have found the Messiah'. Andrew then actually brought his brother Simon (Peter) to Jesus. Imagine every member of your PCC bringing one other person to a faith in Jesus. Could it be the aim of every PCC member - to try to bring one new person into church membership per year? It requires patience, prayer, and waiting for the right moment to present itself. Perhaps only a few words will be required for this to happen, such as 'Let me tell you how I first came to the Church'.

*Mission and evangelization*    What is the difference?

Mission is the whole outreach of the Church in its many forms and at many different levels in the parish. Mission can be divided into four areas - pastoral, evangelistic, social and ecumenical. It includes such trivial things as coffee mornings, committee meetings, clubs and countless things, inside and out-side the traditional structures of the church community. It involves meeting human need in society.

Evangelization is much more specific and definite. It is the proclaiming or telling of the gospel - the good news - of Jesus Christ.

There may be a large 'evangelistic rally' when an evangelist proclaims the gospel to a crowd of people. This is a very specialized field, and perhaps not every PCC is able to gather a crowd of non-Christians together to hear the gospel.

For most PCC members, evangelization will take place quietly with another person, or perhaps in a small group. You may think that it is difficult and complicated, but in fact, it can be very simple: 'This is how I came to belong to the Church'. Then tell your faith story in a straightforward, sensitive and gentle way.

Once a person starts to respond, then appropriate help and training is needed - perhaps with another person. Careful thought and planning is vital, and Christian formation should not be left to chance. Perhaps a nurture group or starter group is needed?

The local church is in the long-term business of mission and evangelization. A free magazine delivered to every home in the parish - say, eight times per year - will sometimes produce some quick results. But on the whole, it is a question of sowing seeds for the future. Seeds usually take some time to germinate in the darkness of the soil, and your parish may, or may not, be difficult ground for the seeds of the gospel (*see* **Magazine** on page 109). What are the long-term alternatives? In what other way can the gospel message be delivered regularly to every home in the parish?

Door to door visiting by PCC members every third year may be appropriate in some parishes. It is certainly a challenge for PCC members, as well as for the parishioners. But it can be effective and useful. Training is needed, and a letter or leaflet can be left in each home.

***Renewal and mission*** The willingness of the PCC to be involved in mission and evangelization depends to a considerable extent on the spiritual health of the PCC and the congregation. This seems to go in cycles, and it is perhaps not unconnected with the ministries of successive priests in the parish. The renewal or the conversion of the congregation is the first step in many parishes.

What is involved in renewal? It involves repentance, a turning afresh to Christ, a call to holiness of life, taking the spiritual life seriously (*see* **Spiritual life of PCC members** on page 182). It is the Holy Spirit who calls us, and it is the Holy Spirit who teaches us and enables us to use the gifts which he has given to each PCC member for the work of the Church.

A praying community is a vital base for the continuing mission of the Church in the parish. PCC members are called to form the nucleus of that praying community. Elderly and housebound members of the Church can take part in front-line mission by praying regularly in their own homes for evangelism in the parish.

***Inward and outward journey of the PCC*** Mission and evangelization involves PCC members travelling in two directions. The first is the inward and spiritual journey towards God. Spiritual renewal starts with individuals, and in time, the congregation grows in maturity towards the full stature of Christ himself. This can involve change, and perhaps surrendering something to God?

The outward journey into the parish is both spiritual and physical. The inward and the outward are perhaps inseparable, and one will not be fruitful unless progress is made in the other.

Renewal, evangelization and mission are the work of the Holy Spirit. They do not depend on human ingenuity, perseverance and goodwill alone – although these are vital ingredients. PCC members are channels for the work of the Holy Spirit. This they can frustrate or even oppose. Far better if they work in co-operation. God does not force himself on people in the majority of cases. There are of course exceptions, e.g. St Paul on the Damascus Road. God is looking for a free response to his love in Jesus Christ – and he is looking for this response first in PCC members, and then in the people of the parish.

In order to see the parish from God's point of view, we have to think about the nature of God. Long ago, the prophet Isaiah had a vision of God in the Temple (Isaiah 6). That vision was a turning point in his life. Today we have a fuller understanding of God, because we have what Isaiah did not have – the knowledge of the Resurrection of Jesus Christ. Isaiah waited on God in the stillness of the Temple. Jesus waited on God on the Mount of Transfiguration and elsewhere. The disciples waited on Jesus in the upper room after the Resurrection. The disciples waited for the coming of the Holy Spirit at Pentecost. This waiting on the Holy Spirit in stillness and quietness is an important part of renewal.

Christ entrusts the privilege and responsibility of continuing his mission on earth to ordinary PCC members (and others too), with all their hopes, fears, human weaknesses, and expectations. The task was completely beyond the Apostles, until they waited for the coming of the Holy Spirit. It will be beyond us too, unless we learn to wait for the guidance and help of the Holy Spirit.

The question is asked in the Revelation of St John: 'What is the Spirit saying to the Churches?' What is the Holy Spirit saying to the PCC and to the church in your parish?

It is helpful for the PCC to work out a parish policy about evangelization, to show what the PCC is trying to do in terms of evangelization. At what stage should the congregation be involved in this process? How can this include all organizations connected with the Church?

A high percentage of people are converted to Christianity because a friend or relative persuades them to come to a service or meeting at church. The appropriate words have to be chosen carefully. The telling of the faith story is the first step. This has to be followed by an invitation – 'Come and see'. 'Would you like to come with me?'

*The mission and evangelism committee*   The aims of this committee are:

1. To meet regularly (monthly?) to study, pray, and engage in evangelization.
2. To help and encourage all members of the congregation and the PCC to engage in mission and evangelization on a

117

long-term basis, as a normal part of church life, and to try to use every opportunity which is presented to further the work of the Church.

3. To report regularly to the PCC.
4. To study diocesan and national material about mission and evangelization, and to invite the diocesan missioner to the parish/PCC when appropriate.
5. To organize appropriate evangelization events, where members of the Church can bring friends and neighbours – special service, concert, party, etc.
6. How can the PCC work together with any other Christian Churches in the area?
7. What arrangements are there in the parish to nurture the faith of those who come forward?

The Church of God is like a ship of salvation. We all come on board through the waters of Baptism. At first we are passengers, and then in due course we start to help the crew with their work. Then we come to realize that God wants everyone who is baptized to become a member of his crew on the ship.

We can put this another way. One definition of the Church: it is the eucharistic community which gathers together for worship. When people go out through the doors at the end of the service, it becomes the scattered Church – the 'Church on legs'.

*Questions for discussion*

1. Has your PCC discussed our Lord's call – 'Seek ye first the Kingdom of God'?
2. What is the quality of worship and fellowship like in your church? Is it something worth sharing with others? Could either be improved?
3. How should the PCC think about this difficult subject of evangelization? Could PCC members talk more about the Church to their friends?
4. How can the PCC be regularly renewed for its work?
5. Is it possible to co-operate with other Christian denominations in mission and evangelization?
6. It really is a great privilege – as well as a great responsibility – to share in Christ's mission to the world. How far is your PCC willing and able to take part in it?
7. What human factors in the local church can be used to

co-operate with the Holy Spirit to bring people into the Church community?

*Mission audit*   This is a time of great opportunity for mission and evangelization. How can the PCC respond to this situation? The first thing is to take a penetrating look at all the facts. Careful thought will be needed by the mission and evangelization committee about which facts will be useful for the audit. They will no doubt include communicants at Christmas and Easter, and perhaps the first Sunday in June and October, and also confirmations and baptisms, and other facts as are appropriate. The figures should be updated each year, in order to see if the Church is declining or growing in your parish.

After the facts have been collected each year, careful consideration and reflection is needed, which should lead on to planning and action. The purpose of mission audit is not to provide facts in a comfortable situation. The mission and evangelization committee needs to marshal all the God-given resources on the PCC and in the congregation to face the challenges and the opportunities in the parish.

**Mothers' Union**   The MU is an organization with a worldwide membership within the Anglican Communion. The members are mainly female, but it is open to all, both men and women, whether single, married or divorced, providing they have been baptized with water and in the name of the Holy Trinity, and that they promise to uphold and support the aims and objectives of the Mothers' Union.

The aim of the MU is the advancement of the Christian religion in the sphere of marriage and family life. The MU has high ideals of service to the community in general and to the Church in particular, but it is not easy to translate these high ideals into a regular branch programme. The MU constitution requires that the programmes are arranged so as to further the aims and objectives of the MU.

In parishes where there is an MU branch, there is a great opportunity for it to influence the lives of those who are not yet members, and particularly the young parents. The MU takes pride in regarding itself as the 'handmaiden of the Church'.

The divorce rate in society is very high, and there is an urgent need to provide Christian education about marriage, and for help in bringing up children. The influence of the home

119

and of television is very powerful. All education begins at home, whether for good or ill. So how can the MU help to develop and maintain Christian family life, not just for Church members, but for young families in the community who do not yet belong to the Church? Without the help of the Holy Spirit, that is an impossible task in today's world. If the MU is to be true to its aims, then great care is needed to work out and plan what can be done by the branch in the parish. This has to be translated into a branch programme. It will require discussion to obtain the support and agreement of all the members about the aim of the MU in the parish. The branch programme should always be made with the priest, and not presented to him after it has been drawn up.

It is, in fact, vital that the committee and the priest meet to pray and to plan the programme together. It is good to look carefully at the past, and to reflect on it in a critical way – but with Christian love. In this way, the committee can see how far the aims of the MU have been achieved through past programmes, and to make plans for the future. Areas where the MU can be involved are:

1.  Baptism (preparation) and follow up. A Birthday Card or 'MU Anniversary of Baptism Card' can be delivered by the member who lives nearest to the family. Every baby who is baptized can be 'adopted' by an MU member – whether known or unknown to the family – and regular prayer can be offered for the family. Also friendship.
2.  Sunday School recruitment.
3.  Baby-sitting circle – done in the name of the Church. (Could this be a way to raise money for the branch or an MU overseas worker?)
4.  Running, or involvement in, a mother and toddler group and playgroup, and pram service.
5.  Loneliness of young mothers in the community.
6.  Praying about various problems in the community.
7.  Prayer – make a definite commitment to give a certain amount of time for prayer. The MU has a worldwide fellowship of prayer, and daily prayer should be part of the Rule of Life, including midday prayers offered by every member of the MU.

What a spiritual power could be released in every parish if the MU, with the approval and agreement of the priest, organized daily prayer in the church – say with two

members coming into the church each day on a rota.
The time of prayer should be at the same time each day,
e.g. 12 noon or 3 p.m., and last for ten or fifteen minutes.
(An alternative suggestion – that two MU members
(minimum) conduct Evensong each day of the week?)

8. Family education. There seems to be a desire among young
families for help and guidance in bringing up their children.
The MU has much excellent material on this subject, and
the opportunity to do a great deal of good in the world.
9. Running a prison visitors centre.
10. Organizing Lent hunger lunches.
11. Organizing a drop-in centre for the unemployed.
12. Developing a link with an overseas branch of the MU in a
developing country.

Much of this is an enormous challenge, so how can each branch
be encouraged to accept responsibilities which are included in
the MU's aims and objectives? How can timidity and reluctance be overcome?

What does God want your branch to do for his kingdom?

An MU branch cannot be started in a parish without the
consent of the incumbent, and it should always be run with
his agreement. The incumbent is always instrumental in closing
down a branch, which should only be done after consultation
with the bishop, the PCC and the MU diocesan president.
Obviously much thought, prayer and consultation is needed
before closing a branch. The same is also true before a new
branch is started in a parish.

Details from: The Central Secretary, The Mothers' Union,
Mary Sumner House, 24 Tufton Street, Westminster, London
SW1P 3RB. Tel: 071-222 5533.

**Motivation and morale**  The whole question of motivation is
very important for the life of the local church, but motivation
is not an easy matter to grasp and put into action. Certain basic
factors are needed to motivate people and encourage them to
share in the work and mission of the Church. These include a
friendly and caring atmosphere, and the feeling that it is good
to belong to the Church. Lines of communication are always
important, and the actual worship of the Church must be good
and meaningful. But these things in themselves will not motivate people.

A great deal depends on the vision and quality of leadership of the priest. However, the wardens and PCC members all have their part to motivate and encourage the congregation to do its work. What motivates the priest? It is easy to say that the priest has a vocation (all Christians have a vocation) – but more than that is needed.

As individuals, PCC members (and the priest) need to be secure in their daily lives and work, and to have sufficient money for a reasonable standard of living. People need to belong to a group (which is fulfilled by belonging to the PCC). People like to make progress as a group, and this can include bringing new people into the Church community. How do PCC members as individuals fit into the work of the Church? There needs to be an element of challenge, and a clear idea about what the PCC is trying to achieve. Daily work is not very fulfilling for some people, and the PCC can provide an exciting vision for them. The Church also provides opportunities for individuals to grow in a personal way and as a group, and to find fulfilment. One person said, 'I've done a great deal for the Church, but in return, I've had a great deal out of doing it'.

The actual content of the PCC agenda can have an important role in motivating people.

In addition, we must remember the work of the Holy Spirit, who inspires and motivates PCC members in their work. The extent to which all PCC members are open to the Holy Spirit is a vital factor. The whole question of motivation is not an easy one, but it does need careful consideration in every parish.

*Questions for discussion*

1. How can PCC members help with this whole question of motivation?
2. In what ways can PCC members accept some responsibility for the motivation and morale of the local church?
3. Is the love of God the best source of motivation for the PCC?

**Moving to another parish**   The population is more mobile today than in the past. Moving to another town can be the cause of a family losing touch with the Church. The priest writes to notify the parish about the new family's arrival, but the family itself must make an effort to join the new church, finding out where it is and the service times. Many things will be different: the relationship with the priest will be new, the building will be strange, and the service may not be the same in many ways.

The congregation will all be unknown for a while. Perhaps no one will come forward and speak on the first Sunday.

Transfer your loyalty and adapt yourself to your new spiritual home 'without mental reservation or equivocation of any kind'. The Church somehow manages to make Christians into members of the local instead of the universal (catholic) Church. Joining a new church can be a real test of your spiritual life. All these thoughts bring home the importance of a warm welcome to strangers and visitors, and this will make up for many things which are different.

**Music in worship**  Music can be a very powerful factor in politics, emotions, entertainment and in worship. All the great religions have expressed themselves in song, and music has certainly played an important part in the life of the Christian Church. In the Bible, there are over a hundred references to musical instruments, and over fifty references to singing. Two well-known examples from St Paul on the subject of music: 'Speak to one another in psalms, hymns and spiritual songs; sing and make music in your heart to the Lord' (Ephesians 5.19). The other reference: 'Let the Word of God dwell in you richly as you teach and admonish one another with all wisdom, and as you sing psalms, hymns and spiritual songs with gratitude in your hearts' (Colossians 3.16).

The hymns and the musical sections of the service are a vital part of worship, and it is important that everyone in the congregation should try to do his or her best to make a worthy offering to God in terms of singing. Without music and singing, worship would lose much of its mystery (and 'otherness'). Singing is a powerful medium of communication between us and God, and of course also between God and us. Good singing can arouse awe and wonder in the congregation and it is a means of expressing prayer, penitence, praise and thanksgiving to God. It is also a channel through which the Holy Spirit encourages, rebukes, and exhorts the worshippers. St Augustine said 'He who sings prays twice'.

Good and lively hymn singing is the offering of another of our faculties to God. It can help to unite a congregation, and encourage visitors and fringe members to come again. Dull and uninspiring music, sung badly or played too slowly or too loudly on the organ, can have a bad effect on the worship, and it can be a factor which might keep some people away.

Music and singing are so important for worship that they

should never be left to the choir alone, or to the choir and just those in the congregation who like singing. Worship is the primary concern of every Christian, and each member of the congregation needs to be helped and encouraged to give the very best they can offer to God in terms of music.

The Church of England has a unique musical heritage, particularly in the cathedrals. But in the parish church, it is important to remember that the choir is there to lead the congregation, and not to sing instead of the congregation. As people learn how to join in and 'have a go', so the congregational singing will improve. The more that people join in the singing, the more they will enjoy it. Every congregation needs to give some time (quarterly?) to congregational practices, and the results will soon be apparent.

*A few practical points*

1. Listen carefully while the organist plays the tune, and the speed at which it will be sung. Take careful note of any difficult parts in the tune, and keep up with the organist. Never drag behind the others.
2. Stand up as soon as the hymn number has been announced (or as soon as the organist starts to play over the tune if the hymns are not announced). You cannot be ready to start singing if you are using your energy and concentration on standing up. Be ready and prepared to sing the first note by taking two or three deep breaths before you start to sing. Deep breathing is good for your health, as well as for your singing. Breathe in and fill your lungs fairly quickly, but let it out slowly and in a controlled way as you sing.
3. Always attempt the high notes – even if you sometimes fail to reach them, and the range of your voice will gradually widen. For men with deep voices, try to sing the tune with other people, and not an octave below the rest. Remember that singing requires energy and effort, but it is most rewarding. The Venite (Psalm 95) encourages us – 'O come let us sing out to the Lord. Let us shout in triumph to the rock of our salvation' (Collins Liturgical Psalter). Enjoy your singing, for it is physically and psychologically good – and human voices singing together can make joyful music to the Lord.

**Comfortable hymns?**   To what extent is the congregation content to sing hymns which make them feel too comfortable? Does the congregation need some new hymns from time to time, which might stir them up from set ways? So often the music is a complete contrast with the music enjoyed by many people, and especially by young people. The music can present an enormous cultural barrier which no doubt excludes a large number of people. Should the local church give more thought to this matter? To change to modern 'pop' type music will probably not attract many – if any – to the congregation. It could well drive some of the present regulars away. But on occasions, the music for the Eucharist could be provided by a group of young people – perhaps a folk group formed in the youth club. It needs expertise, proper training and rehearsal, and also the congregation will need encouraging too!

*Questions for discussion*
1. Could the congregational singing be improved?
2. How could the congregation be helped in singing?

**Singing competition**   Music festivals are organized in many areas, and it might be a good opportunity for your church choir to enter each year. When there is no suitable event in the festival for choirs, perhaps your PCC (or the Deanery Synod or a generous individual) could provide a suitable trophy and negotiate for a church choirs event in the local festival.

**Organist and choirmaster**   Music is an important element in the worship of Almighty God, and it is sometimes one of the factors which influence visitors and occasional worshippers in deciding whether or not to return to the Church.

A written agreement with the organist/choirmaster is desirable; *see* pages 129–31 for a suggested form. The main job of the organist is as follows:

1. To play at the main service on Sunday (and at the evening service). The PCC will pay the fees for a relief organist for four (or six) Sundays per year, the relief organist to be found by the organist.
2. To play suitable music for about fifteen minutes before the service begins, in order to set the scene and prepare the congregation for worship. (The name of the composer and the title of the music could be put on the church notice board, or printed in the duplicated weekly notices.) The organist is also asked to play for a suitable time after the service.

3.  To take a weekly choir practice, except during the month of August and in the week following Easter and Christmas.
4.  To recruit new choir members, and to look after the musical development of the choir, corporately and individually (RSCM scheme?), and to motivate the choir.
5.  The organ is known as the king of musical instruments. Many organs have a considerable capacity to produce volume, which is excellent in an appropriate voluntary, but most discouraging when it drowns the singing of the congregation. It is better to err on the quiet side than to overwhelm the congregation.
6.  The organist is probably the best judge of the choir's ability to sing anthems and to choose which would be appropriate and within the ability of the choir. But always consult the priest, and ask him before the choir practises the piece. It is unwise to choose an anthem for an ordinary parish church choir which really calls for the skills of a cathedral choir – the results can be unfortunate.
7.  It is desirable that the organist is a communicant member of the church, who plays a full part in the life of the church family, and encourages the choir to do the same.
8.  The starting and finishing times of every practice should be strictly observed.
9.  A good organist/choirmaster can usually get the best out of the choir without using a long flow of words in explanation. Long-winded pep talks usually succeed in discouraging the choir.
10. It is much to be desired that the priest and the organist can work together in harmony as fellow members of the body of Christ, and it is hoped that disagreements and problems will not arise. When a decision has to be made, it is the priest who has the final decision – after listening carefully to all points of view. (*See Canon Law about music and musicians* on page 128.)

*Suggestions*
Have you tried any of the following – a verse of a hymn sung by the congregation alone – members of the junior choir singing one verse as a solo every Sunday, done by choir members in turn?

**The Psalms**   The Book of Psalms was the hymn book of the Jewish Church, and its lovely poetry has great spiritual value

126

today. It is probably the best prayer book ever written. But the Psalms are difficult for the congregation (and some choirs?) to sing. It is always better to say them, rather than to leave them unused.

Here are two suggestions. Firstly, alternate verses can be said by a reader and the congregation. Secondly, a responsorial version, where the reader says (or a cantor or choir sings) the verses, and the congregation say or sing the simple response. Some hymnbooks, e.g. the *New English Hymnal*, have a selection of responsorial psalms. Many parishes simply give the response on the notice sheet.

*Music as the servant*   Music in church is not an end in itself, but always the servant of the actual worship. It is also right and proper that the choir should sing an anthem or special setting of the Eucharist from time to time. This is an important side of the organist's job, but the other side is to encourage and involve the congregation. Occasionally it may help to have someone standing in front to conduct and encourage the congregation, especially at a congregational singing practice.

*Other musical instruments*   With the modern increase in leisure time, many people play a musical instrument to a reasonable standard. Instead of using the organ – say once per year – would it be possible for the organist to gather together and train some musicians in a small group or orchestra to lead the worship at the family Eucharist? Could the local schools provide young people and adults for this purpose? We certainly need to encourage the Church of the future, as well as the Church of today.

*Food for thought for the organist and the priest*

1. How often is it desirable to have a congregational singing practice? What is the best time to involve as many of the congregation as possible?
2. Musically speaking, what will help the congregation to worship? What are the musical needs of the people in the pews?
3. It is quite an art to accompany the singing of the congregation on the organ – does the diocese or the deanery ever arrange courses or meetings for organists? Refresher courses are arranged. Ask for details from: The Royal School of

Church Music, Addington Palace, Croydon, Surrey CR9 5AD. Tel: 081–654 7676.

## *Canon Law about music and musicians – Canon B20.*

1. In all churches and chapels, other than in cathedral or collegiate churches or chapels, where the matter is governed by or dependent upon the statutes or customs of the same, the functions of appointing any organist or choirmaster (by whatever name called), and of terminating the appointment of any organist or choirmaster, shall be exercisable by the minister with the agreement of the Parochial Church Council, except that if the archdeacon of the archdeaconry in which the parish is situated, in the case of termination of an appointment, considers that the circumstances are such that the requirement as to the agreement of the Parochial Church Council should be dispensed with, the archdeacon may direct accordingly. Where the minister is also the archdeacon of the archdeaconry concerned, the function of the archdeacon under this paragraph shall be exercisable by the bishop of the diocese.
2. Where there is an organist or choirmaster the minister shall pay due heed to his advice and assistance in the choosing of chants, hymns, anthems and other settings and in the ordering of the music of the church; but at all times the final responsibility and decision in these matters rests with the minister.
3. It is the duty of the minister to ensure that only such chants, hymns, anthems and other settings are chosen as are appropriate, both the words and the music, to the solemn act of worship and prayer in the house of God as well as to the congregation assembled for that purpose; and to banish all irreverence in the practice and in the performance of the same.

### *Some questions from the 1992 Report – 'In Tune With Heaven'*

*Questions for everyone*

Are we taking our music seriously enough
    — in our own worship?
    — in our relations with other Christians?
    — in our desire to be with those who are not yet Christians?

## Questions for clergy and musicians

Are we doing our best to make good working relationships?
Are we giving an opportunity to members of our Christian community to talk to us about music and worship?
Are there enough opportunities for everyone to sing, to try something new, to participate?
Are we giving our musicians a chance to perform on their own?
Are we making the best use of silence in worship?
Are we making the best use of old *and* new material?
Is our worship concerned with quality – good language and music, good liturgical principles?
Do the Psalms have a decent place in our worship?
Are we honest about copyright and about supporting simple and fair copyright schemes?
Do we spend enough time and effort planning our worship?

## Questions for clergy

Am I looking for, and training, other worship leaders?
Am I using the musicians in the right way, and giving them enough pastoral care and support?
If we have no competent musicians, should we try taped hymn accompaniments?

## Questions for musicians

Are we good at enrolling new members in our choir or worship group?
Are boy and girl choir members treated equally and fairly?
Should there be more liaison with local schools?
If we only have a choir, should a music group be formed – or if we only have a music group, should a choir be formed? In either case, how would the two groups work together to complement each other?
Should we use instruments other than the organ?

## Questions for PCCs

Do we have a worship committee?
Are we paying our director of music enough, and offering training?
Are we planning our overall expenditure on music, and deciding priorities?

## Specimen agreement for the appointment of an organist (and choir director)

This document has been issued on the authority of the Incorporated Association of Organists, The Incorporated Society of Musicians, The Royal College of Organists, The Royal School of Church Music and the Legal Adviser to the General Synod of the Church of England.

# Music in worship

*Notes*

1. Where an asterisk * appears in the text, delete as necessary.
2. Paragraph 5 should be omitted if the organist is not also to be the director of the choir.
3. Where a priest-in-charge has been appointed, this draft should be adapted.
4. Attention is drawn to the Organists' Guide to Employment, issued by the Incorporated Society of Musicians.

AN AGREEMENT made the . . . . . day of . . . . . 19 . . . . .
between the Reverend . . . . . . . . . . .
Incumbent/Priest-in-Charge of the Benefice of . . . . . . . . . . . . . . . . .
in the Diocese of . . . . . . . . . . . . . . . . (hereinafter called 'The
incumbent') of the first part, the Parochial Church Council of the Parish
of . . . . . . . . . . . . . . . . . . (hereinafter called 'the Council') of the second
part, and . . . . . . . . . . . . . . . . . . . . . . . . . . . . . . . . . . . . . . . . . . . . . . . . . .
of . . . . . . . . . . . . . . . . . . . . . . . . . . . . . . . . . . . . . . . . . . . . . . . . . . . . . . . . .
(hereinafter called 'the organist') of the third part.
WHEREBY IT IS AGREED AS FOLLOWS:

1. THE INCUMBENT (with the agreement of the Council) hereby appoints the organist to act as organist (*and the choir director) of the Church of . . . . . . . . . . . . . . . . . . . in the Parish of . . . . . . . . . . . . . . . aforesaid.
2. (a) THE COUNCIL shall pay to the organist the salary of £ . . . . . . . . per annum to be payable on the usual quarter days the first payment (which may be a proportionate payment) to be made on the . . . . . . . day of . . . . . . . . . One thousand nine hundred and . . . . . . . .
   (b) THE COUNCIL shall review the salary annually.
3. SUBJECT to the general direction of the incumbent the organist shall have the care and control of the music in the above-mentioned church.
4. (a) THE ORGANIST shall play the organ at all the ordinary Sunday services and at services on the Holy Days of the Church listed in the schedule to this agreement.
   (b) When the organ is required for services in addition to those referred to in sub-paragraph (a) hereof the matter shall be agreed between the incumbent and the organist for which an agreed additional fee shall be payable.
5. (a) THE ORGANIST shall also act as the choir director which shall entail the training of the choir and shall arrange regular weekly practices for this purpose.
   (b) Only choristers who have been approved both by the incumbent and the organist shall be admitted to the choir.
   (c) The power to dismiss choristers shall be that of the organist subject to the concurrence of the incumbent.
6. THE ORGAN shall be reserved for the personal use of, and the giving of lessons by the organist, also for the practice of his/her* pupils and for that of a recognized assistant at such times as will not interfere with the services of the Church. The use of the organ shall not be granted to others without the consent of the organist.
7. THE ORGANIST shall have the sole right to play at wedding services, funeral services and other special services, and to be paid the fee for so doing by those who engage him/her* according to the scale in force at the time at the said church. The organist may allow some other competent person to play at any such service but in that event the organist shall be entitled to receive the fee.
8. Where pursuant to the Performers' Protection Acts 1958–72, the

organist agrees to a sound recording or a video recording being made
of a service, he/she* shall be entitled to the payment of an additional
fee or fees.

9. THE ORGANIST shall be entitled to ............. weeks' holiday
   in each year to be taken at such times as shall be agreed between
   the organist and the incumbent. The Council shall defray the cost of
   supplying a deputy for ........ weeks each year.

10. THE ORGANIST when absent other than for reasons of illness or
    holiday shall provide and pay a competent deputy to carry out
    his/her* duties. If the organist shall be incapacitated by illness from
    performing his/her* duties the cost of supplying a competent deputy
    shall be borne by the Council for a period not exceeding .........
    consecutive weeks. Should such incapacity exceed that period the
    Council may decide that the organist shall be on unpaid leave of
    absence.

11. (a) Subject to the provisions of Canon B20 of the Canons of the
        Church of England this AGREEMENT may be terminated either by
        the incumbent with the agreement of the Council giving notice to
        the organist or by the organist giving notice to the incumbent and
        to the secretary of the Council.
    (b) In this paragraph 'notice' means not less than one quarter's notice
        in writing to be given to the other party to expire on one of the
        usual quarter days.

12. THIS AGREEMENT shall automatically terminate when the organist
    attains the age of ........ years unless the incumbent with the
    agreement of the Council decide that he/she* should continue in
    office after that date for a further period not exceeding twelve months
    and thereafter subject to annual review by the incumbent and the
    Council.

13. Any questions or differences whatsoever which may at any time
    hereafter arise between the parties hereto touching this agreement or
    the subject matter thereof arising out of or in relation thereto shall be
    referred to the archdeacon in whose archdeaconry the parish is
    situated or a person nominated by the archdeacon.

AS WITNESS the hand of the incumbent and the organist and, on behalf
of the Council, the hands of the chairman presiding and two other
members present at a meeting of the Council held on the ...........
day of ........... 19.... at which a resolution was passed
authorizing the signature of this agreement

SIGNED by the incumbent                    ..............................

SIGNED on behalf of the
Parochial Church Council of
the Parish of ...........                  ..............................
                                                CHAIRMAN

                                           ..............................

                                           ..............................
                                           TWO MEMBERS OF THE COUNCIL

SIGNED by the organist
(*and choir director)                      ..............................

THE SCHEDULE
Holy Days on which the organist shall play the organ pursuant to
Paragraph 4(a) of this agreement are:

**Never give up**   God in his mercy does not always allow us to see what he is doing through us at a particular time. God sometimes calls individuals, priests and lay people, and also groups of people such as the PCC, to do a job which seems difficult at the time. It is also strange how people will sometimes only hear just what they want to hear. In one sense, God is 'putting us to the time of trial'. Once you have put your hand to the plough, do not give up. God will provide the necessary strength and courage to finish the task.

Life can be difficult for a Christian at work, especially when the majority of people there do not belong to the Church. The same is true of home life and leisure activities. The Christian may meet mockery, hostility, or he may be ignored. Even in Church circles, Christians sometimes speak with malice and without considering the effect of their words on others. Do not give up, whatever the problems, and remember that Christ and other Christians have suffered before you, and finally triumphed in the power of Christ . . . 'Only be thou faithful until death, and I will give thee a crown of life' (Revelation 2.10).

Our Lord met strong opposition, which eventually put him on the cross. When the Church is active and alive, opposition must be expected. 'In all things we are more than conquerors through Him that loved us' (Romans 8.37).

**New members' evening**   It often happens that new members have to find out for themselves about prayer, the Bible, the faith and worship. Would a new members' evening be a help in your parish? Or a nurture group?

**Notice boards**   A notice board is an important means of communication, but it must always be kept neat, regularly painted, and only have up-to-date notices. It is a good idea to use four drawing pins for each notice.

The incumbent alone has the right to decide what notices may be exhibited on church notice boards, 'within and without' the church and in the church hall. The one exception to this is the official notices about rating, parliamentary elections and parish council notices, and these may not cover up nor replace the existing notices.

**Nurses**   *See* **Guild of St Barnabas** on page 90.

**Odd jobs and repairs**   These frequently need doing in the church, the hall, the rectory, the house for the curate or semi-retired priest. Inside and outside painting needs to be done regularly. Lucky the parish which has a man willing and able to do these jobs as his offering of time and talents to the church – but he should always be repaid the cost of the materials which he uses. If no such person is available, then the jobs must be done as soon as possible by a local builder or handyman.

**Ordination**   Many clergy preach every year about vocations, because all Christians have a vocation to seek and to do God's will in daily life. Some have a special vocation or calling to the sacred ministry. Do *you* ever have the feeling that God is calling you to be a priest? It may be as a full-time professional, or as a non-stipendiary minister (sometimes called the auxiliary pastoral ministry) where you continue in your present job during the week. It may be just a niggling feeling somewhere in the back of your mind, which will not go away. Pray about it, and talk it over with your priest, who may suggest that you see the director of ordinands, or the bishop. God often springs surprises on the people he is going to use, and it is not only the 'good' people that he calls to his service. Do not immediately reject the possibility of ordination simply because you feel unworthy for the priesthood.

In 1975, Dr Donald Coggan said at his enthronement as Archbishop of Canterbury – and his words are still relevant today – 'We must have a steady supply of parish priests who will give themselves wholly to this one thing – the thoughtful ministry of the word, the awesome ministry of the sacraments, the visiting of the homes of the people, the ceaseless ministry of intercession, the equipping of the laity for their witness . . . There is no finer life than that of a parish priest. Covet this calling. Train for it. Put your best into it. Glorify in it. Count yourself thrice-blessed if you hear God calling you to it.'

The number of candidates offering themselves for ordination is a good barometer of the spiritual health of the parish.

*Food for thought*
When did your parish last produce an ordination candidate?

**Organist**   *See* **Music in worship** on pages 123–31.

**Outside help** When the PCC is planning a project, e.g. drama, concert, making a video for marriage, baptism or confirmation preparation, or doing a project which involves hard manual work, there is a vast field of skills and resources out there in the local community. When asked to help, many people are willing to give time and skills for the local church, if they think the project is worthwhile, and provided it is explained properly. Outside help is, of course, valuable in itself, but it may well be the beginning of a closer relationship for the people concerned with the Church.

**Parents** One of the most precious things which parents can give to children is their time. They often realize this when it is too late and their children no longer want them. Another precious thing which they can share with their children is their faith. Whether or not the children share the faith of their parents depends to a great extent on the quality of their faith. It is good to teach children how to pray from an early age, and to read something from the gospels before praying. It is much better for both parents to do this with their child each night. Suggestions: (1) 'Glory be to the Father, and to the Son . . .'; (2) Intercessions; (3) Our Father. (It is sad that many children today do not know the Lord's Prayer.)

**Parish policy** There is a saying, 'If you fail to plan – then you plan to fail'. It is so easy for the PCC to muddle along without having any definite policy.

It is helpful to work out and write down a parish policy. It is desirable to invite and encourage all members of the electoral roll and anyone else to take part in forming the parish policy. There are at least two basic questions which need to be considered.

1. What is the Church?
2. What is the Church trying to achieve in this parish?

It is useful to take plenty of time to do this (perhaps with help from the Diocesan Education Office?). The policy should later be written down and a copy given to every member of the church.

Once the aims have been worked out, then it is necessary to consider how to achieve these aims. Targets – or objectives to be achieved – can be worked out by the PCC, and presented to the Annual Meeting (by the churchwarden?). Obviously it is desirable to have as many as possible working to try to achieve the aims of the parish policy.

**Parochial Church Council**   This is a complicated body, even before you take into account the personalities of the members. It is unlike other committees, for it has to carry out a mixture of spiritual, legal, financial, pastoral and missionary functions. The PCC shares the privileges and responsibility of making certain decisions with the priest, and in return it co-operates with the priest in the whole mission of the Church. This is not some clever arrangement worked out by the church lawyers. It is in fact an attempt to channel the teaching of the Bible into the life of the parishes.

*What is the task of the PCC?*   The answer is clearly given in the Synodical Government Measure 1969, which states:

1. It shall be the duty of the incumbent and the Parochial Church Council to consult together on matters of general concern and importance in the parish.
2. The functions of the Parochial Church Council shall include:

   (a) co-operation with the incumbent in promoting in the parish the whole mission of the Church, pastoral, evangelistic, social and ecumenical;

   (b) the consideration and discussions of matters concerning the Church of England or any other matters of religious or public interest, but not the declaration of the doctrine of the Church on any question;

   (c) making known and putting into effect any provision made by the Diocesan Synod or the Deanery Synod, but without prejudice to the powers of the Council on any particular matter;

   (d) giving advice to the Diocesan Synod and the Deanery Synod on any matter referred to the Council;

   (e) raising such matters as the Council consider appropriate with the Diocesan Synod or Deanery Synod.

3. In the exercise of its functions the Parochial Church Council shall take into consideration any expression of opinion by any parochial church meeting.

This gives great emphasis on the part played by lay people in the parish, and some further comment may be useful:

*The incumbent and the PCC shall 'consult together'.* The word 'consult' is a legal process whereby the priest is required by law to discover the PCC's views on all matters of importance in the parish. He does this without prejudice to his own rights and powers as incumbent, and he does not necessarily have to carry out the wishes of the PCC after it has been consulted. In a similar way, PCC members cannot meet without the priest being present, so that they may know his views. (The priest can withdraw from a meeting, and the PCC can meet without a priest during the interregnum).

Consulting together should bring to light any different opinions which exist, but progress in the parish cannot be made without consultation and discussion. Putting forward reasons for and against a proposal will help to clarify what is best for the church.

***Rights and responsibilities*** Managing the boundaries between the rights of the priest and the PCC is not an easy area. Rules protect the Church from powerful individuals – whether ordained or lay – from misusing authority. Rules exist to help the Church to do its work more effectively. There will be occasions when the priest has to be firm, and occasions when the PCC will prevent something from happening. Hopefully, those occasions will be rare.

It is so easy for the priest and for the PCC to overreach their lawful authority. For this reason, everyone – especially the PCC secretary and wardens – should know and understand the rules. This prevents minor irritations, or perhaps worse. Those who created the rules have made a careful and wise balance of power between priest and PCC, and when the system is used rightly, exciting horizons are opened up in every parish.

***Rights and responsibilities of the PCC*** The following have been gathered together by the author from different sources:

1. The PCC has the right to be consulted on all matters of importance in the parish, even though the parish priest, the bishop, the Diocesan Pastoral Committee, or the Church Commissioners may make the final decision in certain matters. The PCC has the right to know what is being proposed, and it has the right to express an opinion about it.
2. It is the duty of the PCC to co-operate with the incumbent in promoting in the parish the whole mission of the Church, pastoral, evangelistic, social and ecumenical.

3. The PCC and the priest decide jointly how PCC money is to be used. A dispute is referred to the bishop.
4. It is the responsibility of the PCC to maintain and repair all church buildings, the contents, the churchyard and surrounding walls or hedges. The PCC is responsible for providing adequate insurance cover, particularly for paid and voluntary workers and public liability.
5. The PCC has the right to be consulted about any proposed sale, demolition, or purchase of a parsonage house, or the building of a new one. The Church Commissioners must consider the views or objections of the PCC (made within 21 days) before they make a decision.
6. The PCC has the right to be consulted about the appointment of a new incumbent. The PCC can state what kind of priest they would like to have, in view of the particular needs of the parish. (Remember that priests are human, and that angels and saints are not normally available.)
7. The PCC has the right to receive a copy of the architect's report under the Inspection of Churches Measure (the quinquennial report), which is done every five years. It is the PCC that is responsible for carrying out the recommendations in the report.
8. The agreement of the PCC is required before any change is made in the existing forms of worship in use every Sunday, e.g. the priest cannot change from 1662 to ASB services, nor from Matins to the Eucharist, without the agreement of the PCC.
9. The agreement of the PCC is required before any change is made in the priest's vesture in use in the church, e.g. from surplice and stole to chasuble, or vice versa. Disagreements are referred to the bishop. However, the priest can wear a cope on any suitable occasion without reference to the PCC.
10. The PCC is one of the 'interested parties' and has to be consulted about any pastoral scheme which would affect the parish, e.g. creating a group or team ministry, or altering the boundaries etc. The PCC has the right to meet a representative of the Diocesan Pastoral Committee concerning proposed changes.
11. The PCC can acquire property, but with the permission of the diocese, which acts as Holding Trustees. The PCC can purchase or receive gifts of stocks and shares.

12. The PCC is one of the legal parties in any arrangement for sharing the church with another Christian denomination [the Sharing of Church Buildings Act 1969].
13. The consent of the PCC is required for an incumbent or team vicar to continue in office beyond the retiring age of 70 years.

### Rights and responsibilities of the incumbent

1. The incumbent usually has the freehold of the parish church, which means that he is the legal owner of the church and he is ultimately responsible for it during the time that he is rector or vicar of the parish. He has the control and use of the church and its contents, and he has the 'custody of the key'.

   The incumbent cannot make any structural changes without proper authorization to do so; e.g. he cannot remove a stained glass window, nor put one in, without a faculty. The agreement of the PCC is required for a faculty. An official notice on the church notice board gives details of the proposed changes, and the address of the Registrar so that anyone can send in an objection to the changes proposed.
2. The incumbent has 'absolute control' of the services, the times at which they are held, and whether certain parts are said or sung. Any PCC resolutions about the time and conduct of the services should be worded as recommendations to the incumbent. He must obey the 'rubrics' (instructions printed in service books) but he may make any alteration, variation or choice allowed by the rubrics. But the incumbent cannot change the form of service in use every Sunday without the agreement of the PCC. Obviously a wise incumbent would discuss any changes with the PCC. Disagreements are referred to the bishop.

   The incumbent may hold any other services or events in church in addition to the regular Sunday services, as he deems appropriate. The incumbent decides who will read the lessons and the prayers if he does not do them himself.
3. The incumbent usually has the freehold of the churchyard (including certain ancient rights of herbage!). He decides where graves are to be dug and their depth (it is usually a matter of the next space in the row these days). He

authorizes the erection of any monument and inscription. Churchyard rules may be adopted by the PCC, but the incumbent still remains the legal authority for the churchyard, and the churchyard rules have to be acceptable to him. He acts by ancient custom as the deputy of the Chancellor, and any disputes are referred to the diocesan Chancellor. When there is any difficulty or doubt about procedure, it is wise to seek the advice of the archdeacon as soon as possible.

4. The incumbent has the duty to consult the PCC on all matters of importance in the parish. He need not follow the PCC's views in every case, but obviously a wise priest will attach much weight to the opinions of his PCC. In some matters he alone will be responsible for making the final decision.

5. The priest has clearly defined rights and duties in connection with church music. (*See* **Music in worship** on page 128.)

6. The priest has joint responsibility – or an equal say – with the PCC to decide how PCC money is to be used. No money can be voted for any purpose without his agreement. For this reason, he is normally one of the two people who sign PCC cheques. If a serious disagreement arises, the account is 'frozen' by the bank, and the matter is referred to the bishop.

7. The incumbent is an 'interested party' in any pastoral reorganization scheme, and he is consulted separately about any proposed changes affecting the parish or the living – such as a scheme to unite the parish with a neighbouring parish.

8. The incumbent controls the assistant clergy and, with the bishop, he determines how many curates will be employed in the parish. The priest and the PCC together determine the proportion of money which the PCC shall pay towards the curate's stipend (salary) – but obviously this has to conform with diocesan policy.

9. The parish registers are owned by the churchwardens on behalf of the parishioners, but their custody belongs to the priest.

10. The incumbent has a duty to call at least four meetings of the PCC every year, in addition to the Annual Parochial Church Meeting. He is chairman of these meetings, and as chairman he has to give 'due heed to his own rights

as incumbent'. The chairman is the person who makes decisions about 'points of order' and when a decision has been given, it must be accepted by the meeting.

11. The priest has the right to decide which notices may or may not be placed on all notice boards, inside and outside the church and church halls (apart from official government or local government notices, but these may not cover up or replace any existing notice).
12. The priest allocates the seats in the chancel of the church.
13. The incumbent controls the bells.
14. The incumbent must reside in the parsonage house of the benefice, and he must also reside in the parish, unless he has an episcopal dispensation.

(Some of these items have been mentioned elsewhere in the *ABC*.)

Further details are given in *A Handbook for Churchwardens and Parochial Church Councillors*, published by Mowbray.

*To co-operate with the incumbent*   The church lawyers did not include this as some kind of joke! Priest and PCC do co-operate and work together happily in many parishes, and this co-operation releases much energy and power for God's work. Other parishes experience difficulties in co-operating, for one reason or another. So what is needed to enable this process of co-operation to take place?

We will assume that the priest has learned, among other things, the necessary skills of a chairman, and that he has a certain understanding of human nature and of how people function in a group situation. People often act completely out of character when in a group – but there is always a reason for this (*see* **Groups – discussion groups and the PCC** on page 87). We also assume that that the priest is willing to allow others to share in God's work.

What, then, is required of priest and PCC members to enable this process of co-operation to take place? The answer includes a healthy spiritual life, a sense of humour, a willingness to listen to the point of view of others, a willingness to try to find out what God wants in the parish, imagination, foresight, commitment, humility, courage, a willingness to learn. Alertness to prevent the parochial blinkers obscuring the vision. Add to these an ability to see issues from a spiritual point of view; willingness to join in, to take part, and to be a full member;

willingness to take responsibility; love and respect for other people.

It is vital to have a clear understanding of the aims of the PCC, which have been discussed and accepted by the PCC and congregation. The church is clearly God's instrument for bringing about his kingdom in the parish, and the PCC is the nucleus of the task force to help in this work. It is clear from the Old and New Testaments, and from the formulas and documents of the Church, that the Church is a community with a message. Those who allow their names to be put forward for election to the PCC need to be aware of the nature of the work to which they are committing themselves.

*Co-operating with the incumbent in promoting in the parish the whole mission of the Church, pastoral, evangelistic, social and ecumenical.*
Some PCC members may be worried by this clause, and even wish that it had not been included in the legislation about church councils. Others will be aware of the potential which exists, because two can achieve far more than one on his own. When twelve or twenty or more are involved, then the possibilities are enormous. Many vicars work on their own without a curate, but they are not alone if there is a good partnership with the PCC. There is a long tradition of putting responsibility on to one person, so that the rest do not have to bother. This happens most frequently at a subconscious level, and it reminds us of the saying, 'It is expedient for you that one man should die for the people'. There are many implications in that saying.

Mission is not an optional extra for those who like that kind of thing. Mission is part and parcel of the work of every PCC, and it is clearly written into the constitution of the PCC. The local church exists to worship God and to continue Christ's mission in the parish. Each person has his or her own unique contribution to make in the continuous mission of the Church, bringing their strengths, weaknesses, and possibly some hidden talents. Each person has some special skills from God. But there is only one ministry in the parish – the ministry of Christ himself, carried out through PCC members. Apart from Christ, PCC members can do nothing. Serving on the PCC is a call from God not just to co-operate with the priest, but to co-operate with the Lord Jesus Christ himself. There are no short cuts in mission, and it requires permanent commitment both 'in season and out'. This is dealt with more fully under the section **Mission – Evangelism – Renewal** on page 115.

# Parochial Church Council

*Suggestions for PCC members*

1. Study the agenda before coming to the meeting. Try to put God's will before your own likes and dislikes, especially when speaking or voting at the meeting.
2. In your prayers, ask God to bless and guide all members of the PCC and your priest.
3. Arrive in plenty of time, so that you can relax and chat to others before the meeting begins.
4. Keep to the point in a discussion, and address your remarks to the chairman. (Some PCCs find it helpful to arrange the seating in a circle, rather than in straight rows.)
5. The priest gives thought and prays about the business of the meeting. If he makes suggestions, it is because he believes that will be best for the parish. He will not always be right, but he will probably have a good idea of what is needed in the situation. Support his suggestions, unless there is a better alternative.
6. After the meeting, support the decisions made by the PCC and help to put them into effect (even if you voted against them).

**A committee system for the PCC** Every PCC is required to appoint a standing committee, which transacts business between PCC meetings. Many PCCs appoint other committees, so that there is more time to discuss certain subjects thoroughly in detail. The lay chairman can report and make a recommendation for action to the full meeting of the PCC. Sub-committees can co-opt people who will be helpful, and each sub-committee needs a secretary and minute book. The priest is *ex officio* a member of every committee in the parish, but he may feel it is not necessary to attend the meetings of committees. Close liaison with the priest is vital for the smooth running of the whole system.

Sub-committees of the PCC may be formed for the following: (a) finance, (b) stewardship, (c) education and youth, (d) mission in the parish, (e) the Church overseas, (f) the church building, (g) the church hall, (h) the churchyard, (i) communications, (j) worship, (k) prayer fellowship, (l) Bible study.

**Arranging PCC meetings** One method is to meet on the same day every month, e.g. the second Tuesday of every month (except August). Dates can then be entered into diaries at the beginning of the year.

142

Those who agree to serve should regard PCC meetings as top priority over other engagements. If you are unwilling to make such a commitment, is it right to stand again at the next election?

With an efficient sub-committee system, the PCC might hold a business meeting alternately with a discussion on a spiritual or biblical subject.

**Husband and wife**  It is usually better for the church not to have both husband and wife serving together on the PCC – not in case they disagree in public, but in order to involve another family in the work of the church.

**Confidential business**  It is fairly unusual for business of a confidential nature to appear on the PCC agenda. When it does, obviously it has to be treated as absolutely confidential.

In the normal course of events, it is helpful if PCC members do not gossip about who said what at the meeting with those who are not members of the Council. On the other hand, it may be a good idea occasionally to invite the congregation to a special meeting.

It is desirable to give wide publicity to the work of the PCC. One way is to display the minutes on the church notice board, and to make a report in the magazine.

**Resolutions – opinions and action**  Action is only required if a resolution on the agenda is formally passed by the PCC. Action does not have to be taken simply because someone has expressed an opinion at a meeting. It is only necessary to record the wording of the resolution, the proposer and seconder, and the voting in the minutes. Views 'for' and 'against' should not be recorded.

After the vote is taken, the PCC should then spend time deciding who will take the necessary action, and by what date (and record both in the minutes).

PCC members are responsible for the decisions made by the PCC, and for carrying out any action needed as a result of their vote. When, for example, the PCC decides to have a concert, play, discussion, social event, Sunday lunch, etc., then all PCC members (and not the priest alone) are responsible for organizing the event, supporting it themselves and actively encouraging others, organizing the selling and printing of tickets, etc. Corporate responsibility involves much more than sitting in a chair and voting 'for' or 'against' a resolution.

*Sense of urgency*   Mormons and Jehovah's Witnesses have a great zeal for winning converts to their faith. Sadly, neither of them are Christian. The Communists worked hard to achieve their objectives. Why is it that some people are fired with a strong zeal for their cause? How do PCC members get a similar zeal for God's work? The PCC often gets stuck in the rut of the past, ignoring burning issues of the day which are their proper concern. When the PCC wastes time on irrelevant and unimportant issues, then we should not be surprised if the Church is ignored by the rest of the world. Time is precious, and surely each PCC is a team with an urgent job to do in the parish. Is this reflected on the agenda, and is mission given priority?

*Questions for discussion*

1. What are the six most important things done by the PCC (as distinct from the priest)?
2. How can the PCC achieve a greater sense of dedication and urgency in its work?
3. How far do PCC meetings remind you of St Paul's words about being a 'new creation in Christ'?
4. How can the PCC help to make the truths about God more real in the parish?
5. Does the PCC rely too much on human methods, rather than on the power of the Holy Spirit?
6. One of the responsibilities of the bishop is the pastoral care of the clergy. Is it possible for the PCC to help?
7. Does the PCC try to do too many things at the same time? Would it be better to concentrate more effort on one matter for a year?
8. Are there any geographical areas of the parish which are neglected by the PCC?
9. To whom is the PCC responsible?
10. Would it be helpful to co-opt two young people to the PCC, and with full voting rights?
11. Is being a PCC member a call from God to grow in holiness?
12. To what extent is your PCC and church living off the financial and spiritual 'capital' created by Christians in the past?

*Agenda*   A well thought-out and carefully planned agenda is not only necessary to get the work done, but it also helps to motivate PCC members.

Each meeting is an opportunity to think about God's will for the parish, and to learn how members can co-operate with the Holy Spirit to extend God's kingdom in the Church and in the area. God speaks through all members, and in one sense, the PCC is a school of applied Christianity.

From a legal point of view, a notice is put on the notice board ten days before the meeting to give its date, time and place. The agenda is sent to every member seven days before the meeting. This should list all the items to be discussed, and give any information which will be helpful in making a decision. Some people can make a decision quickly, while others need more time to think carefully about the pros and cons of each item. Thus the agenda has to be sent out seven clear days before the meeting.

Much more is needed than these two legal notices. Forward planning is vital, particularly if the standing committee is to be involved in drawing up the agenda. It is wise to plan the dates for the whole year in January, or earlier. For each PCC meeting, the following dates need to be reserved:

1. Date of standing committee – three weeks before the PCC meeting.
2. Notice put up about place, time and date of PCC meeting – ten days before the PCC meeting.
3. Agenda sent to every PCC member – seven clear days before the PCC meeting.
4. PCC minutes circulated to every PCC member – about ten days after the PCC meeting. (The sooner the better, as this reminds people not only of decisions, but of the actions to be taken, and by whom.)

The priest obviously plays a major part in the preparation of the agenda for every PCC meeting. It is a good idea for the standing committee to share fully in this preparation, and to work out who will introduce each item. The order of business is important, also making sure that there is enough business for the meeting (and not too much!).

Every PCC member is entitled to suggest items for the agenda. It is helpful if this is done in writing, and made available for the standing committee which arranges the PCC meeting. Items should never be brought on to the agenda through 'Any Other Business' – because proper thought and discussion cannot be given before a decision is made. The PCC is always responsible under God to give adequate and careful attention to each item, and this cannot be done if a surprise item is suddenly brought up through AOB. See *Any Other Business* below.

Certain items need to be put on every agenda. These include reports from the evangelization committee (or whatever it is called in your parish); the Deanery Synod report and future business; financial report and fabric report. It is good to keep mission and evangelism constantly before the PCC, even if only a short time is allotted to it on the agenda of each meeting. Many PCCs keep these reports brief, and sometimes the person may say, 'Nothing to report, Mr Chairman, for this meeting'. It is helpful to have a main item or subject on the agenda, perhaps with an outside speaker, or recorded talk or video.

It is wise to work out a proposed timetable for the PCC meeting, and include it on the agenda. Some PCCs have a definite time for ending PCC meetings. This helps to clarify thoughts and stop things dragging on endlessly.

*Food for thought*
What are the priorities of the PCC? Do these priorities appear regularly on the PCC agenda?

**Any Other Business**   No business which is not on the agenda shall be transacted at a PCC meeting unless three-quarters of those present agree to this. Even when this agreement is given, 'the Chairman might reasonably, when the matter is important, rule that it is adjourned to a future meeting' (quoted from *Handbook for Churchwardens and Parochial Church Councillors*, published by Mowbray).

Any Other Business allows a genuine matter of urgency to be discussed, which has arisen since the agenda was sent out to PCC members. However, AOB is definitely not an occasion for PCC members to bring up additional items of business at the end of the meeting when everyone is tired. It is unwise and undesirable that any item should be brought to the PCC in this last-minute way. The PCC has a responsibility under God to consider all the options carefully and prayerfully, and then to make a responsible decision. This cannot be done on the spur of the moment and without adequate time and thought being given to the matter. There is a proper channel for every PCC member to bring an item to the agenda, and exceptions should not be made to this procedure. When something urgent arises, an exception can be made, and it can be dealt with at the meeting; or alternatively, an emergency meeting of the PCC could be arranged.

Many PCCs do not include Any Other Business on their agenda, and people soon get into the habit of using the proper channel for bringing something to the PCC.

### General Provisions relating to PCCs
### Synodical Government Measure 1969
### 1. Officers of the Council

(a) The minister of the parish shall be chairman of the Parochial Church Council (hereinafter referred to as 'the Council').

(b) A lay member of the Council shall be elected as vice-chairman of the Council.

(c) During the vacancy of the benefice and when the chairman is incapacitated by absence or illness or any other cause or when the minister invites him to do so, the vice-chairman of the Council shall act as chairman and have all the powers vested in the chairman.

(d) The Council may appoint one of their number to act as secretary of the Council. If no member is appointed so to act the Council shall appoint some other fit person with such remuneration (if any) as they think fit. The secretary shall have charge of all documents relating to the current business of the Council except that, unless he is the electoral roll officer, he shall not have charge of the roll. He shall be responsible for keeping the minutes, shall record all resolutions passed by the Council and shall keep the secretary of the diocesan synod and deanery synod informed as to his name and address.

(e) The Council may appoint one or more of their number to act as treasurer solely or jointly. Failing such appointment, the office of treasurer shall be discharged jointly by such of the churchwardens as are members of the Council, or, if there is only one such churchwarden, by the churchwarden solely. No remuneration shall be paid to any person in respect of this appointment as treasurer.

(f) The Council shall appoint an electoral roll officer, who may but need not be a member of the Council and may be the secretary, and if he is not a member may pay to him such remuneration as it shall think fit. He shall have charge of the roll.

(g) If auditors to the Council are not appointed by the annual meeting, or if auditors appointed by the annual meeting are unable or unwilling to act, auditors (who shall not be members of the Council) shall be appointed by the Council. The remuneration (if any) of the auditors shall be paid by the Council.

2. *Meetings of the Council* The Council shall hold not less than four meetings in each year. Meetings shall be convened by the chairman, and if not more than four meetings are held they shall be at quarterly intervals so far as possible.

3. *Power to call meetings* The chairman may at any time convene a meeting of the Council. If he refuse or neglect to do so within seven days after a requisition for that purpose signed by not less than one-third of the members of the Council has been presented to him, those members may forthwith convene a meeting.

4. *Notices relating to meetings*

(a) Except as provided in paragraph 8, at least ten clear days before any meeting of the Council notice thereof specifying the time and place of the intended meeting and signed by or on behalf of the chairman of the Council or the persons convening the meeting shall be posted at or near the principal door of every church, or building licensed for public worship in the parish.

(b) Not less than seven days before the meeting a notice thereof specifying the time and place of the meeting signed by or on behalf of the secretary shall be sent to every member of the Council. Such notice shall contain the agenda of the meeting including any motion or other business proposed by any member of the Council of which notice has been received by the secretary.

(c) If for some good and sufficient reason the chairman, vice-chairman and secretary, or any two of them, consider that a convened meeting should be postponed, notice shall be given to every member of the Council specifying a reconvened time and place within fourteen days of the postponed meeting.

5. *Chairman at meetings*   Subject to the provisions of rule 18, the chair at a meeting of the Council shall be taken

(a) by the chairman of the Council if present;
(b) if the chairman of the Council is not present, or his office is vacant, by the vice-chairman of the Council if he is present:
(c) in the case of a parish in the area of a benefice for which a team ministry is established, by the rector in that ministry if he is present, and both the vicar in that ministry who would if he were present be entitled, by virtue of a provision in a pastoral scheme on the bishop's licence, to preside and the vice-chairman of the Council are not present:

provided that at any such meeting the chairman presiding shall, if he thinks it expedient to do so or the meeting so resolves, vacate the chair either generally or for the purpose of any business in which he has a personal interest or for any other particular business.

Should neither the chairman nor, where sub-paragraph (c) above applies, the rector be available to take the chair for any meeting or for any particular item on the agenda, during a meeting, then a chairman shall be chosen by those members present from among their number and the person so chosen shall preside for that meeting or for that particular item.

6. *Quorum and agenda*   No business shall be transacted at any meeting of the Council unless at least one-third of the members are present thereat and no business which is not specified in the agenda shall be transacted at any meeting except by the consent of three-quarters of the members present at the meeting.

7. *Order of business*   The business of a meeting of the Council shall be transacted in the order set forth in the agenda unless the Council by resolution otherwise determine.

8. *Short notice for emergency meetings*   In the case of sudden emergency or other special circumstances requiring immediate action by the Council, a meeting may be convened by the

chairman of the Council at not less than three clear days' notice in writing to the members of the Council but the quorum for the transaction of any business at such meetings shall be a majority of the then existing members of the Council and no other business shall be transacted at such meeting except as is specified in the notice convening the meeting.

9. *Place of meetings*   The meeting of the Council shall be held at such place as the Council may direct, or in the absence of such direction, as the chairman may direct.

10. *Vote of majority to decide*   The business of the Council shall be decided by a majority of the members present and voting thereon.

11. *Casting vote*   In the case of an equal division of votes the chairman of the meeting shall have a second or casting vote.

12. *Minutes*

(a) The names of the members present at any meeting of the Council shall be recorded in the minutes.
(b) If one-fifth of the members present and voting on any resolution so require, the minutes shall record the names of the members voting for and against that resolution.
(c) Any member of the Council shall be entitled to require that the minutes shall contain a record of the manner in which his vote was cast on any resolution.
(d) Members of the Council shall have access to the minutes of all meetings, but no other person other than the bishop or the archdeacon, or a person authorized by either of them in writing, shall have access to the minutes without the authority of the Council.

13. *Adjournment*   Any meeting of the Council may adjourn its proceedings to such time and place as may be determined at such meeting.

14. *Standing committee*

(a) The Council shall have a standing committee consisting of not less than five persons. The minister and such of the churchwardens as are members of the Council shall be *ex-officio* members of the standing committee, and the Council shall by resolution appoint at least two other members of the standing committee from among its own members and may remove any person so appointed.

(b) The standing committee shall have power to transact the business of the Council between meetings thereof subject to any directions given by the Council.

15. *Other committees*  The Council may appoint other committees for the purpose of the various branches of church work in the parish and may include therein persons who are not members of the Council. The minister shall be a member of all committees *ex officio*.

16. *Validity of proceedings*  No proceedings of the Council shall be invalidated by any vacancy in the membership of the Council or by any defect in the qualification or election of any member thereof.

17. *Interpretation*  Any question arising on interpretation shall be referred to the bishop of the diocese and any decision given by him or by any person appointed by him on his behalf shall be final. (Acknowledgement: Her Majesty's Stationery Office.)

**Pastoral care**  Difficulties and personal problems arise from time to time in any community. Friends and neighbours often provide care and support but sometimes a talk with a responsible person outside the immediate circle of friends is helpful. A wide variety of problems arise, including family and marital problems, depression and anxiety, guilt, bereavement and loneliness.

*Pastoral care of the congregation*  Is there an awareness among PCC members of the pastoral needs of the congregation? And by whom are these needs met? Traditionally, people through the centuries have brought their problems to their parish priest, in confidence that whatever they say to him will not be repeated to anyone without their express permission. The pastoral care of the congregation and of the PCC is still an important part of the priest's work, but he surely needs help. For example, he may not have noticed that the little old lady who sits near the back of the church has not come for four or five weeks. A PCC member could ask the vicar 'Do you know how Mrs X is - she hasn't been to church recently?'

Quite often, the only help that is required is for someone to call and have a friendly chat. A pastoral care group in the parish can keep an eye open for people who are ill, lonely or who have a problem. They can visit as appropriate, and call in the priest when necessary.

***Pastoral care of the people in the parish*** The Church of England is in a unique position to help in many ways through a street warden system. This provides a communication link between the people in need and the church. The simple act of calling at a lonely person's home is important in itself. Often the street warden can deal with many problems, but if not, other help can be found.

***Pastoral care of the priest and his family*** Who looks after the shepherd? Traditionally, this is the work of the bishop, but most bishops have many other problems to deal with, and it is not always possible for the bishop to know when a priest is under extra pressure and stress. Today, far too many clergy have breakdowns, heart attacks or marital problems, all largely due to long working hours every week, and pressures and problems in their work. Apart from prayer and an awareness of the problem - in what ways can the PCC help?

*Food for thought*
Is there an effective pastoral care system in the parish?

**Pastoral reorganization** What is pastoral reorganization? It covers all changes connected with the reorganization of parishes, the abolition or suspension of livings, creation of team or group ministries, new parishes, boundaries and making a church redundant. It is a subject which causes much emotion, and consumes a great deal of time.

Why does the diocese want pastoral reorganization from time to time? There may not be enough clergy to run the parishes, or not enough money to pay and house them, or a church may be situated away from the population of the parish, or the state of the building may be so bad that the parish cannot raise the money to save the church.

The whole situation has to be considered both from the

circumstances in the parish, and also from the point of view of the diocese as a whole. When a parish falls vacant, representatives of the Diocesan Pastoral Committee usually consider the situation in the parish. What is the size of the electoral roll? The spiritual health of the congregation? Has the parish paid its quota in full and on time? Is the building such a burden that there is no time and energy left for spiritual work? Some dioceses use three categories when considering the future. Is the parish healthy – sick – or terminally ill? Having a new vicar can often save a church from being closed, and bring new life to the parish.

When a major change is proposed for your parish, the PCC will be consulted in the initial stages. Perhaps the PCC may wish to consult the archdeacon or his representative, or the diocesan registrar. The Church Commissioners (Address: 1 Millbank, Westminster, London SW1P 3JZ) handle all major changes, and they send the draft proposals to all 'interested persons and parties'.

When the PCC is not happy about the plans, an amendment should only be sent if there is a better alternative available. The PCC can obtain a copy of the Pastoral Measure 1969 and the 1975 Code of Practice. The PCC would be well advised to make its views and suggestions known at the beginning of the negotiation procedure, and not when matters are about to be finalized. It is as well to remember that formal 'appeals' can be very costly, and they always involve many people in a considerable amount of extra work. Quite obviously the PCC must make its views and wishes known, but a scheme is always put forward for the good of the Church, after the Diocesan Pastoral Committee, the archdeacon and the bishop have considered the matter carefully, and consider that the proposed course of action is the best one available.

**Pilgrimages**  A pilgrimage is a journey to a holy place, and it plays an important part in many of the great religions of the world. In one sense, every Christian is on a pilgrimage throughout life, following in the steps of the Lord. In fact, Jesus went on a pilgrimage to Jerusalem when he was only 12 years old. Since very early times, Christians have made special journeys to the Holy Land to see and pray at those places connected with our Lord's earthly life.

Pilgrimages had become quite popular by the Middle Ages. The Crusades (1095–1291) were both pilgrimages to the country where God chose to become man, and also 'holy wars' to recover Jerusalem and other holy places from the Muslims. During the Reformation in England (which started in 1534) the spiritual value of pilgrimages was rejected. The Blessed Virgin Mary was closely connected with many holy places, and the reformers were unhappy with this special association. It is impossible to prove or disprove the truth concerning the visions of Mary which people claim to have seen, but whatever your views about visions, Mary was given a privileged part to play in God's plan of salvation for mankind.

During the twentieth century, the Church of England has rediscovered the joy and spiritual value of a pilgrimage, which is both a holy day and a holiday, and often with a joyful carnival atmosphere. It is an occasion when Christians metaphorically stand up to be counted. As pilgrimages become increasingly popular, it is encouraging to see Christians gather together in such large numbers – and return again, year after year.

Some questions, however, have to be faced. Is there any spiritual value in a pilgrimage? Prayer and devotion, penitence and intercession, and an element of self-sacrifice are important parts of every pilgrimage. Prayer is always answered, but not always in the ways we hope or expect. A pilgrimage is both an outward and physical journey, and also an inward and spiritual journey, lifting heart and mind to God.

Another question: Can one place be more holy than another? God became flesh, and Christianity (more than any other religion) attaches importance to both the physical and the spiritual side of life. Bethel is a holy place in the Bible, where a pile of stones became for Jacob the meeting place of earth and heaven. The command was given to Moses at the burning bush: 'Take off your shoes, for the place where you are standing is holy ground'. T.S. Eliot in his play *Murder in the Cathedral* wrote:

For wherever a saint has dwelt, wherever a martyr has given his blood
    for the blood of Christ,
There is holy ground, and the sanctity shall not depart from it
Though armies trample over it, though sightseers come with guide-books
    looking over it.

Is it true, then, to say that a place of pilgrimage is even more holy than your own parish church? Just as God calls and sets apart individuals to do special work for him, so it seems that God also uses certain places for special purposes.

The Church is on a pilgrimage, in a similar way to the

individual on his or her pilgrimage through life. The pilgrim Church (and the parish church?) has moved from one stage of spiritual and doctrinal development to the next one, through succeeding centuries. Changes take place in individual Christians as well as in the Church. And for both the individuals and the Church, the pilgrim way is always along the path trodden by the Lord himself, who is the way, the truth and the life.

Two of the main places of pilgrimage in England are Walsingham and Glastonbury.

*Walsingham* The Anglican shrine is open for private and parish pilgrimages throughout the year – except for four weeks at Christmas. The National Pilgrimage is held each year with a Eucharist at 1 p.m. on the last Monday in May (Spring Bank Holiday Monday) in the ruined abbey grounds. There is also a pilgrimage for the sick and disabled on the last Monday in August at 12 noon.

Details about pilgrimages at Walsingham, accommodation, the Pilgrim Manual and the Society of Our Lady of Walsingham for individual membership, and parish groups, from: The Shrine Office, Shrine of Our Lady of Walsingham, The Common Place, Walsingham, Norfolk NR22 6EE. Tel: 0328-820225.

*Glastonbury* The main pilgrimage is held on the last Saturday in June with a concelebrated Eucharist at 12 noon in the grounds of the ruined abbey.

Details about this pilgrimage, and about the West of England Pilgrimage Association, from: The Secretary, West of England Pilgrimage Association, The Abbey Gatehouse, Magdalen Street, Glastonbury BA6 9EL. Tel: 0458-832267.

*Food for thought*

1. Where is the nearest place of pilgrimage to your parish?
2. Have you as an individual – or a group from your parish – made a pilgrimage there yet?
3. When did you last read Bunyan's book *Pilgrim's Progress*?

**Playgroup** The appropriate legislation has to be complied with, and a qualified leader is required, in order to start a playgroup in the parish.

An alternative, if there is no one with the appropriate

qualifications, is to have a mother and baby group. No laws or regulations at present affect this, as the babies and toddlers are in the care of their mothers.

Equipment is needed, and space is required for storage; this can be a problem in some halls. (Problems are there to be overcome.)

Whether a playgroup or a mother and baby group is started by the PCC, it is desirable for the group to be a 'church' group, which reports each year to the APCM. Either or both provide a service for the community, and a great pastoral and evangelistic opportunity for the church.

**Poster secretary**   *See* **Publicity and communication** on page 159.

**Prayer**   *See* **Spiritual life of PCC members** on page 182.

**Prayer group**   (*See* **Spiritual life of PCC members** on page 182.) It can be a source of great strength to the individuals concerned and to the local church, when a group of people meet fortnightly or monthly for a time of prayer together. It is desirable to keep the numbers down to about six, and when the numbers increase above this it might be wise to divide into two separate groups. Those who are willing to do so lead each meeting in turn, and the parish priest, the deanery and the bishop should be included in the prayers each time.

There are different methods of prayer suitable for a small group. Here is one example – but of course, there are many other methods:

A preliminary cup of coffee is provided while people arrive, and during this time a list of names and subjects is compiled for the intercessions and thanksgivings. The meeting begins with the Lord's Prayer – said slowly, followed by a short individual prayer from anyone present who wishes to pray aloud. Then there is a devotional reading, e.g. from Cardinal Basil Hume's *To be a Pilgrim* or Mother Mary Clare's *The Prayer that Heals* – to mention but two. The reading is followed by silent meditation (five to ten minutes). The intercessions are then read, followed by another shorter silence, and ending with the grace.

A simple rule of life is desirable for all members, to pray for all the members of the group every day. If there is more than one group, it is a good idea for the groups to meet together once a year to discuss problems and progress.

**Praying the news** A suggestion made by USPG. A silent prayer can be offered to God in the middle of listening to the news on radio or television, or whilst reading the newspaper on the train. The prayer only needs to be short, and offered to God for those injured in some disaster, or for a statesman with a difficult task in hand. Praying the news must never be a substitute for a regular time of prayer each day.

**Priesthood** (*See* **Ordination** on page 133.) There are two types of Christian priesthood – the 'priesthood of all believers' and the ordained priesthood.

*Priesthood of all believers* St Peter wrote this in his first Epistle:
'So come to him, our living Stone – the stone rejected by men but choice and precious in the sight of God. Come, and let yourselves be built, as living stones, into a spiritual temple; become a holy priesthood, to offer spiritual sacrifices acceptable to God through Jesus Christ. For it stands written:

I lay in Zion a choice corner-stone of great worth.
The man who has faith in it will not be put to shame.'
(1 Peter 2.4–6 NEB)

The priesthood of all believers is given to every Christian by virtue of Baptism and Confirmation. This is not something which can be quietly forgotten, for it forms the basis of the ministry of every Christian. We may feel inadequate, but the love and forgiveness of God are more than enough for our weakness.

God calls every Christian to be 'kings and priests unto God the Father' (Revelation 1.6). All Christians are involved in this royal priesthood, and all are mediators between God and men through their daily work, home life and leisure activities.

St Thomas Aquinas (1225–74) developed the idea of the priesthood of all believers at a time when the Church was firmly in the hands of the bishops and clergy. He wrote, 'We are responsible for the working for our own salvation and also by sharing in the priesthood of Christ, to act as his apostle in the salvation of the world' (*Ministry and Sacrament* 1937. Acknowledgement SCM Press).

*The ordained priesthood* The threefold ministry of bishops, priests and deacons has existed in the Church from very early times. Ordained priests are given authority by God, and are set apart as 'ministers of Christ and stewards of the mysteries of God'.

Here is a quotation from *Ministry and Ordination, An Agreed Statement of the Anglican–Roman Catholic International Commission*: 'The Christian community exists to give glory to God through the fulfilment of the Father's purpose. All Christians are called to serve this purpose by their life of prayer and surrender to divine grace, and by their careful attention to the needs of all human beings. They should witness to God's compassion for all mankind, and his concern for justice in the affairs of men. They should offer themselves to God in praise and worship, and devote their energies to bringing men into the fellowship of Christ's people, and so under his rule of love.

'The goal of the ordained ministry is to serve this priesthood of all the faithful. Like any human community, the Church requires a focus of leadership and unity, which the Holy Spirit provides in the ordained ministry.' (Reproduced by permission of SPCK.)

**Priest-in-charge**   When a change is being considered for the existing situation, it is sometimes necessary to appoint a priest-in-charge, instead of a vicar or rector. The priest-in-charge is deemed to be the incumbent of the parish for all purposes of the PCC (Powers) Measure and the Church Representation Rules.

**Prisons and the PCC**   Is there any opportunity for the PCC to be involved in caring for prisoners, their families or the victims of crime, or with young people caught up in a cycle of crime and punishment? There are many problems connected with this whole subject, but crime is certainly on the increase. What would our Lord want his Church to do, apart from learning to forgive?

Prisoners need to have their confidence and self-respect restored by having an opportunity to show that they can do something useful for other people and which the recipients value. When discharged, they often need somewhere to live, otherwise they are usually inside prison again before very long. (Perhaps there is need of a church-sponsored hostel in the area?) Prisoners are increasingly going out to assist in local community activities and in community service of all kinds, including work with the blind and handicapped. Can the PCC help in any way? Even if there is no prison, open prison, youth custody centre, etc. in the vicinity, perhaps the PCC could consider another question – is our local church doing all it can as a serving and caring community to help to prevent people, young and old, from being involved in crime?

**Publicity and communication**   Personal contact is by far the best form of communication. Could the PCC encourage the congregation to chat about the events at the church as much as possible to their friends and neighbours? Obviously, the Church needs other forms of communication, and the PCC might consider how effective are all its forms of communication and publicity.

Notice boards should be fixed in the best possible position, and always kept in good order and well painted. Remove all notices as soon as they are out of date.

Posters should be carefully planned, and well produced. Posters are always much more effective if a number of them are displayed around the parish, all with the same design and colour. Can we learn anything from publicity at a general election in terms of posters? Many notice boards appear in people's gardens and on fences. Thirty or forty small notice boards can easily be made from wood, 18 × 30 in, nailed to a 5-ft stake. These could be used by members of the congregation when publicity is needed. A poster secretary arranges the printing – or produces the posters.

A good relationship with the Press and local radio is desirable.

**Quinquennial report**   *See* **Buildings** on page 28.

**Quota**   *See Treasurer* under **Finance** on page 81.

**Quotations for PCC members**   Here is a random selection:

The unsearchable riches of Christ. (Ephesians 3.8 AV.)

The harvest truly is plenteous, but the labourers are few. Pray ye therefore the Lord of the harvest, that he will send forth labourers into his harvest. (St Matthew 9.37 and 38 AV.)

The Church is the only society which exists for those who do not belong to it. (Archbishop William Temple.)

Seek ye first the kingdom of God. (St Matthew 6.33 AV.)

God loved the world so much that he gave his only Son, that everyone who has faith in him may not die but have eternal life. (St John 3.16 NEB.)

Go ye into all the world, and preach the gospel to every creature. (St Mark 16.15 AV.)

Follow me, and I will make you fishers of men. (St Matthew 4.19 AV.)

You are a chosen race, a royal priesthood, a dedicated nation, and a people claimed by God for his own, to proclaim the triumphs of him who has called you out of darkness into his marvellous light. You are now the people of God, who once were not his people; outside his mercy once, you have now received his mercy. (1 Peter 2.9 and 10 NEB.)

Lo, I am with you always. (St Matthew 28.20 AV.)

The essential equipment of mission is made up of humility, service, sacrifice. Evangelism is essentially one beggar telling another beggar where food may be found. (Bishop Sadiq.)

The world wide task of evangelism is not an 'optional extra'. It is the high calling of every disciple. (Lambeth Conference Encyclical Letter in 1958. Acknowledgement SPCK.)

The evangelization of England . . . is a work that cannot be done by the clergy alone. It can only be done to a very small extent by the clergy at all. There can be no widespread evangelization of England, unless the work is undertaken by the lay people of the Church. (Archbishop William Temple in *Towards the Conversion of England* – 1945 Report.)

Of one thing I am certain; the One who started the good work in you will bring it to completion by the Day of Christ Jesus. (Philippians 1.6 NEB.)

Come to me, all whose work is hard, whose load is heavy; and I will give you relief. Bend your necks to my yoke, and learn from me, for I am gentle and humble-hearted; and your souls will find relief. For my yoke is good to bear, my load is light. (St Matthew 11.28–30 NEB.)

A Christian is either a missionary or a misfortune. (Source unknown.)

Be ye doers of the word, and not hearers only, deceiving your own selves. (James 1.22 AV.)

The Lord appointed other seventy also, and sent them two and two before his face into every city and place, whither he himself would come. (St Luke 10.1 AV.)

You will receive power when the Holy Spirit comes upon you, and you will bear witness for me. (Acts 1.8 NEB.)

Life is only for Love. Time is only that we may find God. (St Bernard.)

Blessed are the pure in heart: for they shall see God. (St Matthew 5.8 AV.)

Attempt great things for God. Expect great things from God. (Inscribed on the Lectern in Westminster Abbey.)

There can be no participation in Christ without participation in his mission to the world. (The Willingen Conference 1952.)

What can I give him, poor as I am?
If I were a shepherd I would bring a lamb;
If I were a wise man I would do my part;
Yet what I can I give him – give my heart.
(Christina Rossetti.)

A handful of men and women, mostly uneducated, mostly poor, but strong in the Lord and in the power of his might, men of the resurrection, men of the Spirit, went out into the pagan world – and won it for Christ. Let them shame our faithlessness! Let them be our example. (The Archbishop of Canterbury's Christmas Sermon, 1977.)

The most important part of your PCC meetings is that unhurried period of quiet thought and prayer which precedes the time you give to consideration of the agenda – when you wait on God to discover His mind and will for the parish. (From *Convictions* by Dr Donald Coggan, acknowledgement Hodder & Stoughton.)

**Racial problems**    This is not always a comfortable subject. The Anglican Communion has many more black members than white ones. General Synod has asked PCCs to consider what can be done to promote better relationships between people of different racial groups. There is a great deal that is wrong in this whole area, and our emotions are often quickly stirred up by it. There is much anger, violence and guilt, both in the world as a whole, and sometimes hostile feelings are only just below the surface even in Church members.

Racism is an ugly sin. The kingdom of God is about justice and peace, and our Lord wants us to 'Love your neighbour as yourself'. We are all equal in the sight of God. We belong to the one human race. We are all made in the image of God. And Christians are all brothers and sisters in Christ.

We need courage to examine our own attitudes. Are they still affected by our past history with all its pains as well as glories? It is said that there is a certain amount of racial prejudice in most (all?) of us. If we can admit that, then we have taken the first step on the path to doing something positive about the problem.

Self-examination is a Godly discipline. Although it is not good to wallow in guilt, we do need to take a cool and steady look at the problem. In this way we become more aware of the sin of racism, and we grow towards unity between the races.

You may protest that the PCC is already a civilized and Christian group, and that the PCC does not act in a racist and discriminating way. If this is true, it is, of course, a good thing. Black people, however, are a disadvantaged group, not because of a deliberate policy, but because of subtle forces and attitudes in society as a whole. There is also such a thing as institutional racism.

The pressures of racism have great consequences, especially for young people. Some black people feel they have no role to play, and that they are of no personal significance. They often have a deep sense of hopelessness, and feel that the Church does not care about the problem.

The eradication of racism is a serious task, and a challenge to all Christians – whether it exists in the heart, in the parish or in the world.

A serious commitment to be involved does require a willingness to listen, to discover the facts, and to pray for racial harmony and unity between different racial groups, both within the Church and in the world. Pray that we may grow towards God's purposes and to work for the establishment of a more just society in the world. We have a long way to go to achieve this.

What can PCC members actually do? Make an opportunity for the PCC, together with the congregation, to discuss this subject. The diocesan office or the archdeacon could suggest an appropriate person to come to a parish meeting to introduce the subject. In this way we can become more racially conscious and sensitive. Each PCC member is capable of effecting some change, however small it may be. We are not alone. Read Ephesians 2, verses 11-16. There are plenty of other relevant references. But the matchless vision of the Church in Revelation is particularly appropriate – 'After this I looked and saw a vast throng, which no one could count, from every nation, of all tribes, peoples, and languages, standing in front of the throne and before the Lamb' (Revelation 7.9 NEB). PCC members have the resources of the gospel to bring healing into this situation.

*Questions for discussion*

1. Who is my neighbour?
2. How can we love God, if we do nothing to help our neighbour in his hour of need?

**Raphael** *See* **Guild of St Raphael** on page 91.

**Readers** The office of Reader is open to men and women, and the selection procedure for Readers is similar to that for the sacred ministry. Each candidate has to be nominated by the priest, and with the support of the PCC. If accepted for training, the candidate embarks on a course of study to take the Central Readers' Conference Certificate. Training is on a part-time basis – usually one evening per week during university 'terms' in many dioceses. The course normally lasts for three years. Readers are examined about both their knowledge and their competence.

With the widespread popularity of the Parish Communion, and with the increased participation of lay people in the Eucharist, the 'liturgical' role of Readers is limited in some parishes, apart from Evensong. Lay people can be authorized to do most of the things which Readers do in the Eucharist, apart from preaching a sermon. Careful preparation is required to prepare a sermon. Preaching is also very closely connected with the spiritual life of the Reader. *See* **Sermon** on page 176.

Readers can conduct funeral services in church, or at a cemetery or crematorium, but they can do this only with the goodwill of the relatives and at the invitation of the priest. During an interregnum, this is at the invitation of the area/rural dean.

Many clergy have been withdrawn from the countryside through pastoral reorganization schemes, and often a number of churches are now grouped together in a team or group ministry. There is a vital role for the Readers in the countryside, to lead the worship and to share in the pastoral work. In other parishes, the way in which Readers exercise their ministry seems to vary enormously. In all cases, this depends on the amount of time which the Reader can offer for this work, the relationship between the Reader and the priest, and the needs of the parish.

***The pastoral and educational role of the Reader*** In addition to the 'liturgical role', a Reader can exercise an effective pastoral ministry in every parish, providing he or she is willing to do this, and the time can be given for this work. The Readers can share with the clergy particularly in the following areas:

1. The pastoral care of the bereaved – *see* **Bereavement** on page 14.
2. Baptism Preparation and follow up after the service – *see* **Baptism** on page 13.
3. An educational role in leading discussion groups and Bible study groups.
4. The preparation of Confirmation candidates.
5. 'Home Communions'. When regular worshippers can no longer come to church to receive Communion, then the sacrament has to be given to them at home or in hospital. Readers can be authorized by the bishop, with the agreement of the PCC, to administer Communion to people at home or in hospital. The wafers and wine are consecrated by the priest in church, and often the wafer is 'intincted' with a very small spot of wine. This avoids the danger of spilling the wine, or passing on infection in cases of sickness. (*See* **Home Communion** on page 98.) With increasing numbers of people requiring Communion at home or in hospital, Readers can exercise a very important role in this ministry. In some parishes, the sacrament is taken out of the church with an appropriate prayer just before the end of the service. Readers sharing in this work can help to relieve pressure on the priest's work-load, and enable those concerned to 'share in the communion of his Body and Blood' in a regular way.
6. The daily offices. The effectiveness of a Reader's work depends to a very large extent on his or her spiritual life. It can be a great help to the Reader to share in saying Matins and Evensong with the clergy in church. This can also be a help to the clergy.
7. It may be appropriate to take part in staff meetings with the vicar and curates etc.
8. To co-operate with the priest in the whole mission of the Church. The involvement of Readers in the mission and

work of the Church will vary considerably from parish to parish. Much depends on time available, willingness and ability to co-operate and work with the priest and to work under the priest's authority, and also on the situation in the parish.

A Reader is not automatically (*ex officio*) a member of the PCC. This depends on the Annual Parochial Church Meeting. Some feel it is a good idea to elect the Readers in the same way and at the same time as other lay people. In other parishes, Readers are elected to the PCC for a certain number of years.

When being admitted to office, every Reader makes a declaration of assent, to give due obedience to the bishop. In the parish, the Reader undertakes to support the priest, and to work under the direction and authority of the priest. The theological, liturgical and pastoral training gives a tremendous potential for the effectiveness of a Reader's ministry. The need is clearly there in every parish, but so much depends on the relationship and the personalities of those concerned.

A Reader's licence does not continue automatically year after year, and it is reviewed periodically. The priest has to sign the form to renew the licence, which is annually in some dioceses. The bishop may revoke or withdraw the licence at any time.

*Two thoughts for Readers*

1. Could a Reader be more involved in the mission and work of the church in your parish?
2. Is God calling you to the ordained ministry?

*A thought for PCC members*
Is God calling you to be a Reader?

**Redundant churches**    The Pastoral Measure 1969 updated the arrangements needed to close a parish church, and quite a number of churches were declared redundant as a result. Now, however, most deaneries have the right number of church buildings, and there should be fewer redundancies in the future, particularly where priest and PCC can work together effectively. Now is the time for the PCC to have confidence in God, and in its ability to co-operate with the work of the Spirit in the parish.

If the diocese does propose a redundancy scheme, there might be a good reason for it. To fight such a proposal could be a costly business, and the question has to be asked – Who will pay the costs? Details about redundancy procedures can be obtained from the diocesan secretary or from the diocesan registrar (address and telephone number in the local telephone directory).

Now is the time to fight off any possible redundancy scheme, by repairing the roof, keeping gutters and drains in good order, and paying the quota by monthly instalments, co-operating with the priest, and getting on with the rightful work of the PCC before it is too late.

**Redundant Churches Fund** Certain churches of historic or architectural interest which are no longer required for worship may be vested in the Redundant Churches Fund for preservation, if no suitable alternative use is available. When this happens, arrangements can be made for the church to be used on special occasions. A church vested in the Fund can be brought back into use as a parish church if there is a major change in the local situation.

**Religious communities of monks and nuns** This section briefly considers the origins and place of communities in the Church today.

Religious communities did not begin with the Christian Church. The Essenes were a Jewish community with a highly organized monastic life at the time of John the Baptist (Dead Sea Scrolls). From very early times, Christian men and women have not married so that they could devote their lives to God in prayer and in works of charity.

Christian communities were started as early as the third century by hermits in the Egyptian deserts. One of them – St Anthony – organized a simple community life about AD 303. The idea spread, and during the later Dark Ages, the light of learning and devotion was only kept alive by the monasteries. By the sixteenth century, many communities had forgotten the high ideals and the rules of their founders. Some were undoubtedly corrupt and in need of reform. King Henry VIII used this excuse to seize the great wealth of the monasteries, and he ordered them to be 'dissolved' (1534–39). The spiritual life of the Church of England was undoubtedly poorer as a result of this action, but during the nineteenth century religious communities were refounded within the Church as a result of the Oxford Movement. Many obstacles were put in the way of this remarkable growth of religious communities at the time, but happily the situation is very different today. Now there are ten religious orders for men, 45 for women, and two mixed communities within the Church of England.

The main activities of a religious community are prayer and work. The call of Christ to join a religious community seems to come to people today from all walks of life, and from all shades of churchmanship. Perhaps one of the readers of this *ABC* may have a vocation to the religious life. It usually involves spiritual struggle, sacrifice and self-conquest. But a call to the religious life is an appeal to the highest and the noblest side of human life. Everything worthwhile is often only achieved at a cost.

Is there any value in having a traditional monastic community when so much has changed in modern life? The simple answer is – prayer is just as vital as ever. These communities provide a wonderful powerhouse of regular prayer. Some believe that the next great Christian advance will come through the religious communities.

*Questions for thought or discussion*

1. Where is the nearest Anglican monastery to your parish?
2. Would it be possible for the parish to have a prayer link – parish retreat – and other involvement with the community?
3. What about having a visiting speaker or preacher from one of the religious communities?

Address for enquiries: The Enquiries Secretary, Communities Consultative Council, 9 Stafford Road, Eccleshall, Stafford ST21 6JP. Tel: 0785–850588.

**Repentance**  Sin can be a very real problem in the Church itself. This section is not about personal sins, but about the corporate failures and sins of the local church. No parish is perfect. To mis-use Saint Paul's words: 'all have sinned, and all fall short of the glory of God'. Does your church need to repent, because it does not take mission seriously, or it is indifferent to strangers and visitors, or there is pride, in many forms, lack of charity, unkindness to the priest, lack of preparation before Communion . . .? Perhaps an annual Service of Repentance in Lent or Advent? Repentance is needed before renewal will come.

**Retreat**  Not in a military sense of an army retreating because of pressure from the enemy. We grow primarily in the Christian

# Retreat

communities to which we belong, but there are outside resources such as a retreat, which can help from time to time. A Christian retreat is withdrawing from the pressures of daily life in order to have a period of quiet reflection with a group of people in a shared silence. Usually a retreat conductor gives two – or perhaps three – talks during the course of a day.

Silence is kept for the duration of the retreat, and this can be a wonderful experience which produces inner peace and tranquillity, and refreshes the soul. Daily life is often full of noise, chatter, pressures and distractions. Sometimes even our prayers are full of 'chatter' to God. The silence of a retreat provides a wonderful opportunity for God to talk to us and for us to listen to him, and to think of his purposes in our lives. This is much easier to do during a retreat than it is at home.

A retreat is an opportunity to pray, and also to learn more about prayer. The conductor usually puts up a list of times when individuals can make an appointment (by an anonymous tick) to talk about any problem, or to talk about prayer itself, or to make a private confession. A retreat is also an opportunity to read, and a time for physical rest, refreshment and a walk in a quiet garden.

Many people are afraid of silence, and thus they always carry a transistor radio playing loud music. The Christian is never alone, for Jesus said, 'Lo, I am with you always, even to the end of the world'. If someone is bursting to talk on retreat, they can always go and talk to the conductor. But it is strange how so many people say at the end of a retreat that they enjoyed the silence, and that they were sorry when it ended.

From time to time, Jesus took his disciples away from the crowds for a time of quietness, rest and prayer. The invitation of Jesus still stands today, 'Come ye apart, and rest awhile'. Could you who are reading this section respond to this invitation? For a retreat is strongly recommended for all PCC members – and people return from retreat in a relaxed state and with a new vision of the faith, and a new zeal for life. Many who are searching for something in life often find it on retreat.

The number of people going on retreat is steadily increasing year by year, and this in itself is a good testimony to their value. Special retreats can be arranged for PCC members, for young people, the MU, or a general one for the congregation.

The National Retreat Association is a federation of Anglican, Roman Catholic and Free Church groups. The aims of the NRA are to foster and develop the rich and diverse expressions of Christian spirituality, and to provide information and resources.

Details about retreats can usually be found in the *Church Times*. Much more detail is given in a journal called *The Vision*. This gives information about all retreats to be held during the year at the 160 retreat houses throughout the country.

Further information from the National Retreat Association, Liddon House, 24 South Audley Street, London W1Y 5DL. Tel: 071-493 3534.

**Routine jobs** (*See* **Verger** on page 199.) Volunteers can help in a variety of ways, just as routine work is shared out in many households today. Help in this way will free the priest for the work for which he was ordained. It is an act of Christian kindness to relieve the priest of some of his heavy work-load. 'Charity begins at home.' Due care needs to be taken with all routine work, and it is wise to consult the priest about methods.

*Church heating* Another routine job which does not need a priest to look after it is the heating system. Surely a lay person can do this, with an understudy for holidays and sickness. An automatic switch can be fitted to many systems which will operate only on Sundays (or as required). It is important to have a warm church – it is so much more encouraging. A cold church will not tempt those with a lukewarm faith.

*Hymn boards* Put up appropriate numbers for the service and take them down afterwards. Never leave the numbers on the board during the week, as this gives the impression of slackness.

*Church cleaning* Instead of paying a cleaner, some churches have a rota of volunteers to clean each week. It is easier if two adults, or a family, work together each time.

**Rural dean** (called area dean in some urban areas). The rural dean was an ancient appointment in the Church, but the duties were gradually taken over by the archdeacon. The office was revived in 1836, and more and more work now seems to come to them.

The rural dean is the chairman at the meetings of the deanery clergy chapter. He presides at meetings of the Deanery Synod if he so wishes, or he may choose to hand over the chairmanship to the lay co-chairman. The rural dean is appointed by the bishop, usually after consultation with the deanery clergy. The appointment is for a period of three or five years, and can be renewed.

The main responsibility is one of leadership. He shares the bishop's pastoral care of the clergy and their families, and he is a vital channel of communication between the bishop, the clergy and the parishes. General Synod and diocesan synods sometimes send matters to the parishes through the rural dean, and he is also involved when PCCs send matters up to the Diocesan Synod.

During an interregnum in any parish in the deanery the rural dean is sometimes appointed as one of the parish sequestrators. He has general oversight of all vacant parishes in the deanery, and he is the co-ordinator of arrangements for the institution and induction service. He also carries out parish visitations (inspections) on behalf of the archdeacon, and he is involved in various deanery committees and events.

The work of a rural dean is demanding, and it always requires attendance at additional meetings outside the parish. In order that the rural dean's parish does not suffer, how can PCC members help to 'fill the gap'?

**Sacrament**   A sacrament is an activity of the Church which expresses the presence of Christ. It is an 'outward and visible sign of an inward and spiritual grace' (BCP). There are two sacraments of the gospel – Holy Baptism and the Eucharist. In addition, there are Confirmation, Penance (personal confession before a priest, who then gives Absolution), Orders (ordination), the Anointing of the Sick, and Matrimony.

There is a distinction between the 'matter' and the 'form' of the sacrament. The bread and wine in the Eucharist are the 'matter', and the 'form' is the use of the correct words. To have a valid sacrament, the right form and matter are needed, together with the right intention. The validity of the sacrament is independent of the worthiness or unworthiness of the minister who celebrates the sacrament.

Canon Law requires that only a priest, duly ordained by a bishop, can celebrate the Eucharist.

**Sacristan**   This is the person who looks after the sacred vessels and vestments, and who prepares the altar for a service of Holy Communion.

There is a saying, 'Cleanliness comes next to Godliness', and perhaps that saying is only partly true. Cleanliness and neatness are certainly needed for all work in the sacristy.

The cruets for the water and wine need cleaning regularly. Any stain on the glass can be removed with tea leaves or grains of rice, and some water, briskly shaken. Never leave the cruets out after the service; always put them away, even if there is a daily Eucharist. Clean them and refill them ready for the next service.

The priest will explain how he likes things to be arranged. When a new priest arrives in the parish, do not be surprised if he makes some changes and asks you to do things in a different way.

After the service, the chalice (cup) and paten (plate) and ciborium (chalice with a lid for the wafers) are washed, dried and locked away in the safe. Never put silver on silver without a purificator between them, as silver is a soft metal which scratches and quickly wears away.

The silver does not need cleaning with silver polish very often, provided it is regularly washed and rubbed with an ordinary soft tea cloth. When silver polish is used, always wash it afterwards with very hot water and washing up liquid, and rinse well. Unless this is done thoroughly, the silver polish can react with the wine to produce a most obnoxious taste. Even the slightest trace of polish can be detected. In addition, unless the washing has been very thorough, small droplets of wine will cling to the side of the chalice during the administration.

The sacristan also looks after the church vestments (if any) and the robes, and also takes action when they need cleaning, repairing or replacing (after consultation with the priest). Perhaps there is another person willing to do the repairs?

The purificators (small cloths used to wipe the chalice) and the small Lavabo towel (used to dry the priest's hands in the middle of the service) all need washing and ironing (with a little starch) each week. The 'fair linen cloth' (as the 1662 Prayer Book describes the altar cloth) and the corporal (the square linen cloth on which the sacred vessels stand) and other cloths need washing from time to time. The altar cover has a dust cover to keep the fair linen cloth clean, and this of course needs laundering from time to time.

The altar frontal(s), the pulpit fall and the priest's vestments are changed to the appropriate colour for the seasons and saints' days of the church year. The appropriate colours are given in a diary called the lectionary. The colour green is shown by a G, red is R, white is W, and violet or purple is V. The lectionary can be purchased from any religious bookshop. Buy a copy in November, when the church year begins.

The sacristan orders fresh supplies of wine, the priest's and people's wafers, candles, and incense (where used). Also new linen as required.

In parishes where there is a daily Eucharist, perhaps it may be necessary to have an assistant sacristan – who would also be able to help during holidays.

In this very secular age, we need to remember that the sacred vessels and vestments are used to further God's kingdom here on earth. Sacristy work is a vital service to the church, and is it not a privilege for the person concerned? One final thought – each time you prepare the altar, could you offer a prayer to God for the priest taking the service, for all who come to it, for the people of the parish, and also for yourself? (*See* **Spiritual life of PCC members** on page 182.)

### Sacristan's traditional prayer

Almighty God, who through thy most holy Son didst ordain and set in order all things in the upper room, that we might receive the inestimable benefits of his most precious body and blood, grant unto us thy servants that in true humility and fervent recollection we may serve thee in thy sanctuary here on earth, and finally adore thee with thy holy angels in heaven, through the merits of the same, our Saviour Jesus Christ. Amen.

**St Luke's Hospital for the Clergy**   This is a small surgical and medical hospital in one of the loveliest squares in London. It has accommodation for 28 patients and provides treatment entirely free for clergy of the Anglican Communion, their wives, widows, dependent children, monks, nuns, deaconesses, overseas church workers, members of the Church Army, theological college students, and all full-time church workers licensed by a bishop.

The main advantage of this hospital is that the date of admission can usually be arranged to fit in with the events in the parish – unless the vicar is rushed to hospital as an emergency case. There is also privacy and the quiet atmosphere of a friendly Christian hospital.

St Luke's Hospital was a gift of the laity to the Church in 1892. Today, over 150 leading London consultants keep up an old tradition and give their time and talents entirely free of charge, which is a wonderful offering to the servants of the Church.

There are over 850 deanery representatives whose task is to remind PCC members from time to time of the great work done by St Luke's Hospital, and to invite PCCs and individuals to make an annual donation for the hospital. Enquiries and donations to: The General Secretary, St Luke's Hospital for the Clergy, 14 Fitzroy Square, London W1P 6AH. Tel: 071-388 4954.

*Food for thought*

1. Who is your deanery representative for St Luke's Hospital?
2. When did the deanery representative last approach your PCC, and with what results? Does your PCC consider making a donation to St Luke's Hospital when considering the annual budget?

**Secretary for the priest**   An endless flow of paperwork comes to the priest's office, and not all of it can go straight in the waste-paper basket. The priest's ministry will be much more effective if too much time is not spent on paperwork and administration. A good secretary can be a tremendous help with much of the routine work, and in this way, free the priest to concentrate on new initiatives and on all the other jobs done by the priest. It is said that a good secretary can be of more use to the priest than a curate – although it would not be wise to pursue that thought.

The secretary is in some respects a personal assistant to the priest. A job description would include the following – someone who is trustworthy, because confidential papers will sometimes be involved; reliable; efficient; methodical; able to deal with routine administration, filing, typing, a word processor and photocopier/duplicator; ability to think and plan ahead, and to remind the priest of things which need to be done.

Some PCCs are able to pay for a secretary for the priest. If this is not possible, then a volunteer may be willing to offer time and secretarial help to the church without charge. In this case, the PCC could give an honorarium.

**Secretary of the PCC**   The PCC elects its secretary at the first meeting after the APCM. The secretary is normally elected

173

from among the PCC membership, but it is possible to appoint someone who is not a member. In the latter case, the person would either have to be co-opted to the PCC, or be a non-voting member.

Much more is involved in the work of the PCC secretary than taking notes at the meeting, and writing the minutes afterwards. The following is a summary of the work involved:

1. Ten clear days before the PCC Meeting, put a notice in the porch, signed by – or on behalf of – the chairman, to announce the date, time and place of the meeting.
2. Seven clear days before the meeting, send a copy of the agenda to every PCC member. *See Agenda* on page 145, *Any Other Business* on pages 4 (para. 3), 8 (para. 18) and 149 (para. 6), and *Standing committee* under **Parochial Church Council** on page 150.
3. During the meeting, take careful notes of the discussions and decisions, and the numbers voting for and against a resolution if the vote is close. Record the names of all present, or circulate an attendance list or attendance book. Record and announce any apologies for absence during the meeting. Be aware of all matters which will arise from the minutes. Consult with the chairman, preferably two or three days before the meeting, about which correspondence is to be read out at the meeting.

   A good secretary can be a great help to the chairman during the meeting, and for this reason it is helpful if they sit next to each other. *See Rights and responsibilities* on pages 136–40.
4. After the meeting, write a draft copy of the minutes as soon as possible, and certainly while they are fresh in the mind. Submit them to the chairman for approval, and then put them in the minute book. They can be pasted in the minute book, and trimmed to size. When the minutes are photocopied and kept in a loose-leaf file, it is wise to initial each page.

   The minutes should be brief, accurate and adequate. They are not a record of a debate, but a record of the decisions made by the PCC. Sometimes it is helpful to have a brief summary of the arguments for and against. Clear headings in capital letters are desirable. The right-hand column of the minutes should have a heading, 'Action'. This is to record who is to take action and by what date the action is to be taken. The wording of all resolutions should be recorded, and whether they were carried or rejected.

5. Circulate the minutes to all PCC members as soon as possible after the meeting. This will be a reminder of who is doing what, as a result of the meeting.

6. There is a whole range of jobs which have to be done before and after the meeting, including letters to write, lists to prepare, and other administrative jobs.

7. The PCC secretary is an obvious candidate to be elected each year to the standing committee. Otherwise, who else will do the agenda, minutes and other paperwork involved? The secretary has an important role in the standing committee in planning ahead and in foreseeing problems which might arise.

8. Work out the dates for the whole year for PCC meetings and standing committee meetings, with the chairman (for approval by the PCC). Also the dates for putting up the legal notices in the porch, and sending out the agenda.

9. Prepare the notice, the agenda and the various reports for the Annual Parochial Church Meeting. Order a supply of the necessary official Synod notices and voting papers in good time. (*See* **Annual Parochial Church Meeting** on page 4.)

   Take notes during the meeting. Prepare a draft of the minutes for the chairman's approval, and then put the final copy in the minute book.

   After the APCM, put on the notice board a list of the names of the new churchwardens, the Deanery Synod representatives, and those elected to serve on the PCC for the coming year.

   Each year, it is wise to read through all the rules governing the PCC and the APCM, and particularly before the APCM. It can be helpful on occasions to remember the appropriate rules, and to quote them when necessary.

10. After each meeting, write a report for the magazine and notice board.

11. Not every parish is lucky enough to have a verger or caretaker. The committee room or church hall has to be prepared, and the heating put on well before the meeting, so that the room is adequately warm. Soon after being appointed as secretary, it is wise to discuss this with the

churchwardens and the priest or standing committee, and also to work out who should deal with the refreshment rota for meetings.

12. The PCC secretary must inform the secretary of the Diocesan Synod and the secretary of the Deanery Synod, of his or her name and address on appointment.

13. The PCC secretary has an important administrative role when a new priest is being appointed. Detailed instructions are sent by the diocese about procedures, but the parish loses its legal rights about the appointment unless all time limits are strictly observed. (*See Appoinment of the new priest* under **Interregnum** on page 106.)

**Security of churches**  A rota of volunteers to look after the church is one method. Another is to form a church neighbourhood watch scheme. All the people living around the building may not want to come to church, but if approached, they may be willing to help with a watch scheme. How about a social evening and slide show to launch it?

Children love to climb on a church roof. If this is a problem in your parish, one answer is to take a photograph of them! It usually works.

**Sequestration**  *See* **Interregnum** on page 105.

**Sermon**  Every preacher has an awesome responsibility. What, then, do you think the preacher is aiming to achieve? To proclaim the gospel – to convert the congregation – to rebuke on occasions – to encourage – to strengthen and build up the faith of the Church – to draw out and expound God's word in the Scriptures?

A former Archbishop of Canterbury, Dr Michael Ramsey, said, 'Preaching creates and re-creates the Church'. Think for a moment how God's living word is at work in your parish, and also at work when the Church gathers together to worship God.

The sermon plays a very important part in our worship each Sunday. A preacher cannot arrive in the pulpit and hope for sudden inspiration! If the preacher is true to this high calling, then much time is needed for careful preparation. Those who are present will to a large extent be the same people in the congregation week by week.

A priest cannot produce good sermons regularly when the work-load is impossibly heavy. The quality of the sermon will play an important part in determining whether the occasional worshipper in church comes again next week.

The preaching of the gospel was made a priority in the lives of the Apostles. 'The Twelve called the whole body of disciples together and said, "It would be a grave mistake for us to neglect the word of God in order to wait at table. Therefore, friends, look out seven men of good reputation from your number, men full of the Spirit and of wisdom, and we will appoint them to deal with these matters, while we devote ourselves to prayer and to the ministry of the word." This proposal proved acceptable to the whole body' (Acts 6.2–5 NEB). See also Acts 2.2–4 and 2 Timothy 4.1–5.

What message is the preacher delivering? Careful listening is important for all present, for PCC members, and especially 'Know the reason for the faith that is within you'.

A suggestion for every PCC member (and for the congregation too): pray for the preacher just before the sermon. A suggested prayer:

Almighty God, bless this your servant,
and open all our hearts to receive your living word,
through Jesus Christ our Lord. Amen.

*Food for thought*

1. A sermon is much more than a lesson or lecture – but is it the only form of Christian education for the congregation week by week?
2. An occasional alternative to a sermon – a dialogue, or a question and answer session between two people, or a discussion after the service about the sermon on a special subject such as Christian stewardship, mission and evangelism, church music, etc.

**Servers**  There are two sayings about trying to keep young people in the Church:

1. 'Use me, or lose me'.
2. 'The boy holds the candle, but the candle holds the boy.'

How many parish priests have discovered their vocation to the sacred ministry through serving at the altar? Quite a thought!

It is a great privilege to serve at the Eucharist, and for this reason, servers should do their utmost to make their part of the worship as perfect as possible.

The hallmark of a good server is to be unobtrusive, and all movements should be carried out quietly, efficiently and with the minimum of fuss. Whenever two servers are required to move together, they should do so in harmony. Careful training is obviously needed to achieve this.

It is helpful if servers are in church at least twenty minutes before the service (ten minutes on weekdays?). The first thing to do on each occasion is to offer a short prayer to God for the priest, for those present, and for yourself. A suggested prayer (to learn by heart?):

Heavenly Father,
your Son is our great High Priest in heaven:
bless us all with the gifts of your Holy Spirit,
make us worthy to serve you in this holy sacrament,
and unite us in your everlasting love,
through Jesus Christ our Lord. Amen.

As a member of the Church community, it is desirable that every server should join in the worship as far as is possible. The offering of the servers, however, is first of all to do the work of serving to the glory of God, and to the best of their ability.

After the service, help to clear away. Always use the extinguisher to put out the candles. Never blow them out, as this spreads the candle wax. It then has to be removed by someone! This is not always an easy task.

A prayer to be used by the server before leaving church (to learn by heart?):

O God, you have given so much to me.
Give me one thing more – a greatful heart,
for Christ's sake. Amen.

*Food for thought*
Does anyone from the parish belong to the Guild of the Servers of the Sanctuary?

**Shoes**   A suggestion: if walking on uncarpeted aisles before or during a quiet service, try to avoid wearing noisy shoes.

**Sidesmen**   In choosing sidesmen, effort should be made to include people from all walks of life, young and old, men and women, rich and poor, black and white. People need to feel included in the life of the Church. What are the duties of sidesmen?

1. About 20 minutes before the service, prepare the books and notice sheets, so that they are all ready to hand to people as they arrive.

2. The greeting and welcome given to people as they come in is the most important part of the sidesmen's job. It is good to look directly at each person as the books are handed over to them. Never turn your back on people when they come in, in order to pick up the books. A smile works wonders. It is a good thing for the sidesmen to learn the names of the congregation so that they can all be greeted by name. Some churches have a special welcome team, who look out for visitors and strangers. If a visitor comes alone, it is helpful and friendly if someone from the welcome team can sit with them during the service. Many visitors are not able to find their place in the numerous books which seem to be needed for modern worship. Perhaps help could be given here too, or a simple guide for the service could be printed. After the service, invite them for coffee, and introduce them to some other members of the congregation.

3. The sidesmen play a vital role in helping to provide the right tone and spiritual atmosphere in the church before the service. A warm and friendly greeting is good, providing it is done quietly. If the sidesmen talk loudly with each person, this will disturb those who are trying to pray and to prepare for worship. Lack of thought and concern for others can very quickly destroy the peace and quietness that are needed. The sidesmen have a great potential for helping the whole church to prepare for its worship, or for destroying the prayerful and quiet atmosphere that is so vital in preparation. 'How awesome is this place. This is the House of God. This is the Gate of Heaven.'

4. When strangers or visitors come to church, try to find out their names and addresses – but always in a tactful way. Write it down later on, and hand it to the visiting committee or to the vicar. Cards are available from church bookshops – 'Visitors and Newcomers' cards.

5. Take the collection during the service – if that is the tradition in your church. It seems to produce more money than leaving the plate at the back of the church! Count the money and open the envelopes, record the amounts in the Register of Services, and sign the book. It is customary to have at least two sidesmen counting the money in this way.

6. In most parishes, the sidesmen are asked to perform other

duties before the service. These usually include putting on the light and heat, lighting the candles, and, if there is no server, preparing the altar. After the service, put out the candles and lights, and turn off the heating once the church is empty.

7. It is important that the sidesmen come early enough to do the jobs properly. It is more important that they prepare themselves spiritually for the service. It is wrong to forget their own spiritual preparation because they are busy doing other jobs. Canon Law states 'It is the duty of the sidesmen to promote the cause of true religion in the parish' (Canon E2(3)). Their own example and practice is an important part of it.

8. It is the duty of the sidesmen to assist the churchwardens in maintaining order and decency in the church and churchyard, especially during an act of worship. Perhaps it is not very common in your parish for the preacher to be booed during the sermon, but a good team of men may be needed to keep out the drunks at the Midnight Service.

9. After each service, most clergy try to shake hands with all members of the congregation as they leave the building. (They are busy praying before the service.) A friendly word from the sidesmen as people leave is a good thing – 'Hope you enjoyed the service, and that we'll see you again next Sunday'. The sidesmen should never turn their backs on people in order to put the hymn books away.

## A prayer for use by the sidesmen before the service

Almighty God,
you have called us to serve you as sidesmen in your Church:
fill us all with your Holy Spirit,
bless all who come to your House this day,
and help us to worship you with reverence and devotion,
through Jesus Christ our Lord. Amen.

If there is an opportunity, read the collect, the appointed Psalm (given in the ASB after the collect) and the three Scripture readings, as part of your own preparation.

## A prayer for use by sidesmen after the service

Heavenly Father,
the hosts of heaven ceaselessly proclaim your glory,
and we have joined with them in praising your holy name:

Make us mindful of all your blessings,
and guide all of us in this coming week,
through Jesus Christ our Lord. Amen.

**Silver**   All silver, gold, brass and pewter vessels are valuable
and it is wise to have them photographed for identification purposes, in case they are stolen. It is a simple matter to have a
parish identification 'mark' engraved, or the police have an
ultra-violet pen (needs re-doing periodically). *See* **Sacristan** on
page 170.

**Singing**   *See* **Music in worship** on page 123.

**Social events**   It is not possible for the priest to know more
than a small percentage of the people in a large parish. Any
social event organized by the church is an opportunity for PCC
members and others to invite fringe members and outsiders.
The PCC – or the entertainments committee – can organize
'open' social events on numerous occasions, e.g. Shrove Tuesday party, New Year party, dance or dinner dance, barn dance,
harvest lunch or harvest supper, wine and cheese party, coffee
morning and so on.

   Much more than social gatherings is required to draw people
into church membership, but these events certainly do help.
How can PCC members help to follow up any contacts apart
from prayer?

**Social responsibility and concern**   The spiritual gospel and
the social gospel are closely linked together, and they are both
an important part of the life and work of the Church. God
created all people, and his Son took flesh for the redemption of
the whole world. This is shown in the sacraments. We demon-
strate his love not only in our words, but also by our deeds. This
includes working for justice and peace in the world, trying to
meet human need, working for the relief of suffering, and trying
to do our share for the whole of God's creation.

   The Church will lose much of its cutting edge if it fails to do
something about the problems of the modern world – apart
from praying about them. What would the prophet Amos say
about modern injustices, poverty, unemployment, depression,
crime, drug addiction, the problems of the elderly and the
young, the lonely, the mentally handicapped, the disabled?

   The state has done much to improve the lot of many people,

when compared with former years. But the whole system is a partnership between the state and various voluntary organizations, including the Church. Quite often, the system needs prodding, questioning, a new vision and encouragement. It is part of being a Christian in the world to take an active interest in society, and to help whenever possible. The parable of the good Samaritan shows us who are our neighbours. Who then are the modern equivalent of the despised Samaritans? The parable also shows how Christians should be involved, and Jesus himself was constantly helping other people.

The PCC as a Christian organization responds because of its understanding of what God is like. God does not love only the rich and the privileged. He also loves the poor, the oppressed and those who are the outcasts of society today. When God entered the human scene, it was among the poor of the earth that he came. It is so easy for a PCC to be preoccupied with the actual life of the church. It is so easy for Christians to be detached and isolated from the problems of society in general – or even the problems of the local secular community. The basis of Christian love and concern for others comes from the fount of all love, God our loving creator and redeemer.

General Synod has a Board of Social Responsibility, which produces official reports on issues of concern from time to time. These reports are debated in General Synod and widely reported in the media. The reports can be studied, and then discussed at PCC meetings to give a clearer understanding of the issues involved.

The problems of modern society are large and even frightening. They may well seem beyond the ability of the PCC in a small parish to do anything about them. But a concern for justice, for freedom and truth are surely high ideals which a Christian believes should be enjoyed by everyone. Justice and peace are important parts of the kingdom of God.

**Spiritual life of PCC members**   Prayer has been described as 'the lifting of the heart and mind to God'. There is a saying, 'all activity compared with prayer is as nothing', and this is particularly true for PCC members. This section on the spiritual life is probably the most important part of the *ABC*. Every PCC member can make a far greater contribution to the life of the local church through prayer than through any amount of activity. However efficient, caring and responsible a PCC member may be, he or she is failing unless prayer and Christian love are given high priority in their daily lives.

Some people want religion without discipline. 'God will not accept a divided affection' (William Wilberforce), and Evelyn Underhill reminds us that 'there are no short cuts in the spiritual life'. There are different ways of praying, and each PCC member has to work out which is the best for them. Each has to work at his or her spiritual life, and start again after each failure. Continual discipline is needed, but the day will come when prayer is not so much a duty as a delight. Prayer is about developing a relationship with God, and no one else can do this for you. Prayer is your search for God – but remember that God has been searching for you long before you started your search for God. Prayer is deliberately putting yourself into God's presence, and exposing yourself to his love.

*Personal prayer*   Christians are formed by the way in which they pray. Your views about what God is like will powerfully affect your spiritual life. Jesus taught us to think of God as Father. Whatever faults your earthly father may have had, your Heavenly Father is a God of mercy and love, and he really does love you, and all other people too. How then do you respond to God's love for you on the cross, and how do you develop a personal relationship with someone you cannot see or touch? It can be done, but it requires time and commitment each day. Prayer is a journey of discovery.

Many people find it helpful to say the Lord's Prayer very slowly. Go through it phrase by phrase, and with a definite pause between each phrase. This is a particularly good way of starting – or beginning again in the spiritual life.

Praying for ten minutes on your journey to work each morning is a good habit. It is certainly helpful to be aware of God's presence during the journey. But if you are serious in your desire to pray – (and this must surely include every PCC member) – then you need to make additional time for prayer each day in a quiet place, preferably in your home. It is said that 'silence is the gateway to the spiritual life'.

Still your mind, and relax your body, and only when you have done this, try to put yourself into the presence of God. Each person is a complex being, and our emotional and mental side can have a powerful effect on our prayer life and worship. We usually come to God with what we might call our own special personal baggage – our fears, guilt, hopes, expectations, and a whole host of things which will distract us from

God. In some ways, our prayer time can rapidly change from being 'God-centred' to 'self-centred'. In the Confirmation service, we say, 'I turn to Christ' – and we have to turn to Christ again and again, especially after being distracted. Learn to develop an inner stillness and to focus all your attention on God. Choose a position which you can maintain without moving. Whether you sit, stand or kneel, be still, and be aware of your breathing, which should be deep, regular and slow. Hymns of the Holy Spirit are helpful, or simply ask for God's help: 'Heavenly Father, you sent your Spirit to the Church at Pentecost. Renew your gift of the Spirit in us, and teach us how to pray'.

Learn to wait in silence, and do not be in a hurry to begin your prayers with words. God is always trying to help us to get to know him better. His Spirit is always with us, and we have to try to be open to his suggestions and promptings. Reading books on prayer helps you to find out what other people have discovered about prayer before you. Your aim is to find God in your prayers, so try to find a way of praying which works for you. Each person must try and work out what is best and most helpful.

**Praying with the Bible**   Many people soon come to the end of their own resources in prayer, but God offers us help, for example, through the Bible. By all means use the King James Authorized Version if you glory in good English, but it is helpful to have another more modern translation as well. Compare the old with the new version. Buy a Bible with good clear print. The Bible is one of the important ways in which God's word comes to us today. Become aware of God's presence, and imagine that you are part of the scene in the Bible passage. Reflect on how God is speaking directly to you through the passage. You may feel happiness, sadness, guilt or anger, but try to turn your feelings and thoughts about the passage into prayer.

**Daily with God**   A prayer book, called *Daily with God*, has been produced by the author. It has a page a day: an opening prayer, verses of a Psalm, Old and New Testament readings, and three new prayers mainly based on the readings. Provision is made for Saints' days and Festivals. (Published by the Canterbury Press, St Mary's Plain, Norwich.)

**Praying with a mantra**   A mantra is a word or phrase which is repeated six or more times whenever appropriate during the day or night. It is a very ancient method of prayer from the East, and it quickly makes you aware of God's presence. Choose your own mantra carefully, and then use it as required. Here is a selection to chose from – but there are others:

> Lord Jesus Christ, Son of God, have mercy upon us (The Jesus Prayer).
> Jesus is Lord.
> Jesus Christ is risen indeed.
> My God, I love thee. Help me to love thee more and more.
> I am loved by God more than I can either conceive or understand (Henri de Tourville).

*Using a book of prayers*  Ask your priest for suggestions. (It may be helpful for the PCC to spend a whole meeting, with no other business on the agenda, to discuss the subject of prayer.) When using a book of prayers, it is important actually to *pray* the prayers, rather than just read them. The day will come, as you grow in your prayer life, when you will want to use your own words. Here are some suggestions for prayer books: *When You Pray* compiled by John Gilling and Sister Patricia (Darton, Longman and Todd); *Daily Prayer and Praise* by George Appleton (USCL-Lutterworth); *A Dairy of Private Prayer* by John Baillie (Oxford University Press); and *Daily with God* by the author (see above).

*Praying and breathing*  Pray one line of (say) the Lord's Prayer, with each intake of breath, and with a silent pause as you breath out. It will seen strange at first, but effective when you have mastered it. This can be helpful in the early stages of learning how to pray. Other prayers can be used in this way too.

*Meditation*  Become still, and aware of God's presence. Then spend time thinking about one word only, which describes Jesus or God, e.g. holy Jesus, loving Jesus, merciful Jesus, forgiving Jesus. Each time, use only one of these words. 'If a man love me, he will heed my words and my Father will love him, and we will come and make our dwelling with him.'

*Cross or crucifix*  Some people find it helpful to conduct their prayer time in front of, or near, a cross or crucifix, e.g. in their room. A lighted candle is also helpful.

*Saints' days*  Receiving Communion on the major Saints' days is part of the rule of life of a Christian (a 'day of obligation').

We ask people to pray for us during our life on earth. Do they stop praying for us after they die? Many people (but not all) feel it is right to ask the Saints to pray for us. Probably the most widely used prayer (apart from the Lord's Prayer) is the Hail Mary, which is used in the Orthodox and Roman Catholic Churches, and by many Anglicans too. People do not pray to the Saints, but ask the Saints to pray for them.

*Food for thought*
Which of the Apostles, Saints or Martyrs do you feel are close to you?

*A busy life?* If the answer is yes, then think about Martin Luther's words: 'I have much to do today, therefore I shall have to pray for a long time'.

*Arrow prayers* These are short, quick prayers, offered to God at any time on the spur of the moment. It is important to remember that arrow prayers are always 'extra' prayers, and they must never be used as an alternative for a regular time of prayer. Arrow prayers help you to become aware of God's presence during the day or night, and they help you to seek God's will in every situation. They are also asking for God's help, particularly when there has been an accident, or when you are watching the news on television. Here are a few examples:

> O Lord, bless this person here with me now.
> O Lord, bless all who are travelling on this plane/train/ship/bus.
> Father, forgive me for those unkind words/for that unkind thought.
> Thank you, Lord, for all your blessings, and especially . . .
> Lord, help this person.
> Heavenly Father, bless and help all who are connected with this emergency (at the sound of ambulance, fire engine or police car).
> Lord, help us to see what you want in this situation.

*Making the sign of the cross* Christians make the sign of the cross to remind them of God's whole work of salvation on the cross to save us from our sins. It is a shorthand prayer to bring this to mind. It reminds us that we are turning to Christ, and turning away from ourselves. Thus, with the right hand, we make the letter 'I' from the top to the bottom of the chest, and then cross it out again from left to right. It is traditional to say 'In the name of the Father and of the Son and of the Holy Spirit. Amen' as this is done.

*What to say in your prayers* Prayer is not a time to give a catalogue of your wants and desires to God. Not much of a relationship can be built up if all you do is to say what you want from God. There are different kinds of prayer, and these are represented in the word PACTS. Each letter of the word PACTS stands for a different aspect of prayer. P stands for Preparation for prayer. A stands for our Adoration and praise of God. C stands for Confessing our sins to God. T stands for Thanking God. S stands for the word 'Supplications' – which means praying for others and, lastly, praying for yourself. 'PACTS' reminds us of the different parts of prayer, and some people find they can base their daily prayers on the word PACTS. But it is not easy, and it is perhaps wiser not to try this in the early stages.

Prayer should always be 'God-centred' rather than 'self-centred'. The praise and glory of God is followed by the needs of men and women (as in the Lord's Prayer). Always avoid telling God what you think he should do, as though you know best. It is sufficient to bring the person or situation to God in prayer – and 'kept in your heart' while you are praying.

God's love flows endlessly towards the world, and our prayers for others are one channel of his love. Prayer is about God and his kingdom, his will and his justice.

Pray each day for your bishop and your priest by name. Pray regularly for the mission of the Church in your parish, in your deanery, and in the nearest town or city. Pray for PCC members in the parish and in the deanery – for all who have been baptized and confirmed, and their families – for all who have lapsed – for all on the electoral rolls of the deanery – for diocesan officials – for those who serve on diocesan committees or Diocesan and Deanery Synods – for those who live near to you – for all who live and work in the parish – for all who are ill or dying, the bereaved, those who have died, and for those whose anniversary of death falls during the week.

Include 'outward'-looking subjects such as those who influence public opinion – those who administer the law – the unemployed – homeless people and all refugees – all in authority, locally and nationally – the leaders of the nations – police, probation and prison officers, prisoners and their families – the Royal Family – the disabled and their families – all involved in education, especially Christian education. Could you make your own '31-day cycle of prayer'? Pray for your friends, family, and finally for yourself – including those 'dark corners' in your life (if any exist). Prayer is all about bringing our wishes into line with God's wishes.

One way to conclude your prayers is with the Lord's Prayer, the collect for the day and the Grace. Do not then get up and rush away from God's presence. He is your friend, and he is always with you. If you do want to rush away, then ask yourself what is wrong. Also consider: could my prayers have been better?

*Difficulties in prayer*    Prayer is sometimes joyful and peaceful, while at other times you may not feel like praying. Your thoughts wander or you do not even want to start praying. At such times, keep on praying 'as a duty', even though it is difficult and God does not seem to be there. He is always there, even though you are not aware of his presence. Always try to pray before you are too tired, because you cannot offer your best to God when you are half asleep. However, a prayer last thing at night, in addition to your regular time of prayer, is a good thing.

One way to deal with difficulties in prayer is to try to turn them into prayer – even your wandering thoughts. You may well experience difficulties in the early stages, and also in later stages too. Perhaps the difficulties indicate that you need to change your method of praying. Consult your spiritual adviser about it.

*Sin and forgiveness*    We all have to learn the difficult lesson of how to forgive other people. 'Forgive us our trespasses (sins) as we forgive those who trespass against us.' This is vital for your spiritual life, and it will also teach you something about God's love and mercy and forgiveness for you.

Any form of sin kills spiritual growth, and separates you from God. Every Christian needs God's forgiveness regularly, and it can be received in three different ways. First, by asking God in your own private prayers to forgive you. Secondly, you can confess your sins Sunday by Sunday in the general confession at church, and the priest pronounces God's absolution. Thirdly, you can make a private confession to a priest, if you feel this is necessary. The 1662 Book of Common Prayer states, in the visitation of the sick: when a person's 'conscience is troubled with any weighty matter' he is to make a private confession to a priest, who will absolve him with the authority of Christ, and in his name. Sacramental confession gives us the assurance of God's forgiveness. There is a saying in the Anglican Church about confession – 'None must, all may and some do'.

Whatever the priest hears during confession is always kept with absolute secrecy.

**Parish days of prayer**    Ask people to spend 30 minutes in prayer in church on a rota list through the day. Just because one person is in church e.g. from 1 to 1.30 p.m., it does not mean that others cannot be present at the same time. The important thing is to have the chain through the day. There is usually a special 'intention' for the prayers, e.g. the mission of the Church in the parish, and prayer material can be provided for those who wish to use it. How often should a day of prayer be held? Four times a year? Monthly? Opportunity should be provided for those who work to come in the early evening.

**Parish prayer fellowship**    This is arranged with a daily list of intercessions for each month, and a teaching letter on prayer for use by people at home. Each member prays each day for all the other members of the prayer fellowship, and for the priest and the parish. Could this be organized by a lay person?

**Three-parish prayer links**    Each parish prays for the other two parishes every day. A town parish, a country one and an inner city parish? Dare one say – an evangelical (low Church) linked with a catholic (high Church) parish?

**Husband and wife**    What a strong team if husband and wife can pray together! This is not always easy. An alternative – to read a passage from the Bible together each day or night, followed by silent prayer (or saying the Lord's Prayer together). The Psalms may be added, one saying even verses and the other doing the odd verses.

**Parish library**    A collection of books about the spiritual life is a good resource for every local church. Every PCC member should aim to read one book on prayer each year (during Lent?).

**Spiritual director (soul friend)**    Whatever name is used, it is helpful to talk about your prayer life with another person at least once a year. Have you fallen back or made progress in your prayer life during the year? What are the problems? Spiritual blockages?

Choose someone steeped in prayer, whether ordained or lay, but someone you can trust and with whom you would be happy to share the secrets of your spiritual life. 'Spiritual direction' is at the heart of spiritual growth. The way you live your life during the day affects your relationship with God and your whole prayer life. Your body is a 'temple of the Holy Spirit'.

*A retreat*  An annual retreat forms part of the life of many PCC members. What about a PCC retreat or quiet day? (*See* **Retreat** on page 167.)

*God's will*  Prayer is not offered to God to try to persuade him to change his mind, and to alter the course of events. You pray to discover God's will, and to bring your will into line with God's will. 'Thy kingdom come, thy will be done, on earth as it is in heaven.' How far do you really mean that, when you say the Lord's Prayer?

*Regular worship*  The Church is the eucharistic community, which gathers together on its knees to receive the body and blood of Christ in the Eucharist. Then it becomes the 'Church on legs' as PCC members and others go out into the world to love and serve God during the coming week. Worship is not a question of going to church only when you feel like it. Your presence shows how much God is worth to you (worship means worthship). Invite visitors to come with you, and allow nothing to keep you away, except illness or an accident. PCC members should set an example to the congregation in this matter of regular worship, which is essential for personal growth and the growth of the congregation. God wants you to worship him and to show your love to him in this way. If you stay away, you are rejecting his love, and also causing weakness in his body the Church. Your absence shows that you do not appreciate the cost of God's love for you on the cross. Jesus said, 'You shall love the Lord your God with all your heart, with all your mind, with all your soul and with all your strength'. In the ten commandments, we are exhorted to 'keep holy the Sabbath', i.e. by worshipping God. See also St John 15.5.

*Holy Communion*  During the week a parish is fortunate if it can have a daily celebration of our Lord's death and resurrection. 'Give us this day our daily bread.' Without any shadow of doubt, a daily celebration of the Eucharist makes a tremendous difference for the spiritual life of the priest. It is also good for the parish to have a daily celebration of the Eucharist. After all, the Church is the Eucharistic community. Receiving Communion regularly is a vital part of Christian formation.

*Preparation for Holy Communion*   Noise before the service seems to be a problem in some congregations. ASB Rite A, Note 1 states: 'Careful devotional preparation before the service is recommended for every communicant' (proposed at General Synod by the author). St Paul puts this in a different way: 'Anyone who eats the bread or drinks the cup of the Lord unworthily will be guilty of desecrating the body and blood of the Lord. A man must test himself before eating his share of the bread and drinking from the cup' (1 Corinthians 11.27–28 NEB).

Traditionally, Christians do three things before the service to prepare for Holy Communion:

1. Thank God. The Eucharist means The Thanksgiving. Decide before the service which of his many blessings you will thank God for during the service.
2. Confess your sins. Before the service, go back over the past week and work out exactly what you will confess to God in the service. Remember, we only receive God's forgiveness if we forgive those who sin against us. The cross is about our sins. Penitence (sorrow for sin) is needed for spiritual growth. 'Drink this, all of you; this is my blood of the new covenant, which is shed for you and for many for the forgiveness of sins. Do this, as often as you drink it, in remembrance of me.'
3. Pray for someone or something. Offer the Eucharist with that 'intention' in mind.

Many people find it helpful to get into the habit of doing these three things before each service.

Arrive early, and if possible about fifteen minutes before the service. As a PCC member, you have a responsibility to give a lead to the congregation in prayer and preparation. By arriving early, you can make your own preparations in an unhurried and worthy way, and learn to grow in the spiritual life. It is not easy to put yourself in the presence of God especially if you arrive in a hurry or late. Obviously, it is much more difficult for a family with young children.

Are there other Christians kneeling and praying in church when you arrive? If so, what secret about the spiritual life have they discovered that you have not yet learned?

Another suggestion. Very quietly say 'Hello' to the sidesmen, but do not chatter before the service. You are there to worship your Creator and Redeemer, and you need to prepare yourself to come into the presence of the King of Kings. To chatter before the service is harmful to the spiritual life of the Church, and it prevents you and others from making careful preparations. Voices carry in a church building, and your talking, however quiet, will disturb those who are trying to pray. Noise certainly lessens the spiritual effectiveness of the Church. Two old sayings: 'Silence is the gateway to the spiritual life.' 'Before the service, talk to God. During the service, listen to God. After the service, talk to each other.'

In former years, people had a greater respect for the Church. Today, this respect seems to be much less evident, even among Church members. Jesus said, 'My house shall be called a House of Prayer'. Perhaps we need to rediscover a sense of awe and mystery for what is sacred and set apart for God in a building consecrated to his holy name. God said to Moses, 'Take off your sandals, for the place where you are standing is holy ground'. Muslims take this literally. Is there a message which we can learn from this? A church building often has an atmosphere of prayer, and many find it is a good place for their own private prayers. People come early not only to make their own preparation, but also to say their prayers in the peace and quietness of God's house.

When you have made your preparation – whether using the three points mentioned above, or some other method – then read the Scripture readings appointed for the day. Think about their meaning, and what God is wanting to say to you through them. Work out what is the common theme of the readings. Can you turn any parts of the Scripture passages into prayer?

The hymn 'Come, Holy Ghost, our souls inspire' is good for personal preparation. Could you learn it by heart and use it for every Eucharist? Some of the Communion Hymns are good for personal preparation.

The Book of Psalms is the greatest prayer-book ever written, and the Psalms were loved and used by Jesus. They are excellent for our preparations. Each 'day' has an appointed psalm for use with the set readings, found in the ASB after the collect for the day. Use the Psalms and get to know them, and work out which are helpful in preparation.

Another suggestion: pray for all who are near you in the building, the priest, and all who will lead the worship. Pray for the whole congregation at this and the other services today. If you have offended anyone, or if you have been offended by anyone, or you find it hard to like someone, then pray for God's healing love, and for his blessing on them and on you. Pray for the deepening of the spiritual life of the congregation, and for an extension of God's kingdom in the church and in the parish.

Another thought – as you walk up to the church door, say a prayer to yourself. 'Lord, bless us and all who will worship in your house today.' Or the well-known prayer, 'Lord, teach us how to pray'.

In one sense, we receive from the service in proportion to what we put into it in terms of personal preparation. In another sense, we receive everything, unworthy though we are, through the grace and love of God.

A powerful way to help the mission of the Church is through prayer – and to make our worship a spiritual powerhouse.

Worship means 'worthship' – how much God is really worth to us. Jesus asked Peter, 'Do you love me?' If God asked you to what extent do you love him, how would you answer? One way we show our love for God is by the care and effort with which we prepare for our worship.

*Before receiving Communion*   Many people, as they walk up to receive Communion, repeat to themselves the words: 'Lord, I am not worthy to receive you, but only say the word, and I shall be healed'.

*After the service*   Kneel quietly and thank God for all the benefits you have received, and particularly the gift of his Son in the sacrament.

*Rule of life for PCC members*   PCC members are all at different stages of their spiritual journey. Whatever stage you have reached, you need to think about what you are doing and why. Prayer is difficult, and if you find you have stopped for a few days, then start again, and ask God to help you to persevere. The basic principles of the spiritual life remain unchanged, despite all other modern changes.

Think about what God has done for you through his Son on the cross, and base your rule of life on those thoughts. We try to respond to God's love in definite areas of our lives. We give our time to acknowledge that all our time is a gift from God.

1. *To receive Communion every Sunday.* Make Sunday a 'day of

obligation', and prepare carefully for it. In some ways, that is the easy part of the rule of life.

2. *Daily prayer*. Some PCC members may find this more difficult than others. Prayer is not easy, but PCC members should try to give time to God each day for a time of silent prayer. How could you improve the quality of your prayers?

3. *Bible reading*. Once you get into the habit of reading the Bible each day, this becomes an easy part of your rule. The important thing to remember each day is the question – What does God want to say to me through this Scripture reading?

4. *Money*. In Christian stewardship parishes, PCC members will no doubt work out what is a responsible proportion of their income to give back to God, in thanksgiving for his many blessings, and for all that he has given to us. Those PCC members who have not considered this subject as a spiritual matter could perhaps read about Christian *Stewardship of money* on page 38.

5. *Time and talents*. Again, it is good to thank God for the time and the skills he has given to each of us, and how we can offer them back to God for his work on earth. *See Stewardship of time and of skills and abilities* on page 38.

6. *Daily life*. Are you satisfied with the part which your faith plays in your life and your work?

It is helpful to write down your rule of life under these six headings, and with the date. Later you may want to revise your rule.

*Questions for discussion*

1. Do you make adequate preparation before you receive Communion?
2. Do you read the Bible each day? Do you try and work out how it is relevant for you?
3. Are you satisfied with the progress you are making in your spiritual life?
4. Do you have a spiritual director (soul friend)?

**Spring cleaning**  The church building, and the hall, need to be thoroughly cleaned once a year, apart from their regular weekly or daily cleaning. Members of the congregation can be invited to help. If this is done in the evening, or on Saturday, it enables those who are at work to help. Do not forget the tower and those dark corners where things are 'dumped', and especially on top of cupboards in the vestry. Someone is needed to organize the spring cleaning. (Is it a good time to think about timber treatment after the spring clean?)

**Stewardship**   *See* **Christian stewardship** on page 37.

**Street wardens**   A warden system has been adopted in many parishes. There are different ways of doing this, but always the whole of the parish is divided into areas. Each area has its own warden, who is the church representative for that area. The warden's job is to be the communication link to take information from the church to every home, and this can be done verbally or by duplicated letter (or both). The warden is also the communications link between the home and the church, and particularly to report back sickness, someone in hospital, death, a problem, departures and new arrivals. With the considerable reduction in the number of clergy and the vast increase in population in this century, it is essential for the church to have this kind of help through a warden scheme if the church is to be a caring and serving church, relevant to modern life. (*See* **Pastoral care** on page 151.)

**Sunday School**   *See* **Children and toddlers of the Church** on page 32.

**Synods of the Church**   The word 'synod' comes from two Greek words which mean 'the way' and 'together'. Synodical government is built on the principle of a partnership between bishops, clergy and lay people. Synodical government does not mean that the Church is a democracy in the full and more usual sense of the word. It is sometimes called 'government by discussion'. The bishop exercises a guardianship of the Church, and to a lesser extent this guardianship is also one of the functions of the parish priest.

*Deanery Synod*   This is made up of two 'houses' – the house of clergy (all incumbents, assistant clergy, clergy holding the bishop's licence, and semi-retired clergy who are 'resident and working') and also the house of laity. The Deanery Synod has at least one lay representative from each parish (depending on the numbers on the electoral roll) who is elected for three years by the Annual Parochial Church Meeting. Deanery Synod members are *ex-officio* members of their own Parochial Church Councils.

It is important that the lay representatives make a report on the proceedings of Deanery Synod at every PCC meeting. When a PCC representative cannot attend a Deanery Synod meeting, it is important to arrange for an observer to attend the meeting.

A PCC can send a resolution to the Deanery Synod, or to the Diocesan Synod, or indeed to the local government council if appropriate.

**Diocesan Synod**  This has three 'houses' and the house of bishops forms one of these houses. The house of clergy forms another house, which includes the dean or provost, archdeacons and the clergy elected by Deanery Synods. The house of laity forms the third house, and it is elected by the lay members of the Deanery Synods. On important matters, a resolution has to be carried in all three houses, voting separately by houses. In other words, each house has the power of veto. Items on the Diocesan Synod agenda are normally discussed and voted upon by all three houses sitting together in full synod, and require only a simple majority vote.

**General Synod**  This has three 'houses', bishops, clergy and laity. General Synod is a legislative assembly, a financial authority, and an administrative centre for the Church of England. It was created by the Synodical Government Measure 1969. The houses of clergy and laity are elected mainly by Deanery Synod members. They are elected for five-year periods.

**Convocations**  The two ancient Convocations of Canterbury and York are much older than Parliament itself. Convocation has two houses – bishops and archbishops, and secondly the clergy. General Synod has taken over most but not all of the functions of the Convocations, and meetings of the Convocations are now held only occasionally.

**The Anglican Consultative Council**  The Anglican Church came into existence mainly through the work of the missionary societies of the Church of England in the different continents of the world. The Anglican Church has no legislative body, and the Church in each province is constitutionally independent.

As recently as 1971, the Anglican Consultative Council was created. Three representatives from each province throughout the world meet every other year. The Council has no power to make any laws, and its functions are mainly advisory, and a platform to exchange opinions and information.

**Team ministry**  *See* **Group and team ministries** on page 86.

**Telephone**  Is your church listed in the directory under the name of your Church?

**Terrier and inventory**  A terrier is a list of lands, goods and possessions of the parish church and any chapels. Every parish is required to have an up-to-date terrier and inventory.

The archdeacon or rural dean inspects the terrier every three years, and it has to be signed by the archdeacon (or rural dean) and the churchwardens, two members of the PCC and the minister. This is to ensure that a proper inspection is made to check that nothing is missing. A copy of the terrier and inventory can be obtained from any religious bookshop.

**Transport**  Elderly and disabled people often need transport to and from church and for other journeys too. This can often be organized with volunteer help from the congregation. A transport organizer is required, with his or her name, address and telephone number clearly in the magazine, and on the notice board. He enlists the drivers and arranges lifts as and when needed. The demand will vary from time to time. Each driver is advised to check his insurance policy.

**Treasurer of the PCC**  *See* **Finance** on page 81.

**Trouble-maker**  Occasionally, there is someone in the parish whose main aim is to cause trouble. There is strong legislation to deal with a priest who 'goes off the rails'. The situation has recently been balanced with legislation to deal with a lay person who is a persistent and deliberate trouble-maker. The bishop now has the power to ban such a person or persons from holding office for a number of years. It is wise to consult the archdeacon at an early stage when a problem of this nature arises.

**Uniformed organizations**  A major part of Church youth work is done through uniformed organizations. But how much thought does the PCC give to this most important aspect of

Church life? Does the relationship of the uniformed organization depend entirely – or largely – on the relationship of the priest with them? If so, would it not be wise for the PCC to be involved?

The largest groups are the Scout Association (Baden-Powell House, Queen's Gate, London SW7 5JS. Tel: 071–584 7030), and the Guide Association (17/19 Buckingham Palace Road, London SW1W 0PT. Tel: 071–834 6242). Each member is required to make a formal promise . . . 'to do my best, to do my duty to God . . .'.

The Church Lads' Brigade and the Church Girls' Brigade (2 Barnsley Road, Wath upon Dearne, Rotherham S63 6PY. Tel: 0709–876535) are the only specifically Anglican uniformed organizations, and they are based in parishes, within a diocesan structure. Perhaps it is a pity that the Church does not make more use of these two organizations. The PCC has similar aims to all these organizations, in helping young people to develop, and particularly in the Christian faith. It is a good vision, and it often works well in practice.

One difficulty is how to find suitable leaders who are competent to take charge of young people, and who also have a strong Christian faith. Some uniformed organizations have departed from the original intentions of their founders in respect of the Christian faith. This is partly due to the problem of finding Christian leaders.

Another problem is how to encourage young people to come to church parade without too much pressure (assuming the worship is bright and attractive). Many will come from families with little or no connection with the Church, but a church parade may well sow seeds which will flourish later on in life.

How much should the PCC expect from church-sponsored organizations – bearing in mind their stated aims? The church provides a hall. It is good, of course, to provide a service for the community in this way too. But apart from the hall, is anything further required from the PCC? What about a meeting of the leaders with the PCC – followed by refreshments? The encouragement, support and interest of the PCC and congregation are surely vital to build up good relationships with the uniformed organizations. Involvement of young people in worship and in parish activities is also helpful, so that they feel that it is their church, and that they belong to it.

*Food for thought*

Could more be achieved with the uniformed organizations by the PCC?

**Verger**   The person who carries the verge or mace (staff of authority) in processions, and also looks after the church. Most churches no longer enjoy the luxury of a paid verger. They either have a paid cleaner, or church members help to clean the church on a rota system.

A schoolboy definition of a verger – 'someone who minds his keys and pews'.

**Vestry Meeting**   Until 1894, the Vestry Meeting was a meeting of parishioners (ratepayers) who fixed the rates for the coming year. They appointed the churchwardens (or overseers), who administered relief to the poor of the parish. In 1894, all the civil functions of the Vestry were transferred to the local government authorities. The church functions of the Vestry were transferred to the PCC by the Parochial Church Council (Powers) Measure 1956. The churchwardens are now appointed under the Churchwardens' (Appointment and Resignation) Measure 1964. (*See* **Churchwardens** on pages 52–3.)

**Vicarage maintenance**   The most important assets and resources of the Church in the parish (apart from the committed members of the congregation) are surely the church building, the church hall and the vicarage. It is important to remember that the vicarage is the private home of the priest and his family, as well as his place of work. If the house seems large for a bachelor priest, the next one may have three or four children. The ownership of the vicarage is vested in the priest while he is the incumbent of the parish. It is his responsibility to maintain it in a proper state of repair. An architect or the diocesan surveyor gives it a thorough inspection every five years and submits a report on the work which needs to be done. This report is not sent to the PCC, as the diocese deals with the work and pays the bills. Money for the repairs and maintenance of the vicarage comes partly from a proportion of the quota which is paid by every parish to the Diocesan Board of Finance.

In the period between the quinquennial inspections, regular inspections and checks are needed on the vicarage. When a priest is overworked, it is so easy to forget about gutters and gullies. Certain things need regular attention, such as cleaning gutters and drains, clearing roof valleys and gullies, checking for missing tiles, and repairing or replacing leaking gutters. Dampness and a lack of ventilation quickly cause problems and dry rot. It is wise to carry out appropriate repairs as soon as possible, and the longer the delay in taking action, the larger the eventual bill will be. Lucky the parish which has someone able and willing to help in these vital matters.

A draughty vicarage can be considerably improved by secondary or double glazing of the windows. If they do not already exist, building front and back porches with doors much improves heat retention. This is important when there are many callers.

*Food for thought*

1. Can the PCC help with any improvements in the vicarage?
2. Does the kitchen need modernizing? Most PCCs have a vicarage repair and improvement fund. Does your parish allocate a reasonable sum each year for this purpose in the budget? (Before making any alterations, it is wise to consult the archdeacon to see if the alterations are acceptable to the diocese, and also to inquire whether the diocese could provide any money to help.)
3. Is there a vicarage log book to record alterations, repairs and plans?

**Vicarage – sale of**   The PCC does not own the vicarage (nor the church). The ownership is vested in the priest for the period when he is vicar of the parish. Any scheme to sell or alter the vicarage requires his formal consent. The PCC also has to be notified of any proposal to sell or to demolish the parsonage house, or to buy or build a new one. The PCC is given 21 days in which to object – but in practice this is usually much longer. The diocese takes professional advice, but it is possible that, with the benefit of local knowledge, or by seeking another opinion, a better scheme could be found. Christians have to be as 'wise as the children of this world' in their property dealings.

Certain questions need consideration: Is the vicarage in a good position? Next to the church is ideal. If it is old and has stood the test of time, it will probably outlast any new building. Most of the large and rambling parsonages have now been replaced.

It is the Church Commissioners who have the final responsibility of upholding or overruling any objections. The

Commissioners fortunately have much experience and wisdom in this whole subject.

**Videos**    There is a wide range of religious subjects available for church use. Many parishes have a video recorder and screen installed in the hall or committee room. A parish library of videos and audio cassettes needs a well organized index.

Religious videos are available from a wide range of sources. The diocesan education team usually have lists of videos available for borrowing or hiring. Also the Church Army (see page 42) and CPAS (see page 44).

Also: The Churches VT Centre, Beeson's Yard, Bury Lane, Rickmansworth, Herts WD3 1DS. Tel: 0923–777933.

And The National Society, Religious Education Development Centre, 23 Kensington Square, London W8 5HN. Tel: 071–937 4241.

**Visiting**    The old saying is still true today – 'a house-going priest makes for a church-going people'. Nothing can replace personal contact; but it is an impossible task for one person to do single-handed, although many priests aim to do at least three visits per day. But the vicar is surely not the only person who can do visiting on behalf of the Church? Roman Catholic congregations often do a great deal of visiting on behalf of the Church, and so too do the Mormons and Jehovah's Witnesses. At general election time, think how many people visit homes in the constituency. What a difference if such numbers from the Church did visiting to extend the kingdom of God!

Many congregations and PCCs do in fact undertake visiting. The magazine distributor, for example, can knock on the door of a lonely person and say, 'Hello, I've called to deliver your church magazine and to see how you are today'. An annual visit can be made to the homes of the Sunday School children, the choir, the uniformed organizations, the youth club, etc., to invite parents and children to special functions at the church. The churchwarden, or whoever is in charge of the sidesmen's rota, could visit fringe people in their homes to recruit new sidesmen. The church is the whole baptized membership, and there is great value in the church going out into the community in these and other ways.

When visiting a home, knock boldly three times, and as you do so, say to yourself 'In the name of the Father, and of the Son, and of the Holy Spirit. Amen'. Another silent prayer may be appropriate, e.g. 'Peace be to this house and to all who live here.'

There is much value in a general visitation of the parish, undertaken every five years – if there are sufficient people willing to undertake this work. A final thought: Remember the call of the prophet Isaiah, 'Whom shall I send?' 'Here I am', I answered, 'send me.'

**Where to sit**   Unless allocated a seat by the churchwarden or his representative, worshippers can choose where to sit in church, and it is strange how people will sit near the back. Are Christians afraid of each other? Is the love of God locked so firmly in their hearts that it cannot radiate out even to fellow Christians? God wants the 'ice' to melt so that Christians can be friendly with other Christians, and so that his love can go to non-Christians. The outside world is desperately crying out for fellowship and (Christian) love, and the Holy Spirit wants to create a friendly family atmosphere especially in the congregation.

At the last supper, Jesus was not at one end of the upper room with his back to the twelve, and they were not scattered over the length of a long building. The best conditions for worship will be created if the congregation is the 'gathered community' because it is gathered and not scattered around a large building. The disciples gathered around a table for a meal in the upper room.

PCC members can set an example by always sitting in the front pews.

**Will and Testament**   *See* **Finance** on pages 82–3.

**Work**   Daily work is not simply a way to earn a living. Many take a pride in their work and offer and dedicate it to God, whether it is in office, factory or home.

Christians sometimes keep quiet at work about their membership of the Church, in case they meet hostility or ridicule. Your place of work is a testing ground for your faith. It is also an opportunity for the outward penetration of the Church into the world by your words and example.

*Questions for discussion*

1. How can the PCC support members of the church who meet with hostility at work because of their Christian faith?

2. Can the PCC help in any way with the problem of unemployment in the area?
3. Could the PCC organize a pre-retirement or post-retirement course?

**Yoga and Christians**   Some Christians may be suspicious of this ancient Hindu art of mental and bodily relaxation and control. However, the Christian Church has taken over many pagan things and 'Christianized' them. Many Christian monks and nuns practise yoga. The value of yoga for a Christian is that it teaches you how to relax, and sit still or kneel without fidgeting and wanting to move. That surely is very important in learning how to pray. Apart from individuals, a group of people may benefit from yoga, using Christian meditations. Some specifically Christian books on yoga include:

1. *Exploration into Contemplative Prayer* by Fr Herbert Slade (a Church of England monk of the Society of St John the Evangelist). It is published by Darton, Longman & Todd, and it goes quite deeply into the subject.
2. *Everyday Yoga for Christians* by the Revd Eric W. Hayden (a Baptist minister). Published by Arthur James Ltd, Evesham, it is a very practical book and easy to follow.
3. *Christian Yoga* by Fr Dechanet (a French Roman Catholic priest). Published by Search Press. This is for those who wish to take yoga beyond its basic stages.

**Youth work and the PCC**   The children of church members do not automatically become regular worshippers as adults. Whether they remain members of the Church depends to a considerable extent on the quality of the Christian lives of their parents. They are much more likely to remain as members of the Church if the local church provides opportunities for young people to meet together regularly. The responsibility of the PCC surely goes beyond the children of church members. If the PCC is a group of people with a mission to the whole parish, then all young people should definitely be included in the PCC's plans. Many young people do not belong to the Church now, but they may become part of the Church of tomorrow through the activities of youth work done by the local church.

Some PCCs will see youth work in terms of service to the community, without any intention of trying to bring the young people into Church membership. Other PCCs will feel that the

*Youth work and the PCC*

Church is 'in business' for a definite purpose – namely to extend the kingdom of God among young people. In former generations, the Church has done magnificent things in terms of youth work, but now many others compete with the Church for the allegiance of the young. The Church certainly has to be involved, even if there are no obvious leaders available. Prayer, the diocesan youth adviser, looking for help outside the church community, or perhaps asking the next parish if they could 'lend' someone to run your youth club. The diocesan youth adviser can provide suggestions for starting youth work, or new ideas for work which has been going for some time. The diocese will probably provide training courses for youth leaders.

Leaders need selecting with care. People can sometimes volunteer to help with youth work for the wrong reasons, and many problems are caused if the wrong person is in charge. Youth work can be demanding, and the (adult) youth committee is wise to make sure that there are sufficient leaders to share the load properly. Leaders need much understanding and insight, as they are the people who are out in front for others to follow. A leader needs to be able to exercise discipline, but at the same time to be friendly. Young people need someone who is stable, knows the principles on which he or she stands, and will not deviate from those standards. The ability to communicate with young people is important, especially when so many parents cannot or will not give the time for communicating with their children. Time is perhaps the most valuable thing a parent can give a child.

*Questions for discussion*

1. What are the aims of the PCC in youth work?
2. Each generation of young people has to be persuaded afresh of the relevance of the Christian faith. How is the PCC attempting to do this?
3. What resources are available from the diocese?
4. Is the PCC aware of the courses and holidays run by the diocese for young people?
5. Would a good time to hold the church youth club be on a Sunday morning after the Parish Communion service?

**Zeal** – 'Where is thy zeal and thy strength?' (Isaiah 63.15).

204

# Christian Bookshops

| | |
|---|---|
| **BIRMINGHAM** | Mowbrays Bookshop, 12 Ethel Street. Tel. 021–643 2617. |
| **BRADFORD** | SPCK Bookshop, 14 North Parade, BD1 3HY. Tel. 0274–728669. |
| **BRIGHTON** | SPCK Bookshop, Chapel Royal, North Street, BN1 1EA. Tel. 0273–28767. |
| **BRISTOL** | SPCK Bookshop, 79 Park Street, BS1 5PF. Tel. 0272–273461. |
| **CAMBRIDGE** | Mowbrays Bookshop, 14 King's Parade, CB2 1SR. Tel. 0223–358452. |
| **CANTERBURY** | SPCK Bookshop, 7 St Peter's Street, CT1 2EF. Tel. 0227–462881. |
| **CARDIFF** | SPCK Bookshop, 26 Morgan Arcade, CF1 2AF. Tel. 0222–227736. |
| **CARLISLE** | The Cathedral Bookshop (SPCK), Fratry Undercroft, The Cathedral, CA3 8TZ. Tel. 0228–43498. |
| **CHESTER** | SPCK Bookshop, 7–11 Werburgh Street, CH1 2EJ. Tel. 0244–323753. |
| **CHICHESTER** | SPCK Bookshop, St Olave's Church, North Street, PO19 1LQ. Tel. 0243–782790. |

| | |
|---|---|
| **DURHAM** | SPCK Bookshop, 55–57 Saddler Street, DH1 3EJ.<br>Tel. 091–384 2095.<br>The Cathedral Bookshop (SPCK), Durham Cathedral, DH1 3EQ.<br>Tel. 091–386 2972. |
| **EXETER** | SPCK Bookshop, 1–2 Catherine Street, Cathedral Yard, EX1 1EX.<br>Tel. 0392–73640. |
| **GLOUCESTER** | SPCK Bookshop, 27 Southgate Street, GL1 1TP.<br>Tel. 0452–22805. |
| **GUILDFORD** | SPCK Bookshop, St Mary's Church, Quarry Street, GU1 4AU.<br>Tel. 0483–60316. |
| **HEREFORD** | Palace Yard Bookshop (SPCK), Palace Yard, HR4 9BJ.<br>Tel. 0432–266785. |
| **LEEDS** | SPCK Bookshop, Holy Trinity Church, Boar Lane, LS1 6HW.<br>Tel. 0532–442488. |
| **LEICESTER** | SPCK Bookshop, 68 High Street, LE1 5YP.<br>Tel. 0533–626161. |
| **LINCOLN** | SPCK Bookshop, 36 Steep Hill, LN2 1LU.<br>Tel. 0522–527486. |
| **LONDON** | Dillons (Mowbray), 28 Margaret Street, Oxford Circus, W1N 7LB.<br>Tel. 071–580 2812.<br>Faith House Bookshop (Church Union), 7 Tufton Street, Westminster, SW1P 3QN.<br>Tel. 071–222 6952.<br>Church House Bookshop, 31 Great Smith Street, Westminster, SW1P 3BN.<br>Tel. 071–222 5520/9011. |
| **MANCHESTER** | SPCK Bookshop, 14 St Mary's Street, Deansgate, M3 2LA.<br>Tel. 061–834 0257. |
| **NEWCASTLE-UPON-TYNE** | SPCK Bookshop, 8 Ridley Place, NE1 8JW.<br>Tel. 091–232 3466. |

**NORWICH**          SPCK Bookshop, 19 Pottergate, NR2 1DS.
Tel. 0603–627332.

**OXFORD**           Newman–Mowbray Bookshop, 87 St Aldates, OX1 1RB.
Tel. 0865–244654.

**SALISBURY**        SPCK Bookshop, 51 High Street, SP1 2PE.
Tel. 0722–334535.

**SHEFFIELD**        Cathedral Bookshop (SPCK), Campo Lane, S1 2EF.
Tel. 0742–723454.

**TRURO**            SPCK Bookshop, 8 St Mary's Street, TR1 2AF.
Tel. 0872–72771.

**WINCHESTER**       SPCK Bookshop, 24 The Square, SO23 9EX.
Tel. 0962–866617.

**WORCESTER**        SPCK Bookshop, 105 High Street, WR1 2HS.
Tel. 0905–24396.

**YORK**             SPCK Bookshop, 28 Goodramgate, YO1 2LG.
Tel. 0904–654176.

# Useful Addresses and Telephone Numbers

**Actors' Church Union** The Senior Chaplain, St Paul's Church, Bedford Street, Covent Garden, London WC2E 9ED. Tel. 071–836 5221.

**Additional Curates Society** The Secretary, Gordon Browning House, 8 Spitfire Road, Birmingham B24 9PB. Tel. 021–382 5533.

**Anglican Society for the Welfare of Animals** The Hon Secretary, 10 Chester Avenue, Hawkenbury, Tunbridge Wells TN2 4TZ. Tel. 0892–25594.

**Anglican Young People's Association** The Administration Secretary, Chi Rho House, 53 Cedar Drive, Keynsham, Bristol BS18 2TX. Tel. 0727–864306.

**Association for Promoting Retreats** The Secretary, National Retreat Centre, 24 South Audley Street, London W1Y 5DL. Tel. 071–493 3534.

**Bible Reading Fellowship** The Director, Peter's Way, Sandy Lane West, Oxford OX4 5HG. Tel. 0865–748227.

**Bible Society** Executive Director, Stonehill Green, Westlea, Swindon SN5 7DG. Tel. 0793–513713.

**Central Board of Finance Investment Department** St Alphage House, 2 Fore Street, London EC2Y 5AQ. Tel. 071–588 1815.

**Christian Aid** PO Box No 100, London SE1 7TR. Tel. 071–620 4444.

**Christians Abroad** General Secretary, 1 Stockwell Green, London SW9 9HP. Tel. 071–737 7811.

**Church Army** Church Army Headquarters, Independents Road, Blackheath, London SE3 9LG. Tel. 081–318 1226 /3916.

**Church of England Enquiry Centre** Church House,

Great Smith Street, Westminster, London SW1P 3NZ. Tel. 071-222 9011 (ask for Enquiry Centre).

**Church Lads' Brigade and Church Girls' Brigade** General Secretary, 2 Barnsley Road, Wath upon Dearne, Rotherham S63 6PY. Tel. 0709-876535.

**Church Missionary Society** Partnership House, 157 Waterloo Road, London SE1 8UU. Tel. 071-928 8681.

**Church of England Children's Society (The Children's Society)** Edward Rudolph House, Margery Street, London WC1X 0JL. Tel. 071-837 4299.

**Church Pastoral Aid Society** 32 Fleet Street, London, EC4Y 1DB. Tel. 071-353 0751.

**Church Union** The General Secretary, Faith House, 7 Tufton Street, Westminster, London SW1P 3QN. Tel. 071-222 6952.

**Church Urban Fund** The Secretary, 2 Great Peter Street, Westminster, London SW1P 3LX. Tel. 071-222 7010.

**Churches' Council for Health and Healing** St Marylebone Parish Church, Marylebone Road, London NW1 5LT. Tel. 071-486 9644.

**Ecclesiastical Insurance Group** Beaufort House, Brunswick Road, Gloucester GL1 1JZ. Tel. 0452-28533.

**Guild of St Barnabas** (for nurses and others in the caring professions) Organizing Secretary, 16 Copperwood, Ashford TN24 8PZ. Tel. 0233-635334.

**Guild of St Raphael** The Secretary, St Cyprian's Church, Clarence Gate, Glentworth Street, London NW1 6AX. Tel. 071-724 7352.

**Historic Churches Preservation Trust and Incorporated Church Building Society** The Secretary, Fulham Palace, London SW6 6EA. Tel. 071-736 3054.

**Institute of Religion and Medicine** The Secretary, St Marylebone Parish Church, Marylebone Road, London NW1 5LT. Tel. 071-935 6374 Ext 132.

**Intercontinental Church Society** The General Secretary, 175 Tower Bridge Road, London SE1 2AQ. Tel. 071-407 4588.

**Jerusalem and The Middle East Church Association** The General Secretary, The Old Gate House, Castle Hill, Farnham GU9 0AE. Tel. 0252-726994.

**Missions to Seamen** The General Secretary, St Michael Paternoster Royal, College Hill, London EC4R 2RL. Tel. 071-248 5202.

**Mothers' Union** The Mary Sumner House, 24 Tufton Street, Westminster, London SW1P 3RB. Tel. 071-222 5533.

*Useful Addresses & Telephone Numbers*

**National Society (C of E) for Promoting Religious Education** The General Secretary, Church House, Great Smith Street, Westminster, London SW1P 3NZ. Tel. 071-222 1672.

**Prayer Book Society** The Secretary, St James Garlickhythe, Garlick Hill, London EC4V 2AL. Tel. 081-958 8769.

**RADIUS (Religious Drama Society of Great Britain)** The Administrative Secretary, Christ Church and Upton Chapel, Kennington Road, London SE1 7QP. Tel. 071-401 2422.

**Royal School of Church Music** Addington Palace, Croydon CR9 5AD. Tel. 081-654 7676.

**St Luke's Hospital for the Clergy** The General Secretary, 14 Fitzroy Square, London W1P 6AH. Tel. 071-388 4954.

**Scripture Union** Scripture Union House, 130 City Road, London EC1V 2NJ. Tel. 071-250 1966.

**South American Missionary Society**, Allen Gardiner House, Pembury Road, Tunbridge Wells TN2 3QU. Tel. 0892-38647/8.

**United Society for the Propagation of the Gospel (USPG)** The General Secretary, Partnership House, 157 Waterloo Road, London SE1 8XA. Tel. 071-928 8681.

**Women's World Day of Prayer** The Administration Secretary, Commercial Road, Tunbridge Wells TN1 2RR. Tel. 0892-541411.